MYSQL

IN A NUTSHELL

Other resources from O'Reilly

MYSQL

IN A NUTSHELL

Russell J. T. Dyer

O'REILLY®

Beijing • Cambridge • Farnham • Köln • Paris • Sebastopol • Taipei • Tokyo

MySQL in a Nutshell
by Russell J.T. Dyer

Copyright © 2005 O'Reilly Media, Inc. All rights reserved.
Printed in the United States of America.

Published by O'Reilly Media, Inc., 1005 Gravenstein Highway North, Sebastopol, CA 95472.

O'Reilly books may be purchased for educational, business, or sales promotional use. Online editions are also available for most titles (*safari.oreilly.com*). For more information, contact our corporate/institutional sales department: (800) 998-9938 or *corporate@oreilly.com*.

Editor:	Andy Oram
Production Editor:	Sarah Sherman
Cover Designer:	Ellie Volckhausen
Interior Designer:	David Futato

Printing History:

May 2005:	First Edition.

 This book uses RepKover™, a durable and flexible lay-flat binding.

ISBN 0-596-00789-2
[M]

*To my friend Richard Stringer, for
encouraging me in literature, liberalism,
and writing, and for helping me to
become the person I was meant to be.*

—Russell J.T. Dyer

Table of Contents

Preface

MySQL is the most popular open source database system available. Although it's free, it's still very dependable and fast, and is being employed increasingly in areas that used to be the province of Oracle or MS SQL Server. Thanks to a variety of utilities packaged with MySQL, administration is fairly effortless. And with its several application programming interfaces (APIs), it's easy to develop your own software to interface with MySQL.

This book provides a quick reference to MySQL statements and functions, the administrative utilities, and the most popular APIs. The first few chapters are designed to help you get started with MySQL. Each chapter on an API also starts with a tutorial.

When this book was written, Version 4.1 of MySQL was released, and early releases of the development Version of 5.0 were available but not yet stable. As a result, you will find mostly features from Version 4.x, along with some from Version 5.x, in this book. Features that appear only in newer versions are noted as such.

The Purpose of This Book

The purpose of this book is to provide a quick reference to:

- MySQL statements and functions
- The most popular APIs used to access MySQL databases
- Command-line options and configuration information for the MySQL server and utilities

Several chapters start with tutorials, but the central purpose of the book is to fill in the gaps for people who are already comfortable with relational databases.

The format that I've followed for a description of each statement or function is to move from curt memory-joggers to more leisurely explanations. If you know the function that you're looking up, but can't quite remember the syntax, you'll find that first. If you need a bit more information to jog your memory or to clarify the possibilities available with the function, you can find this in the first sentence or so of the explanation. If you require more clarification concerning a function's use, you can continue with the slower-paced material that follows. Examples of usage are provided for most functions.

In summary, the goal is to be brief but fairly complete, and to increase the level of detail as you read on.

How This Book Is Organized

This book is broken up into fourteen chapters and three appendixes, as follows:

Chapter 1, *Introduction to MySQL*, explains the major components of MySQL and useful guidelines for getting information and dealing with the MySQL community.

Chapter 2, *Installing MySQL*, describes how to get MySQL running on all the systems supported by MySQL AB. It is necessary to read this chapter only if your system does not already have MySQL installed.

Chapter 3, *MySQL Basics*, introduces SQL and use of the *mysql* command-line utility. It is no replacement for learning SQL and relational database design, but can be useful to orient you.

Chapter 4, *SQL Statements*, is the major chapter in this book, a comprehensive listing of all SQL statements supported by MySQL and their subclauses.

Chapter 5, *String Functions*, covers SQL functions for manipulating text data.

Chapter 6, *Date and Time Functions*, covers SQL functions that manipulate the various data and time formats supported by MySQL.

Chapter 7, *Mathematical and Aggregate Functions*, covers mathematical SQL functions and functions used for combining information in columns, such as MAX() and COUNT().

Chapter 8, *Flow Control Functions*, covers SQL functions, such as CASE and IF.

Chapter 9, *Miscellaneous Functions*, covers SQL functions that can be used to control or get information about the database engine, and do other miscellaneous tasks.

Chapter 10, *MySQL Server and Client*, covers the options for the *mysqld* daemon, the *mysql* command-line client, and related commands.

Chapter 11, *Command-Line Utilities*, covers other commands for administering MySQL and its data.

Chapter 12, *Perl API* presents the Perl DBI module, used to access MySQL databases from Perl.

Chapter 13, *PHP API*, presents the PHP functions used to query and manipulate MySQL databases.

Chapter 14, *C API*, covers the data types and functions provided by MySQL's basic C library.

Appendix A, *Datatypes*, lists all the data types supported by MySQL.

Appendix B, *Operators*, lists all MySQL operators, such as arithmetic signs and the LIKE and IS NULL comparison operators.

Appendix C, *Environment Variables*, lists the operating system's environment variables consulted by the MySQL server, client, and other utilities.

Conventions Used in This Book

The following typographical conventions are used in this book:

Plain text
> Indicates menu titles, menu options, menu buttons, and keyboard accelerators (such as Alt and Ctrl).

Italic
> Indicates new terms, URLs, email addresses, usernames, hostnames, filenames, file extensions, pathnames, directories, and utilities.

Constant width
> Indicates elements of code, configuration options, variables, functions, modules, the contents of files, or the output from commands.

Constant width bold
> Shows commands or other text that should be typed literally by the user.

Constant width italic
> Shows text that should be replaced with user-supplied values.

Using Code Examples

This book is here to help you get your job done. In general, you may use the code in this book in your programs and documentation. You do not need to contact us for permission unless you're reproducing a significant portion of the code. For example, writing a program that uses several chunks of code from this book does not require permission. Selling or distributing a CD-ROM of examples from O'Reilly books does require permission. Answering a question by citing this book and quoting example code does not require permission. Incorporating a significant amount of example code from this book into your product's documentation does require permission.

We appreciate, but do not require, attribution. An attribution usually includes the title, author, publisher, and ISBN. For example: "*MySQL in a Nutshell* by Russell J.T. Dyer. Copyright 2005 O'Reilly Media, Inc., 0-596-00789-2."

If you feel your use of code examples falls outside fair use or the permission given above, feel free to contact us at *permissions@oreilly.com*.

Request for Comments

Please address comments and questions concerning this book to the publisher:

O'Reilly Media, Inc.
1005 Gravenstein Highway North
Sebastopol, CA 95472
(800) 998-9938 (in the United States or Canada)
(707) 829-0515 (international or local)
(707) 829-0104 (fax)

The examples in this book are professionally written and have been tested, but that does not mean that they are guaranteed to be bug-free or to work correctly with your version and your platform's implementation of MySQL 2.1. If you have problems, find bugs, or have suggestions for future editions, please email them to:

bookquestions@oreilly.com

There's a web page for this book that lists errata, examples, and any additional information. You can access this page at:

http://www.oreilly.com/catalog/mysqlian

For more information about books, conferences, Resource Centers, and the O'Reilly Network, see the O'Reilly web site at:

http://www.oreilly.com

Safari Enabled

 When you see a Safari® Enabled icon on the cover of your favorite technology book, that means the book is available online through the O'Reilly Network Safari Bookshelf.

Safari offers a solution that's better than e-books. It's a virtual library that lets you easily search thousands of top tech books, cut and paste code samples, download chapters, and find quick answers when you need the most accurate, current information. Try it for free at *http://safari.oreilly.com*.

Acknowledgments

Thanks to Andy Oram, my editor, for his guidance and editing, and for helping me to be the person fortunate enough to write this book. Thanks also to Kasia Trapszo, Rick Rezinas, and others for reviewing the manuscript for technical accuracy. Their assistance is greatly appreciated. I also appreciate the chances that Rikki Endsley (editor of *Unix Review*) took with me at the start of my writing career, and the help that she, chromatic (editor of *ONLamp.com*), and several other magazines editors gave me in developing my skills. Special thanks to Kathryn Barrett (publicist for O'Reilly) for her moral support and advice over the past couple of years. Finally, thanks to my friends Rusty Osborne for listening to me through it all and Michael Zabalaoui for buying me lunch almost every weekday while I worked on this book in lieu of a regular job.

Introduction to MySQL

MySQL is an open source, multithreaded, relational database management system created by Michael "Monty" Widenius in 1995. In 2000, MySQL was released under a dual-license model that permitted the public to use it for free under the GNU Public License (GPL); this caused its popularity to soar. The company that owns and develops MySQL is MySQL AB (the AB stands for *aktiebolag*, or stock company). Currently, MySQL AB estimates that there are more than 4 million installations of MySQL worldwide, and reports an average of 35,000 downloads a day of MySQL installation software from its site and from mirror sites. The success of MySQL as a leading database is due not only to its price—after all, other cost-free and open source databases are available—but also its reliability, performance, and features.

The Value of MySQL

Many features contribute to MySQL's standing as a superb database system. Its speed is one of its most prominent features. In a comparison by *eWEEK* of several databases—including MySQL, Oracle, MS SQL, IBM DB2, and Sybase ASE—MySQL and Oracle tied for best performance and for greatest scalability (see *http://www.mysql.com/it-resources/benchmarks* for more details). For a database long dismissed by many people, MySQL is remarkably scalable, and is able to handle tens of thousands of tables and billions of rows of data. Plus, it manages small amounts of data quickly and smoothly.

The storage engine, which manages queries and interfaces between a user's SQL commands and the database's backend storage, is the critical software in any database management system. MySQL offers several storage engines—previously called *table types*—with different advantages. Some are transaction-safe storage engines that allow for rollback of data. Additionally, MySQL has a tremendous number of built-in functions that are detailed in several chapters of this book.

MySQL is also very well-known for rapid and stable improvements. Whenever you visit MySQL AB's site to download MySQL, you will see a stable release that has been thoroughly tested. You will also see a distribution that has undergone testing, but contains components that have not been tested as thoroughly as the standard version. This version contains everything in the latest standard version plus new features that eventually will be rolled into the standard version. Each new release comes with speed and stability improvements, as well as new features.

The MySQL Package

The MySQL package comes with several programs. Foremost is the MySQL server, represented by the *mysqld* daemon. The daemon listens for requests on a particular port (3306 by default) by which clients submit queries. The standard MySQL client program is simply called *mysql*. With this text-based interface, a user can log in and execute SQL queries. This client can also accept queries from text files containing queries, and thereby execute them on behalf of the user or other software. However, most MySQL use is done by programs using a variety of languages. The interfaces for Perl, PHP, and C are discussed in this book.

A few wrapper scripts for *mysqld* come with MySQL. The mysqld_safe script is the most common way to start *mysqld*, because the script can restart the daemon if it crashes. This helps ensure minimal downtime for database services. The script mysqld_multi is used to start multiple sessions of mysqld_safe, and thereby multiple *mysqld* instances, for handling requests from different ports and different Unix socket files, and to make it easier to serve different sets of databases. For MS Windows NT and 2000 servers, there's mysqld-nt. It supports the named pipes that some Windows systems use instead of socket files.

MySQL also comes with a variety of utilities for managing a MySQL server. *mysqlaccess* is used for creating user accounts and setting their privileges. *mysqladmin* can be used to manage the MySQL server itself from the command line. This interaction includes checking a server's status and usage, and shutting down a server. *mysqlshow* may be used to examine a server's status, as well as information about databases and tables. Some of these utilities require Perl, or ActivePerl for Windows, to be installed on the server. See *http://www.perl.org* to download and install a copy of Perl on non-Windows systems, and *http://www.activestate.com/Products/ActivePerl* to download and install a copy of ActivePerl on Windows systems.

MySQL also comes with a few utilities for importing and exporting data from and to MySQL databases. *mysqldump* is the most popular for exporting data and table structures to a plain-text file known as a *dump* file. This can be used for backing up data or for manually moving it between servers. The *mysql* client can be used to import the data back to MySQL from a *dump* file.

mysqlhotcopy can also be used to back up a database or specific tables. It's more effective at data consistency between tables than *mysqldump*, because it locks the tables automatically. The resulting backup files are ready-to-use copies of the databases in the format MySQL uses. To restore them, you can just copy them to MySQL's data directory.

For importing data into MySQL from an external file that was exported in a common database format, MySQL provides *mysqlimport*.

Licensing

Although MySQL can be used for free and is open source, MySQL AB holds the copyrights to the source code. The company offers a dual-licensing program for its software: one allows cost-free use through the GPL under certain common circumstances, and the other is a commercial license bearing a fee. They're both the same software, but each has a different license and different privileges. See *http://www.fsf.org/licenses* for more details on the GPL.

MySQL AB allows you to use the software under the GPL if you use it without redistributing it, or if you redistribute it only with software licensed under the GPL. You can even use the GPL if you redistribute MySQL with software that you developed, as long as you distribute your software under the GPL as well.

However, if you have developed an application that requires MySQL for its functionality and you want to sell your software with MySQL under a nonfree license, you must purchase a commercial license from MySQL AB. There are other scenarios in which a commercial license may be required. For details on when you must purchase a license, see *http://www.mysql.com/company/legal/licensing*.

Besides holding the software copyrights, MySQL AB also holds the MySQL trademark. As a result, you cannot distribute software that includes MySQL in the name.

Mailing Lists

You can receive some assistance with problems that you may have with MySQL from the MySQL community at no charge through several listserv email systems hosted by MySQL AB. There is a main mailing list for MySQL (*mysql*) and several specialized mailing lists where anyone can post a message for help on a particular topic. One list covers questions about database performance (*benchmarks*). Another is for questions on the Windows versions of MySQL (*win32*). There are also lists for problems concerning the Java JDBC drivers (*java*) and for the Perl DBI module (*perl*).

For a complete listing or to subscribe to one or more of these mailing lists, go to *http://lists.mysql.com*. On this mailing list page, you will find links for subscribing to each list. When you click a subscription link, you will see a very simple form on which to enter your email address. Some subscribers, incidentally, like to use a special email address and name representing their online persona. It allows you anonymity and may make sorting emails easier. Others, however, prefer to use their real name and contact information. After you enter your email address, you will receive an automated message to confirm your address. That email will have a link to the MySQL site with some parameters identifying your address. Click the link, and it will open your web browser and confirm your subscription.

The page from which you can subscribe to a list also has links for unsubscribing from lists, as well as links to archives of previous listserv messages for each list. You can search these archives for messages from others who are describing the same problem that you are trying to resolve. It's always a good idea to search archives before posting anything of your own, to find out whether your topic has been discussed before. If you can't find a solution in the documentation available to you or in the archives, you can post a message to a particular mailing list by sending an email to that list on *lists.mysql.com*. For example, if you have a problem with the Perl DBI module in relation to MySQL, you would send a message to *perl@lists.mysql.com*. Just be sure to send the message from the email account that is registered with the list to which you're submitting your question.

Books and Other Publications

Besides the mailing list archives mentioned in the last section, MySQL AB provides extensive online documentation of the MySQL server and all of the other software it distributes. You can find documentation at *http://dev.mysql.com/doc*. You can read the material online or download it in a couple of formats (e.g., HTML or PDF). It is also available in hardcopy format: *MySQL Language Reference* and *MySQL Administrator's Guide*, both from MySQL Press.

In addition to this book, O'Reilly Media publishes a few other books on MySQL worth buying and reading. O'Reilly's mainline MySQL book is *Managing & Using MySQL* (2002) by George Reese, Randy Jay Yarger, and Tim King (with Hugh E. Williams). George Reese has compiled a smaller version called *MySQL Pocket Reference* (2003). For common practical problem solving, there's *MySQL Cookbook* (2002) by Paul DuBois. For advice on optimizing MySQL and performing administrative tasks, such as backing up databases, O'Reilly has published *High Performance MySQL* (2004) by Jeremy D. Zawodny and Derek J. Balling.

O'Reilly also publishes several books with regard to the MySQL application programming interfaces (APIs). For PHP development with MySQL, there's *Web Database Applications with PHP and MySQL* (2004) by Hugh E. Williams and David Lane. For interfacing with Perl to MySQL and other database systems, there's *Programming the Perl DBI* (2000) by Alligator Descartes and Tim Bunce. To interface to MySQL with Java, you can use the JDBC and JConnector drivers and George Reese's book, *Database Programming with JDBC and Java* (2002).

In addition to published books on MySQL, a few web sites offer brief tutorials on using MySQL topics. The O'Reilly Network often publishes articles on MySQL and the APIs for Perl, PHP, and Python in its online publication ONLamp.com (*http://www.onlamp.com/onlamp/general/mysql.csp*). Incidentally, I've contributed a few articles to that publication on MySQL and related topics. I've also written many articles on MySQL for my column on Unix Review.com (*http://www.unixreview.com/mysql*). MySQL AB also provides some in-depth articles on MySQL. You can find them at *http://dev.mysql.com/tech-resources/articles*. Many of these articles deal with new products and features, making them ideal if you want to learn about using the latest releases available even while they're still in the testing stages. Developer Shed (*http://www.devarticles.com/c/b/MySQL*) and Web Monkey (*http://search.hotwired.com/webmonkey/?query=mysql*) are additional educational resources. All of these online publications are subscription-free.

2

Installing MySQL

The MySQL database server and client software work on several different operating systems, notably Linux, FreeBSD, and a wide range of Unix systems: Sun Solaris, IBM AIX, HP-UX, and so on. MySQL AB has also developed a Mac OS X version, a Novell NetWare version, and several MS Windows versions. You can obtain a copy of MySQL from MySQL AB's site (*http://dev.mysql.com/downloads*) or from one of its mirror sites (*http://dev.mysql.com/downloads/mirrors.html*).

This chapter briefly explains the process of installing MySQL on Unix, Linux, Mac OS X, NetWare, and Windows operating systems. For some operating systems there are additional sections for different distribution formats. For any one platform, you can install MySQL by reading just three sections of this chapter: the next section, "Choosing a Distribution"; the section that applies to the distribution that you choose; and the "Postinstallation" section at the end of the chapter.

Choosing a Distribution

Before beginning to download an installation package, you must decide what version of MySQL to install. The best choice is usually the latest stable version recommended by MySQL AB on its site. It's not recommended that you install a newer version unless you need some new feature that is contained only in a newer version. It's also not recommended that you install an older version unless you have an existing database or an API application that won't function with the current version.

When installing MySQL, you also have the option of using either a source distribution or a binary distribution. It's easier, and recommended, for you to install a binary distribution. However, you may want to use a source distribution if special configuration must be performed during installation or at compile time. You may also have to use a source distribution if a binary distribution isn't available for your operating system.

For some distributions, you can download a Standard version, a Max version, or a Debug version. The Standard version is recommended for most users and developers, as it has been thoroughly tested.

Unix Source Distributions

The steps for installing MySQL on all Unix types of operating systems are basically the same. This includes Linux, Sun Solaris, FreeBSD, IBM AIX, HP-UX, etc. It's recommended that you install MySQL with a binary distribution, but as explained in the previous section, sometimes you may want to use a source distribution. To install a source distribution, you will need copies of GNU *gunzip*, GNU *tar*, GNU *gcc* (at least Version 2.95.2), and GNU *make*. These tools are usually included in all Linux systems and in most Unix systems. If your system doesn't have them, you can download them from the GNU Foundation's site (*http://www.gnu.org/*).

Once you've chosen and downloaded the source distribution files for MySQL, enter the following commands as *root* from the directory where you want the source files stored:

```
groupadd mysql
useradd -g mysql mysql
tar xvfz /tmp/mysql-version.tar.gz
cd mysql-version
```

The first command creates the user group *mysql*. The second creates the system user *mysql* and adds it to the group *mysql* at the same time. The next command uses the *tar* utility (along with *gunzip* via the *z* option) to unzip and unpack the source distribution file you downloaded. You should replace the word *version* with the version number—that is to say, you should use the actual path and filename of the installation file that you downloaded for the second argument of the *tar* command. The last command changes to the directory created by *tar* in the previous line. That directory contains the files needed to configure MySQL.

This brings you to the next step, which is to configure the source files to prepare them for building the binary programs. This is where you can add any special build requirements you may have. For instance, if you want to change the directory where MySQL is installed from the default, use the --prefix option with a value set to equal the desired directory. To set the Unix socket file's path, you can use --with-unix-socket-path. If you would like to use a different character set from the default of *latin1*, use --with-charset. Here is an example of how you might configure MySQL with these particular options before building the binary files:

```
./configure --prefix=/usr/local/mysql \
            --with-unix-socket-path=/tmp \
            --with-charset=latin2
```

You can also enter this command on one line without the backslashes.

Several other configuration options are available. To get a complete and current listing of options permitted, enter the following from the command line:

```
./configure --help
```

You may also want to look at the latest online documentation for compiling MySQL at *http://dev.mysql.com/doc/mysql/en/Compilation_problems.html*.

Once you've decided on any options that you want, run the configure script with these options. It will take quite a while to run, and it will display a great deal of information, which you can ignore usually if it ends successfully. After the configure script finishes, the binaries will need to be built and MySQL needs to be initialized. To do this, enter the following:

```
make
make install
cd /usr/local/mysql
./scripts/mysql_install_db
```

The first command builds the binary programs. If it's successful, you need to enter the second line to install the binary programs and related files in the appropriate directories. In the next line, you're changing to the directory where MySQL was installed. If you configured MySQL to be installed in a different directory, you'll have to use that one instead. The last command uses a script provided with the distribution to generate the initial privileges or grant tables.

All that remains now is to change the ownership of the MySQL programs and directories. You can do this by entering the following:

```
chown -R mysql /usr/local/mysql
chgrp -R mysql /usr/local/mysql
```

The first command changes ownership of the MySQL directories and programs to the *mysql* user. The second command changes the group owner of the same directory and files to *mysql*. These file paths may be different depending on the version of MySQL you installed and whether you configured MySQL for different paths.

With the programs installed and their file ownerships properly set, you can start MySQL. You can do this in several ways. To make sure that the daemon is restarted in the event that it crashes, enter the following from the command line:

```
/usr/local/mysql/bin/mysqld_safe &
```

This starts the *mysqld_safe* daemon, which will in turn start the MySQL server *mysqld*. If the *mysqld* daemon crashes, *mysqld_safe* will restart it. The ampersand at the end of the line instructs the shell to run the daemon in the background.

To have MySQL started at boot time, copy the *mysql.server* file, located in the *support-files* subdirectory of */usr/local/mysql*, to the */etc/init.d* directory. To do this, enter the following from the command line:

```
cp support-files/mysql.server /etc/init.d/mysql
chmod +x /etc/init.d/mysql
chkconfig --add mysql
```

The first line follows a convention of placing the startup file for the server in the server's initial daemons directory with the name *mysql*. The second command makes the file executable. The third sets the run level of the service for startup and shutdown.

Now that MySQL is installed and running, you need to make some postinstallation adjustments that are explained in the last section of this chapter.

Unix Binary Distributions

Installing MySQL with a binary distribution is easier than using a source distribution and is the recommended choice if a binary distribution is available for your platform. The files are packaged together into an archive file and then compressed before being placed on the Internet for downloading. Therefore, you will need a copy of GNU *tar* and GNU *gunzip* to be able to unpack the installation files. These tools are usually included on all Linux systems and most Unix systems. If your system doesn't have them, though, you can download them from the GNU Foundation's site (*http://www.gnu.org*).

Once you've chosen and downloaded the installation package, enter something like the following from the command line as *root* to begin the MySQL installation process:

```
groupadd mysql
useradd -g mysql mysql
cd /usr/local
tar xvfz /tmp/mysql-version.tar.gz
```

The first command creates the user group *mysql*. The second creates the user *mysql* and adds it to the group *mysql* at the same time. The next command changes to the directory where the MySQL files are about to be extracted. In the last command, you use the *tar* utility (along with *gunzip* via the *z* option) to unzip and unpack the source distribution file that you downloaded. The word "version" in the name of the installation file is replaced with the version number—that is to say, use the actual path and name of the installation file that you downloaded as the second argument of the *tar* command. For Sun Solaris systems, you should use *gtar* instead of *tar*.

After running the previous commands, you need to create a symbolic link to the directory created by *tar* in */usr/local*:

```
ln -s /usr/local/mysql-version /usr/local/mysql
```

This creates */usr/local/mysql* as a link to */usr/local/mysql-version*, where *mysql-version* is the actual name of the subdirectory that *tar* created in */usr/local*. The link is necessary, because MySQL is expecting the software to be located in */usr/local/mysql* and the data to be in */usr/local/mysql/data* by default.

At this point, MySQL is basically installed. Now you must generate the initial privileges or grant tables, and change the file ownership of the MySQL programs and datafiles. To do these tasks, enter the following from the command line:

```
cd /usr/local/mysql
./scripts/mysql_install_db
chown -R mysql /usr/local/mysql
chgrp -R mysql /usr/local/mysql
```

The first command changes to the directory containing MySQL's files. The second command uses a script provided with the distribution to generate the initial privileges or grant tables, which consist of the *mysql* database with MySQL's *root* user. The third command changes the ownership of the MySQL directories and programs to the *mysql* user. The last command changes the group owner of the same directory and files to *mysql*.

With the programs installed and their ownerships properly set, you can start MySQL. This can be done in several ways. To make sure that the daemon is restarted in the event that it crashes, enter the following from the command line:

```
/usr/local/mysql/bin/mysqld_safe &
```

The *mysqld_safe* daemon, started by this command, will in turn start the MySQL server *mysqld*. If the *mysqld* daemon crashes, *mysqld_safe* will restart it. The ampersand at the end of the line instructs the shell to run the command in the background.

To have MySQL started at boot time, copy the *mysql.server* file located in the *support-files* subdirectory of */usr/local/mysql*, to the */etc/init.d* directory. To do this, enter the following from the command line:

```
cp support-files/mysql.server /etc/init.d/mysql
chmod +x /etc/init.d/mysql
chkconfig --add mysql
```

The first line follows a convention of placing the startup file for the server in the server's initial daemons directory with the name *mysql*. The second command makes the file executable. The third sets the run level of the service for startup and shutdown.

Now that MySQL is installed and running, you need to make some postinstallation adjustments that are explained in the last section of this chapter.

Linux RPM Distributions

If your server is running on a version of Linux that installs software through the RPM package format (where RPM originally stood for RedHat Package Manager), it is recommended that you use a package instead of a source distribution. The differences between RPM versions are based not on the Linux distribution (e.g., SuSE or Mandrake), but on the Linux kernel or the type of libraries installed on the server. For each version of MySQL, there are a few RPM files that you can download. The primary two contain the server and client files. Their naming scheme is *MySQL-server-version.rpm* and *MySQL-client-version.rpm*, where *version* is the actual version number. In addition to these main packages, you may also want to install some of the other RPM files that are part of a distribution. There's an RPM for client-shared libraries (*MySQL-shared-version.rpm*), another for libraries and C API include files for certain clients (*MySQL-devel-version.rpm*), and another for benchmarking and other MySQL performance tests (*MySQL-bench-version.rpm*).

To install the RPM files after downloading them to your server, enter something like the following from the command line in the directory where they're located:

```
rpm -ivh MySQL-server-version.rpm \
       MySQL-client-version.rpm
```

If an earlier version of MySQL is already installed on the server, you will receive an error message stating this problem, and the installation will be canceled. If you want to upgrade the existing installation, you can replace the *i* option in the example with an uppercase "U."

When the RPM files are installed, the *mysqld* daemon will be started or restarted automatically. Once MySQL is installed and running, you need to make some postinstallation adjustments that are explained in the last section of this chapter.

Macintosh OS X Distributions

On recent versions of Mac OS X, MySQL is usually installed already. However, in case it is not installed on your system or you want to upgrade your copy of MySQL by installing the latest release, directions are included here.

As of Version 10.2 of Mac OS X and Version 4.0.11 of MySQL, binary package (PKG) files are available for installing MySQL. If your server is using an older version of Mac OS X, you need to install MySQL using a Unix source or binary distribution, following the directions described earlier in this chapter for those particular packages.

If an older version of MySQL is already installed on your server, you will need to shut down the MySQL service before installing and running the newer version. You can do this with the *MySQL Manager Application*, which is a graphical user interface (GUI) application. It's typically installed on recent versions of Mac OS X by default. If your server doesn't have the MySQL Manager Application, enter the following from the command line to shut down the MySQL service:

```
mysqladmin -u root shutdown
```

Incidentally, if MySQL isn't already installed on your system, you may need to create the system user, *mysql*, before installing MySQL.

To install the MySQL package file, use the *Finder* utility to locate the disk image file (the *.dmg* file) that you downloaded, and mount it by double-clicking it. This reveals the disk image file's contents. Look for the PKG icon, and double-click it to begin the installation program. The installer will take you through the installation steps from there. The default settings are recommended for most users and developers.

Once you've finished installing MySQL, start the service by entering the following from the command line:

```
sudo /usr/local/mysql/bin/mysqld_safe
[Ctrl-z]
bg
```

On the second line, hold down the Ctrl key and then press the Z key. Finally enter **bg** to send the daemon's process to the background.

To have MySQL started at boot time, add a *StartupItem*. Within the disk image file that you downloaded, you should see an icon labeled *MySQLStartupItem.pkg*. Just double-click it, and it will create a *StartupItem* for MySQL. Once it's created, instead of using the method shown previously to start the service, enter the following from the command line:

```
sudo /Library/StartupItems/MySQL/MySQL start
```

Once MySQL is installed and running, you need to make some postinstallation adjustments that are explained in the last section of this chapter.

Novell NetWare Distributions

If your server is using Novell NetWare 6.0 or above, and the required Novell support packs have been installed, you can install MySQL on it. For Version 6.0 of NetWare, you need to have Support Pack 4 installed and updated along with the current version of LibC. For Version 6.5 of NetWare, Support Pack 2 needs to be installed and updated along with the current version of LibC. You can obtain support packs from Novell's site (*http://support.novell.com*). You can find the latest version of LibC at *http://developer.novell.com/ndk/libc.htm*. Another requirement for installing MySQL is that the MySQL server and data be installed on an NSS volume.

If an older version of MySQL is already installed and running on your server, you need to shut down the MySQL service before installing and running the newer version. You can do this from the server console like so:

```
mysqladmin -u root shutdown
```

Next you need to log on to the server from a client that has access to the location (SYS:MYSQL) where MySQL is to be installed. Unpack the compressed binary package to that location. When the zip file has finished unpacking, you can establish a search path for the directory that holds the MySQL NLM's by entering the following from the server console:

```
SEARCH ADD SYS:MYSQL\BIN
```

At this point, MySQL is basically installed. Now you need to generate the initial privileges or grant tables. You can do this by entering the following from the server console:

```
.\scripts\mysql_install_db
```

The *mysql_install_db* utility is a script provided with the distribution to generate the initial privileges or grant tables (i.e., the *mysql* database). Once this is done, MySQL is ready to be started. To do this, just enter the following from the server console:

```
mysqld_safe
```

To have MySQL started at boot time, you must add the following lines to the server's *autoexec.ncf* file:

```
SEARCH ADD SYS:MYSQL\BIN
MYSQLD_SAFE --autoclose --skip-external-locking
```

The first line establishes the search path for MySQL. The second line starts the *mysqld_safe* daemon at startup. The first option in this command instructs the server to close MySQL automatically when the server shuts down. The second option instructs the server not to allow external table locking. External locks can cause problems with NetWare Version 6.0. Both of these options are recommended.

Now that MySQL is installed and running, you need to make some postinstallation adjustments that are explained in the last section of this chapter.

Windows Distributions

Installing MySQL on a server using Windows is fairly easy. If MySQL is already installed and running on your server, and you want to install a newer version, you will need to shut down the existing one first. For server versions of MS Windows (e.g., Windows NT), MySQL is installed as a service. If it's installed as a service on your server, you can enter the following from a DOS command window to shut down the service and remove it:

```
mysqld -remove
```

If MySQL is running, but not as a service, you can enter the following from a DOS command window to shut it down:

```
msyqladmin -u root shutdown
```

MySQL AB's site contains three installation packages: a Windows Essential package, a standard Windows package, and a standard Windows package without the installer. The Windows Essential package is the recommended format. It contains only the essential files for running MySQL. This includes the usual command-line utilities and the header files for the C API. The standard Windows package contains the essential files, as well as documentation, the MySQL Administrator, the embedded server, the benchmark suite, and a few other useful scripts. The standard Windows package without the installer contains the same binary files and other related files for MySQL, but not an installer. You'll need to extract and copy the files into the *c:\mysql* directory. Then you must create a *my.ini* file in the *c:\windows* directory. Several examples showing different server usage come with the distribution package.

The Windows Essential package is a file called *MySQL-version.msi*. From the Windows desktop, just double-click this file's icon and the Windows Installer program will start.

The standard Windows installation package is a compressed file from which you have to extract the installation files. To do this, you need a utility such as WinZip (*http://www.winzip.com*) to uncompress the files. One of the files is named *setup.exe*. Double-click it to start the installer for this package. From this point, the installation process is pretty much the same for the packages that use the installer.

Once you've started the installer, a dialog box appears that offers you three general choices. The *Typical* choice is the recommended one, but it will omit the installation of C API include files and other client libraries. For the standard Windows package, this choice will also omit installation of the embedded server, the benchmark suite, and several other scripts. The *Complete* installation choice instructs the installer to install everything that's included in the distribution package that you downloaded. The *Custom* choice allows you to choose from a list of programs and libraries to install. On the same screen is a button labeled *Change* that lets you change the directory in which MySQL will be installed. Older versions of MySQL use *c:\mysql* as the default. Recent versions install MySQL by default in directories like *c:\Program Files\MySQL\MySQL Server version*, where the word *version* is replaced with the version number.

After you choose what to install and where, the files are installed. When the installer is finished, the MySQL Server Instance Configuration Wizard is started. It asks you a series of questions to create a server configuration file (*my.ini*), which, by default, is stored in *c:\windows*. The questions are based on the intended usage of the MySQL server, and your answers determine the contents of the configuration file. You will also be allowed to change the default location of the datafiles, the TCP/IP port used, and a couple of other settings.

To invoke the command-line utilities without having to enter the file path to the directory containing them, enter the following from the command line:

```
PATH=%PATH%;c:\Program Files\MySQL\MySQL Server version\bin
```

You should replace the word *version* with the version number—that is to say, you should enter the path to the MySQL installation. If you changed location when you installed MySQL, you need to use the path that you named. Older versions of Windows may not accept long directory names in the startup file. Therefore, you may need to abbreviate the line shown previously so that it looks something like this:

```
PATH=%PATH%;c:\Program~1\MySQL\MySQLS~1.1\bin
```

The characters ~1 are substituted for the extra characters of a directory name that follow the first seven characters. An S is substituted for any space that occurs in the first seven characters of a directory name. If the directory name ends in a dot and more characters, the last dot and characters are given. For example, a directory named "MySQL Server 4.1" would be entered as "MySQLS~1.1," as shown in the previous command. To make this new path available at boot time, you may want to add it to the *c:\autoexec.bat file*.

Once you've finished installing MySQL and you've set up the configuration file, the installer will start the MySQL server automatically. If you've installed MySQL manually without an installer, enter something like the following from a DOS command window:

```
mysqld-nt --install
net start mysql
```

All that remains are some postinstallation adjustments that are explained in the next section.

Postinstallation

After you've finished installing MySQL on your server, you should perform a few tasks before allowing others to begin using the service. You may want to configure the server differently by making changes to the configuration file. At a minimum, you should change the password for the *root* user and add some nonadministrative users. MySQL is initially set up with anonymous users. You should delete them. This section will briefly explain these tasks.

Although the MySQL developers have set the server daemon to the recommended configuration, you may want to set the daemon differently. For instance, you may want to turn on error logging. To do this, you will need to edit the main configuration file for MySQL. On Unix systems, this file is */etc/my.cnf*. On Windows systems, the main configuration file is usually either *c:\windows\my.ini* or *c:\my.cnf*. The configuration file is a simple text file that you can edit with a plain-text editor, not a word processor. The configuration file is organized into sections or groups under a heading name contained in square brackets. For instance, settings for the server daemon *mysqld* are listed under the group heading [mysqld]. Under this heading you could add something like log = /var/log/mysql to enable logging and to set the directory for the log files to the one given. You can list many options in the file for a particular group. For a complete listing and explanation of these options, see Chapter 10.

You can change the password for the *root* user in MySQL in a few ways. One simple way is to log in to MySQL through the *mysql* client by entering the following from the command line:

```
mysql -u root -p
```

On a Windows system, you may have to add the path *c:\mysql\bin* to the beginning of this line, if you haven't added it to your command path. After successfully entering the command, you will be prompted for the *root* user's password. This is not the operating system's *root* user, but the *root* user for MySQL. Initially there is no password, so press Enter to leave it blank. If everything was installed properly and if the *mysqld* daemon is running, you should get a prompt like this:

```
mysql>
```

This is the prompt for the *mysql* client interface or MySQL monitor. To change the *root* user's password, enter the following at this prompt:

```
SET PASSWORD FOR root@localhost=PASSWORD('password');
SET PASSWORD FOR root@host=PASSWORD('password');
```

Replace the word *password* in quotes with the password that you want to use for *root*. There are two lines here, because typically there are two entries for the *root* user: one with the localhost and another with the system's hostname. On Windows the wildcard % is used instead of this second account, to allow *root* login from any host. After you change these passwords, you need to log out of the *mysql* client and log back in with the new password.

The next security measure to take regarding MySQL users is to delete the anonymous users. You can do this by entering the following from the *mysql* client:

```
DELETE FROM mysql.user WHERE User='';
DELETE FROM mysql.db WHERE User='';
FLUSH PRIVILEGES;
```

The first two commands delete any anonymous users from the *user* and *db* tables in the database called *mysql*—that's where the privileges or grant tables are stored. The last line resets the server privileges to reflect these changes.

The next step regarding users is to set up at least one user for general use. It's best not to use the *root* user for general database management. When you set up a new user, you should consider which privileges to allow the user. If you want to set up a user that can only view data, you should enter something like the following from the *mysql* client:

```
GRANT SELECT ON *.* TO tina IDENTIFIED BY 'muller';
```

In this line, the user is *tina* and her password is *muller*. If you want to give a user more than viewing privileges, you should add additional privileges to the SELECT command, separated by commas. To give a user all privileges, replace SELECT with ALL. Here's another example using the ALL flag:

```
GRANT ALL ON db1.* TO tina IDENTIFIED BY 'muller';
```

In this example, the user *tina* has all basic privileges, but only for the *db1* database. This statement adds the user *tina* to the table *user* in the *mysql* database, if there is already a row for her in it, but with no privileges. It will also add a row to the *db* table in the *mysql* database indicating that *tina* has all privileges for the *db1* database. See the explanation of GRANT in Chapter 4 for more options.

If you have any existing MySQL datafiles from another system, you can copy the actual files to the directory where MySQL data is stored on your server. Just be sure to change the ownership of the files to the *mysql* user and *mysql* group with the *chown* system command after you copy them to the appropriate directory. If your existing datafiles are dump files created by the *mysqldump* utility, see the explanation regarding that utility in Chapter 11. If your data needs to be converted from a text file, see the explanation of the LOAD DATA INFILE statement in Chapter 4. You probably should also check the online documentation (*http://dev.mysql.com/doc/mysql/en/Upgrade.html*) on upgrading from a previous version to a current one, especially if you are migrating across major versions.

With the MySQL installation software downloaded and installed and all of the binary files and data in their place and properly set, MySQL is now ready to use.

3

MySQL Basics

While the bulk of *MySQL in a Nutshell* contains reference information, which you can read in small segments as needed, this chapter presents a basic tutorial on MySQL. It explains how to log in to the MySQL server, create databases, and enter and manipulate data within them. This tutorial does not cover everything about MySQL. Instead, it's more of a sampler; it's meant to show you what's possible and to get you thinking about how to approach tasks in MySQL.

The mysql Client

There are various methods for interacting with the MySQL server and, thereby, developing or working with a database. The most basic interface that you can use, though, is the *mysql* client. With it, you may interact with the server from either the command line or what is sometimes called the monitor.

If MySQL was installed properly on your server, *mysql* should be available to run. If not see Chapter 2. If you used the default installation method, the *mysql* program resides at */usr/local/mysql/bin/mysql*. On Unix systems, be sure that *mysql* is in your path by typing:

```
PATH=$PATH:/usr/local/mysql/bin
export PATH
```

Assuming that everything is working, you will also need a MySQL username and an accompanying password. If you're not the administrator, you must obtain these from her. If MySQL was just installed and the *root* password is not set yet, its password is blank. See Chapter 2 to learn how to set passwords, and to create new users and grant them privileges.

From a shell prompt, log in to MySQL like so:

```
mysql -h host -u user -p
```

If you're logging in locally—that is to say, from the server itself—either physically or through a remote login method, such as Telnet or the SSH secure shell, you can omit the *-h host* argument. This is because the default host is *localhost*, which refers to the system you are on. In other circumstances, where your commands actually have to travel over a network to reach the server, replace the argument *host* with either a hostname that is translatable to an IP address or the actual IP address of the MySQL server.

You should replace the argument *user* with your username. The *-p* option instructs *mysql* to prompt you for a password. You can also add the password to the end of the *-p* option (e.g., enter *-prover* where *rover* is the password); there's no space between *-p* and the password. However, entering the password on the command line is not a good security practice, because it displays the password on the screen and it transmits the password as clear text through the network, as well as making it visible whenever somebody gets a list of processes running on the machine.

To exit *mysql*, type **quit** or **exit**, and press the Enter key.

Creating a Database and Tables

Assuming that you have all of the privileges necessary to create and modify databases on your server, let's look at how to create a database and then tables within a database. For the examples in this chapter, we will build a database for a fictitious bookstore:

```
CREATE DATABASE bookstore;
```

In this brief SQL statement, we have created a database called *bookstore*. You may have noticed that the commands or reserved words are printed here in uppercase letters. This isn't necessary; MySQL is case-insensitive with regards to reserved words for SQL statements and clauses. Database and table names are case-sensitive on operating systems that are case-sensitive, such as Unix systems, but not on systems that are case-insensitive, such as Windows. As a general convention, though, reserved words in SQL documentation are presented in uppercase letters and database names, table names, and column names in lowercase letters.

You may have also noticed that this SQL statement ends with a semicolon. An SQL statement may be entered over more than one line, and it's not until the semicolon is entered that the client sends the statement to the server to read and process it. To cancel an SQL statement once it's started, enter **\c** instead of a semicolon.

With our database created, we can switch the default database for the session to the new database like so:

```
USE bookstore;
```

Next, we will create our first table, in which we will later add data. We'll start by creating a table to contain basic information on books, because that's at the core of a bookstore's business:

```
CREATE TABLE books (
  rec_id INT,
  title VARCHAR(50),
  author VARCHAR(50)
);
```

This SQL statement creates the table *books* with three columns. The first column is a simple identification number for each record. It has an integer type. Incidentally, fields are referred to as *columns* and records as *rows* in MySQL. The datatype for the second and third columns consists of character fields of variable widths—up to 50 characters each. Notice that the list of columns is contained within parentheses.

To see the results of the table we just created, enter a DESCRIBE statement, which displays a table as output:

```
DESCRIBE books;
```

```
+--------+-------------+------+-----+---------+-------+
| Field  | Type        | Null | Key | Default | Extra |
+--------+-------------+------+-----+---------+-------+
| rec_id | int(11)     | YES  |     | NULL    |       |
| title  | varchar(50) | YES  |     | NULL    |       |
| author | varchar(50) | YES  |     | NULL    |       |
+--------+-------------+------+-----+---------+-------+
```

Looking at the resulting table, we realize that we need to add a few more columns for data elements: publisher, publication year, ISBN number, genre (i.e., novel, poetry, drama), description of book, etc. We also realize that we want MySQL to automatically assign a number to the *rec_id* column so that we don't have to bother creating one for each row or worry about duplicates. Additionally, we've decided to change the *author* column from the actual author's name to an identification number that we'll join to a separate table containing a list of authors. This will reduce typing, and will make sorting and searching easier, as the data will be uniform. To make these alterations to the table that we've already created, enter the following SQL statement:

```
ALTER TABLE books
CHANGE COLUMN rec_id rec_id INT AUTO_INCREMENT PRIMARY KEY,
CHANGE COLUMN author author_id INT,
ADD COLUMN description BLOB,
ADD COLUMN genre ENUM('novel','poetry','drama'),
ADD COLUMN publisher_id INT,
ADD COLUMN pub_year VARCHAR(4),
ADD COLUMN isbn VARCHAR(20);
```

After the opening line of this SQL statement, notice that each clause in which we change or add a column is separated from the following one by a comma. On the second line here, we're changing the *rec_id* column. Even though we are keeping the column name and the datatype the same, we have to restate them. We're adding the AUTO_INCREMENT flag, which carries out the task mentioned in the previous paragraph, assigning a unique and arbitrary value to each book in the table. We're also making the column the PRIMARY KEY for indexing, which allows faster data retrieval.

In the third line, we're also changing the *author* column so that its label and datatype align with the *authors* table that we'll create later. The *authors* table will have an indexed column to which we will join in queries. Because that column will have a datatype of integer, so must this one.

The fourth line adds a column for each book's description. This has a datatype of BLOB, which stands for "binary large object." A BLOB is a variable-length datatype that can hold very large amounts of data, up to 64 kilobytes. There are other datatypes that will hold even more data. See Appendix A for a list of datatypes and their limits.

For *genre*, we're enumerating a list of possible values to ensure uniformity. A blank value and a NULL value are also possible, although they're not specified in the command.

Before moving on to adding data to our *books* table, let's quickly set up the *authors* table. The *authors* table will be what is known as a reference table. We need to set it up first, because when we enter data into the *books* table, we will need to know the identification number for the authors of the books:

```
CREATE TABLE authors
(rec_id INT AUTO_INCREMENT PRIMARY KEY,
author_last VARCHAR(50),
author_first VARCHAR(50),
country VARCHAR(50));
```

This table doesn't require too many columns, although we might add other columns to it for an actual bookstore. As mentioned before, we'll join the *books* table to the *authors* table through the *author_id* in the *books* table and the *rec_id* in this table. My style is to name the key column (*rec_id*) of each table the same so that when I'm entering queries, I can easily remember their names without having to enter a DESCRIBE statement for each table.

In this table, we've separated the first and last name of the author into two columns so that we can easily sort on the last name, and search on it. We've also added a column for the author's country of origin so that we can search for works by authors of a particular country when asked by customers.

Show Me

Let's take a moment to admire our work and see what we've done so far. To get a list of databases, use the SHOW DATABASES statement like so:

```
SHOW DATABASES;

+-----------+
| Database  |
+-----------+
| bookstore |
| mysql     |
| test      |
+-----------+
```

The result of the SHOW DATABASES statement lists not only the database that we've created, but also two others. One is the *mysql* database, which contains data on user privileges. This was covered in Chapter 2. The third one listed is the *test* database, which is set up by default when MySQL is installed. It's there as a convenience for you to be able to add tables or run SQL statements for testing.

To see a list of tables in the *bookstore* database, once we select the *bookstore* database with the USE statement shown earlier, we would enter the following statement:

```
SHOW TABLES;
```

```
+--------------------+
| Tables_in_bookstore |
+--------------------+
| authors            |
| books              |
+--------------------+
```

The result of the SHOW TABLES statement provides a list containing our two tables, just as we expected. If you want to see a list of tables from another database while still using the *bookstore* database, add a FROM clause to the previous statement:

```
USE bookstore;
SHOW TABLES FROM mysql;
```

This displays a list of tables from the *mysql* database while still anchoring the client in the *bookstore* database.

Inserting Data

Now that we've set up our first two tables, let's look at how we can add data to them. We'll start with the simplest method: the INSERT statement. With INSERT, we can add one or more records at a time. Before adding information on a book to our *books* table, because it refers to a field in our *authors* table, we need to add the author's information to the latter. We'll do this by entering these SQL statements through the *mysql* client:

```
INSERT INTO authors
(author_last, author_first, country)
VALUES('Vernon','Olympia','USA');
```

After adding an entry for the author, we can insert an entry for the book:

```
INSERT INTO books
(title, author_id, isbn, genre, pub_year)
VALUES('Eden', LAST_INSERT_ID( ),'0802117287','novel','2003');
```

With the first SQL statement, we've added a record or row for Olympia Vernon, an author I love who wrote the book *Eden*. The standard INSERT syntax is to name the columns for which the values are to be inserted, as we're doing here. If you're going to enter values for all of the columns, you don't need to name the columns. In the second SQL statement, we've listed the columns in an order that's different from their order in the table. That's acceptable to MySQL; we just have to be sure that our values are in the same order. We are getting the *author_id* number for the row just inserted in the previous statement by using the LAST_INSERT_ID( ) function.

Selecting Data

Now that we have one row of data in each of our two tables, let's run some queries. We'll use the SELECT statement to select the data that we want. To get all of the columns and rows from the *books* table, enter the following:

```
SELECT * FROM books;
```

The asterisk, which acts as a wildcard, selects all columns. We did not specify any criteria by which specific rows are selected, so all rows are displayed from the *books* table. To select specific columns and rows, we name the columns we want and add a WHERE clause to the end of our SELECT statement:

```
SELECT rec_id, title, description
FROM books
WHERE genre = 'novel';
```

This SQL statement displays just the record identification number, the book's title, and the description of the book from the *books* table for all books where the *genre* column has a value of *novel*. The results will be more meaningful, of course, when we have data on more books in the database. So, let's assume that we've entered data for a few dozen more books, and proceed.

If we want to get a list of novels from the database along with the author's full name, we need to join the *books* table to the *authors* table. We can join the two tables like this:

```
SELECT books.rec_id, title, pub_year,
       CONCAT(author_first, ' ', author_last) AS author
FROM books, authors
WHERE author_last = 'Vernon'
   AND author_id = authors.rec_id;
```

Both tables have columns called *rec_id*, so we need to specify the table to which we're referring whenever we refer to *rec_id* and are joining both tables. We do this by inserting the name of the table followed by a dot as a separator and then the column name. You can see an example of this in the first line, where we're selecting the record identification number for each book. Notice also in the second line that we've employed a string function, CONCAT( ). With this function you can take bits of data and merge them together with text to form more desirable-looking output. In this case, we're taking the author's first name and pasting a space (in quotes) onto the end of it, and then the author's last name onto the end of that. The results will appear in the output display as one column, which we've given a column heading of *author*, as an alias using the keyword AS. In the FROM clause, we've named both tables, separated by a comma. If we had more tables that we wanted to string together, we would just add them to this comma-separated list in any order. In the WHERE clause, we've specified that we want data on books written by authors with the last name "Vernon" and where we're able to join a row for a book to a row for an author. The joining point for this SQL statement is in the last line: we're joining the *author_id* from *books* to the *rec_id* in *authors*. If the table did not contain books by Olympia Vernon, nothing would be displayed. If it did, but we had failed to enter a row of data for her in the *authors* table, we would not have a successful match between the two tables, and nothing would be displayed. The results of the previous query are as follows:

```
+--------+-------+----------+----------------+
| rec_id | title | pub_year | author         |
+--------+-------+----------+----------------+
|      1 | Eden  | 2003     | Olympia Vernon |
|      2 | Logic | 2003     | Olympia Vernon |
+--------+-------+----------+----------------+
```

As you can see, a second book by Olympia Vernon was found and both have been displayed. The column heading was changed for the output of the author's name per the AS. We could change the column headings in the display for the other columns with the keyword AS, as well. The *author* alias can be reused in a SELECT statement, but not in the WHERE clause, unfortunately. You can find more information on AS in Chapter 4.

Ordering, Limiting, and Grouping

For times when we retrieve a long list of data, it can be tidier to sort the data output in a specific order. To do this, we can use the ORDER BY clause. Suppose that we want a list of plays written by William Shakespeare from our database. We could enter the following SQL statement to retrieve such a list and to sort the data by the play title:

```
SELECT books.rec_id, title, publisher
FROM books, authors, publishers
WHERE author_last = 'Shakespeare'
    AND genre = 'play'
    AND author_id = authors.rec_id
    AND publisher_id = publishers.rec_id
ORDER BY title, pub_year;
```

The ORDER BY clause comes at the end, after the WHERE clause. First, we're ordering the data results by the *title* column and then, within *title*, by the *pub_year* column, or the year that the particular printing of the play was published. By default, data is sorted in ascending alphanumeric order. If we want to order the results in descending order for the titles, we can just add a DESC flag immediately after the *title* column in the ORDER BY clause and before the comma that precedes *pub_year*.

A large bookstore will have many editions of Shakespeare's plays, possibly a few different printings for each play. If we want to limit the number of records displayed, we could add a LIMIT clause to the end of the previous SQL statement like so:

```
SELECT books.rec_id, title
FROM books, authors, publishers
WHERE author_last = 'Shakespeare'
    AND genre = 'play'
    AND author_id = authors.rec_id
    AND publisher_id = publishers.rec_id
ORDER BY title, pub_year
LIMIT 20;
```

This addition will limit the number of rows displayed to the first 20. The count starts from the first row of the result set after the data has been ordered according to the ORDER BY clause. If we want to retrieve the next 10, we would adjust the LIMIT clause to specify the number of rows to skip, along with the number of records to retrieve. So, if we want to skip the first 20 rows and list the next 10 rows from our sort, we would replace the LIMIT clause in the SQL statement with this one:

```
...
LIMIT 20, 10;
```

As you can see, in a two-argument clause, the first argument specifies the number of rows to skip or the point to begin (i.e., 20) and the second argument states the number of rows to display (i.e., 10).

If we want to get just a list of titles by Shakespeare, and we are not concerned with which printing or publisher—that is to say, if we want one row for each title and are satisfied with the first row found for each—we could use the GROUP BY clause like so:

```
SELECT books.rec_id, title
FROM books, authors
WHERE author_last = 'Shakespeare'
    AND author_id = authors.rec_id
GROUP BY title;
```

The result of this SQL statement is a list of titles by Shakespeare from the database, with the record identification number displayed for the first one found for each title. Incidentally, GROUP BY will return the same data as ORDER BY on the same column.

Analyzing and Manipulating Data

With MySQL you can not only retrieve raw data, but also analyze and format the data retrieved. For instance, suppose we want to know how many titles we stock by Tolstoy. We could enter a SELECT statement containing a COUNT( ) function like this:

```
SELECT COUNT(*)
FROM books, authors
WHERE author_last = 'Tolstoy'
    AND author_id = authors.rec_id;

+----------+
| COUNT(*) |
+----------+
|       12 |
+----------+
```

As another example, suppose that after setting up our database and putting it to use we have another table called *orders* that contains information on customer orders. We can query that table to find the total sales of a particular book. For instance, to find the total revenues generated from, say, William Boyd's book *Armadillo*, we would enter the following SQL statement in the *mysql* client:

```
SELECT SUM(sale_amount) AS 'Armadillo Sales'
FROM orders, books, authors
```

```
WHERE  title = 'Armadillo'
   AND author_last = 'Boyd'
   AND book_id = books.rec_id
   AND author_id = authors.rec_id;
```

```
+-----------------+
| Armadillo Sales |
+-----------------+
|          250.25 |
+-----------------+
```

Here we are joining three tables together to retrieve the desired information. MySQL is selecting the value of the *sale_amount* column from each row in the *orders* table that matches the criteria of the WHERE clause. Then it adds those numbers and displays the sum with the column heading given. Most column names appear in only one table, so MySQL knows what we mean even if we don't specify the table each column is in; for a couple of columns we need to use the *table.column* format.

For columns that contain date or time information, we can format how the data is displayed using a variety of functions. For instance, suppose that we want to extract from the *orders* table the date that a customer made a particular purchase based on his receipt number (e.g., 1250), which in turn is the record identification number or *rec_id*. We could simply enter the following statement and get the default format as shown in the last line of results:

```
SELECT purchase_date AS 'Purchase Date'
FROM orders
WHERE rec_id = '1250';
```

```
+---------------+
| Purchase Date |
+---------------+
| 2004-03-01    |
+---------------+
```

This format (year-month-day) is understandable. However, if we want the month displayed in English rather than numerically, we would have to use a date function:

```
SELECT CONCAT(MONTHNAME(purchase_date), ' ',
       DAYOFMONTH(purchase_date), ', ',
       YEAR(purchase_date)) AS 'Purchase Date'
FROM orders
WHERE rec_id = '1250';
```

```
+---------------+
| Purchase Date |
+---------------+
| March 1, 2004 |
+---------------+
```

To put the date together in a typical human format used in the United States, we're using the CONCAT( ) function in conjunction with a few date functions. It may be a little confusing at first glance, because we're inserting a space between the month and the day at the end of the first line and a comma and a space after the day at the end of the second line. As for the date functions, the first one extracts the month from the *purchase_date* column and formats it to display it as the full name. The second date function on the second line extracts just the day so that we can put spaces around it and a comma after it. The third date function on the third line extracts just the year. As you can see in the results, this works. However, it's not the cleanest method by which the date can be assembled. We could use the DATE_FORMAT( ) function instead:

```
SELECT DATE_FORMAT(purchase_date, "%M %d, %Y")
       AS 'Purchase Date'
FROM orders
WHERE rec_id = '1250';
```

This is a much more efficient method and it provides the same output as the previous statement. You just have to know the formatting codes to be able to use this function properly. They're listed in Chapter 6, along with several more formatting codes.

Changing Data

You can change data in a database using a few different methods. The most basic and perhaps the most common method is to use the UPDATE statement. With an UPDATE statement, you can change data for all rows or for specific records based on a WHERE clause. Looking back on the results displayed from an earlier query, we can see that Olympia Vernon's book *Logic* has a copyright year of 2003. That's not correct; it should read 2004. To change or update that bit of information, enter the following SQL statement:

```
UPDATE books
SET pub_year = '2004'
WHERE rec_id = '2';

Query OK, 1 row affected (0.00 sec)
Rows matched: 1  Changed: 1  Warnings: 0
```

First, name the table that's being updated. Next, issue the SET keyword with the column to change and its corresponding new value. If we want to change the values of more than one column, we would provide a comma-separated list of each column along with the equals-sign operator and the new respective values. SET is declared only once, by the way.

This statement has a WHERE clause in which we're limiting the rows that will change by specifying a condition the row must meet. In this case, our condition is for a specific value of a unique column, so only one row will be changed. The results of the query show that one row was affected, one row was matched, one row was changed, and there were no errors to generate warnings.

Sometimes inserting data into a table will cause a duplicate row to be created because a row for the data already exists. For instance, suppose that we want to run an SQL statement that inserts data on a few books into the *books* table and one of the books is already in the table. If we use INSERT, we'll end up with a duplicate row. To prevent this, we can use the REPLACE statement, which inserts new rows and replaces existing rows with new data. From MySQL's perspective, duplicates occur only when unique columns would contain the same value. Because the *rec_id* column is assigned automatically, it's unlikely that we would duplicate it, because we wouldn't tend to assign its value when adding records. What's unique about each book is its ISBN number, which is the bar-code number on the back of the book. To ensure that we do not have rows with the same ISBN number, we'll alter our *books* table again and change the *isbn* column to a UNIQUE column, a column that requires a unique value. This way we won't be able to enter data inadvertently on a book more than once.

```
ALTER TABLE books
CHANGE COLUMN isbn isbn VARCHAR(20) UNIQUE;
```

Now we're ready to begin inserting data for more books without worrying about duplicate rows for books with the same ISBN number. Here is an example in which we're attempting to add two more books by Olympia Vernon, one of which is already in the table:

```
REPLACE INTO books
(title, author_id, isbn, genre, pub_year)
VALUES('Eden','1000','0802117287','novel','2003'),
      ('Hiro','1000','0802117289','novel','2004');
```

The syntax for the REPLACE statement is the same as the INSERT statement. Notice that we've added two rows here in one statement. This is the same syntax that you would use if you want to add more than one row using INSERT. Just list each row's data within parentheses and separate them by commas, as shown earlier. In this example, there is already a row for the book containing the ISBN number 0802117287 (i.e., *Eden*), so it will be replaced and not added. There isn't one for her new book *Hiro*, though, so it will be added.

Deleting Data

To delete specific rows of data, you can use the DELETE statement. For example, if we want to delete all rows of data from our *books* table for the author J.K. Rowling, because we've decided not to carry *Harry Potter* books (we just don't want that kind of business), we could issue the following statement:

```
DELETE FROM books
WHERE author_id =
    (SELECT authors.rec_id FROM authors
     WHERE author_last = 'Rowling'
        AND author_first = 'J.K.');

DELETE FROM authors
WHERE author_last = 'Rowling'
    AND author_first = 'J.K.';
```

Here, we're deleting only rows from the *books* table where the author identification number is whatever is selected from the *authors* table based on the specified author's last name and first name. That is to say, the *author_id* must be whatever value is returned by the SELECT statement, the subquery contained in the parentheses. This statement involves a subquery, so it requires Version 4.1 or later of

MySQL. To delete these same rows with an earlier version of MySQL, you would need to run the SELECT statement shown here separately (not as a subquery), make note of the author's identification number, and then run the first DELETE statement, manually entering the identification number at the end instead of the parenthetical SELECT statement shown.

An alternative to the previous SQL statement would be to utilize user-defined variables. Here is the same example using variables:

```
SET @potter =
   (SELECT rec_id FROM authors
      WHERE author_last = 'Rowling'
         AND author_first = 'J.K.');

DELETE FROM books
WHERE author_id = @potter;

DELETE FROM authors
WHERE rec_id = @potter;
```

In the first stanza, we use the SET statement to establish a variable called @potter that will contain the results of the SELECT statement that follows in parentheses, another subquery. Incidentally, although this subquery is not available before Version 4.1, user-defined variables are. The second SQL statement deletes the rows from *books* where the author identification number matches the value of the temporary variable. Next we delete the data from the *authors* table, still making use of the variable. A user-defined variable will last until it's reset or until the MySQL session is closed.

Searching Data

Once our database is loaded with large amounts of data, it can be cumbersome to locate data by simply scrolling through the results of SELECT statements. Also, sometimes we don't have the exact or complete text for a column in which we're looking. For these situations, we can use the LIKE operator. Suppose that our *books* table now has thousands of entries. Suppose further that a customer says he's looking for a specific book. He can't remember the author or the title, but he does remember that the words *traveler* and *winter* are in the title. We could enter this statement to search the database based on this minimal information:

```
SELECT books.rec_id, title,
       CONCAT(author_first, ' ', author_last) AS author
FROM books, authors
WHERE title LIKE '%traveler%'
   AND title LIKE '%winter%'
   AND author_id = authors.rec_id;

+--------+-------------------------------+--------------+
| rec_id | title                         | author       |
+--------+-------------------------------+--------------+
|   1400 | If on a winter's night a traveler | Italo Calvino |
+--------+-------------------------------+--------------+
```

With the LIKE operator, we use the percent-sign wildcard twice to indicate that we're searching for all rows in which the title column's data starts with zero or more characters before the pattern of *traveler* is found, and then zero or more characters may follow. Put another way, the word *traveler* must be contained somewhere in the column's data to have a pattern match. Also, *winter* must be found in the column. Incidentally, the LIKE keyword is an operator. For more information on operators, see Appendix B.

If another customer asks us to search the database for a book with either the word *Ford* or *Chevrolet* in the title, we could use the OR operator within an expression like so:

```
SELECT books.rec_id, title,
       CONCAT(author_first, ' ', author_last) AS author
FROM books, authors
WHERE title LIKE '%Ford%' AND author_id = authors.rec_id
OR title LIKE '%Chevrolet%' AND author_id = authors.rec_id;
```

You can find more examples and possibilities for searching data in Chapter 4.

Importing Data in Bulk

While the INSERT and REPLACE statements are useful, they can be time-consuming when you're entering a large number of rows, because they're somewhat manual methods of entering data. Often, when setting up a new database, you will need to migrate data from an old database to MySQL. In the case of our bookstore, let's suppose that a vendor has sent us a disk with a list of all of their books in a simple text file. Each record for each book is on a separate line and each field of each record is separated by a vertical bar. Here's how the fictitious vendor's data text file looks:

```
ISBN|TITLE|AUTHOR LAST|AUTHOR FIRST|COPYRIGHT DATE|
067973452X|Notes from Underground|Dostoevsky|Fyodor|August 1994|
...
```

Obviously, an actual vendor file would contain more fields and records than are shown here, but this is enough for our example. The first line contains descriptions of the fields in the records that follow. We don't need to extract the first line; it's just instructions for us. So, we'll tell MySQL to ignore it when we enter our SQL statement. As for the data, we must consider a few problems: the fields are not in the order that they are found in our tables. We'll have to tell MySQL the order in which the data will be coming so that it can make adjustments. The other problem is that this text table contains data for our *books* table and our *authors* table. This is going to be a bit tricky, but we can deal with it. What we'll do is extract the author information only in one SQL statement, then we'll run a separate SQL statement to import the book information. To start, we will copy the vendor's file called *books.txt* to the */tmp* directory, and then we will run a LOAD DATA INFILE statement from the *mysql* client:

```
LOAD DATA INFILE '/tmp/books.txt' REPLACE INTO TABLE authors
FIELDS TERMINATED BY '|' LINES TERMINATED BY '\r\n'
TEXT_FIELDS(col1, col2, col3, col4, col5)
SET author_last = col3, author_first = col4
IGNORE col1, col2, col5, 1 LINES;
```

First, I should point out that the TEXT_FIELDS and the IGNORE clause for columns are not available before Version 4.1 of MySQL. The IGNORE *n* LINES clause has been around for awhile, though. With IGNORE 1 LINES, the first line of the text file containing the column headings will be ignored. Going back to the first line in the SQL statement here, we've named the file to load and the table in which to load the data. The REPLACE flag has the effect of the REPLACE statement mentioned earlier.

In the second line, we specify that fields are terminated by a vertical bar and that lines are terminated by a carriage return (\r) and a newline (\n) to terminate each line. This is the format for an MS-DOS text file. Unix files have only a newline feed. In the third line, we create aliases for each column. In the fourth line, we name the table columns to receive data and set their values based on the aliases given in the previous line. In the final line, we tell MySQL to ignore the columns that we don't want, as well as the top line, because it doesn't contain data.

If you're using an older version of MySQL that doesn't have this new feature of being able to ignore unwanted columns, you will have to perform a couple of extra steps. There are a few different ways of doing this. One simple way, if the table we're loading data into isn't too large, is to add three extra, temporary columns to *authors* that will take in the unwanted fields of data from the text file and drop them later. This would look like the following:

```
ALTER TABLE authors
ADD COLUMN col1 VARCHAR(50),
ADD COLUMN col2 VARCHAR(50),
ADD COLUMN col5 VARCHAR(50);

LOAD DATA INFILE '/tmp/books.txt' REPLACE INTO TABLE authors
FIELDS TERMINATED BY '|' LINES TERMINATED BY '\r\n'
IGNORE 1 LINES
(col1, col2, author_last, author_first, col5);

ALTER TABLE authors
DROP COLUMN col1,
DROP COLUMN col2,
DROP COLUMN col5;
```

These statements will work, but they're not as graceful as the more straightforward statement shown earlier. In the second SQL statement here, notice that the IGNORE clause specifies one line to be ignored. The last line of the same statement lists the columns in the *authors* table that are to receive the data and the sequence in which they will be imported. In the third SQL statement, having finished importing the data from the vendor's text file, we now delete the temporary columns with their unnecessary data by using a DROP statement. There's usually no recourse from DROP, no undo. So, take care in using it.

Once we manage to copy the list of authors into the *authors* table from the text file, we need to load the data on the books and find the correct *author_id* for each book. We do this through the following:

```
LOAD DATA INFILE '/tmp/books.txt' IGNORE INTO TABLE books
FIELDS TERMINATED BY '|' LINES TERMINATED BY '\r\n'
TEXT_FIELDS(col1, col2, col3, col4, col5)
```

```
    SET isbn = col1, title = col2,
      pub_year = RIGHT(col5, 4),
      author_id =
        (SELECT authors.rec_id
          WHERE author_last = col3
          AND author_first = col4)
    IGNORE col3, col4, 1 LINES;
```

In this SQL statement, we've added a couple of twists to get what we need. On the fifth line, to extract the year from the copyright field, which contains both the month and the year, we're using the string function RIGHT( ). It captures the last four characters of col5 as specified in the second argument. Starting on the sixth line, we're using a subquery to determine the *author_id* based on data from the *authors* table where the author's last and first names match what is found in the respective aliases. The results of what is selected within the parentheses will be written to the *author_id* column. Finally, we're having MySQL ignore col3 and col4, as well as the column heading line. Doing this maneuver with earlier versions of MySQL will require temporary columns or a temporary table along the lines of the previous example. The IGNORE flag on the first line, incidentally, instructs MySQL to ignore error messages, not to replace any duplicate rows, and to continue executing the SQL statement.

Command-Line Interface

It's not necessary to open a MySQL monitor to enter SQL statements into the MySQL server. In fact, sometimes you may have only a quick query to make in MySQL, and you'd rather just do it from the shell or command line. For instance, suppose we have a table called *vendors* in our database, and we want to get a quick list of vendors in Louisiana and their telephone numbers. We could enter the following from the shell in Linux (or an equivalent operating system) to get this list:

```
mysql --user='tina' --password='muller' \
-e "SELECT vendor, telephone FROM vendors \
    WHERE state='LA'" bookstore
```

The *mysql* command or interface is called on, although we're not entering monitor mode. Next, we provide the username *tina* and the password *muller*. This line ends with a backslash to let the Unix shell know that there are more parameters to come. Otherwise, we would need to put all of this on one line. On the second line we use the -e switch to indicate that what follows it in quotes is to be executed by the *mysql* client. Notice that what's in double quotes is the same SQL statement in the same syntax as we would enter it in monitor mode. Finally, we provide the name of the database to be used.

Other command-line options and command-line utilities are available. You can use some of these utilities for backing up the database or for performing server maintenance and tuning. These are covered in Chapter 11.

Conclusion

Obviously, you can do plenty more with MySQL. This tutorial was designed to give you an idea of how to create a database and manage the data in some very basic ways. The remaining sections of this book provide details on all of the MySQL statements, clauses, arguments, options, and functions. If you're new to MySQL, you can begin with the statements and clauses highlighted in this chapter, and refer to the chapters that follow for more options and to learn about other functions and features as needed.

4

SQL Statements

This chapter provides brief but comprehensive explanations of the clauses, flags, and options in MySQL's extensive implementation of SQL. While this chapter covers some new material in Version 5.0 of MySQL, some features are left out, because they were not firm at the time of this writing.

This chapter starts with a list of statements grouped by type, as a quick reference. Following this, the statements are listed in alphabetical order. For the more complex statements, to simplify their presentation, the syntax is broken into several sections according to the different uses of the statement.

Some general elements of MySQL's SQL syntax include the following:

- SQL statements may span multiple lines, but must end with either a semi-colon or \G.
- When values are enclosed in parentheses, multiple values usually can be specified, separated by commas.
- Strings and dates must be specified within single or double quotes.
- Elements of a statement's syntax are case-insensitive. However, on Unix-type systems, database and table names, as well as filenames, are case-sensitive.

Statements Grouped by Type

The following is a quick list of SQL statements grouped by type. Some statements are listed in more than one group, because they have more than one use relative to the groups listed.

Data Manipulation

DELETE, DO, HANDLER, INSERT, JOIN, LOAD DATA INFILE, REPLACE, SELECT, SELECT... UNION, TRUNCATE, UPDATE, USE

Database and Table Schema

ALTER DATABASE, ALTER TABLE, ALTER VIEW, CREATE DATABASE, CREATE INDEX, CREATE TABLE, CREATE VIEW, DROP DATABASE, DROP INDEX, DROP TABLE, DROP VIEW, RENAME TABLE

Database and Table Properties

DESCRIBE, SHOW CHARACTER SET, SHOW COLLATION, SHOW COLUMNS, SHOW CREATE DATABASE, SHOW ENGINES, SHOW ERRORS, SHOW GRANTS, SHOW INDEX, SHOW INNODB STATUS, SHOW LOGS, SHOW PRIVILEGES, SHOW PROCESSLIST, SHOW STATUS, SHOW TABLE STATUS, SHOW TABLES, SHOW VARIABLES, SHOW WARNINGS

Table Administration

ANALYZE TABLE, BACKUP TABLE, CACHE INDEX, CHECK TABLE, CHECKSUM TABLE, LOAD INDEX INTO, OPTIMIZE TABLE, REPAIR TABLE, RESET, RESTORE TABLE, SET, SHOW INDEX, SHOW TABLE STATUS

User Administration

DROP USER, GRANT, REVOKE, SET PASSWORD, SHOW GRANTS, SHOW PRIVILEGES, FLUSH

Server Administration

SET, SHOW ENGINES, SHOW ERRORS, SHOW INNODB STATUS, SHOW LOGS, SHOW PROCESSLIST, SHOW STATUS, SHOW VARIABLES, SHOW WARNINGS, FLUSH, KILL

Replication

CHANGE MASTER TO, LOAD DATA FROM MASTER, PURGE MASTER LOGS, RESET SLAVE, RESET MASTER, SET GLOBAL SQL_SLAVE_SKIP_COUNTER, SET SQL_LOG_BIN, SHOW BIN_LOG_EVENTS, SHOW MASTER LOGS, SHOW MASTER STATUS, SHOW SLAVE HOSTS, SHOW SLAVE STATUS, START SLAVE, STOP SLAVE

Statements and Clauses in Alphabetical Order

The following is a list of MySQL statements and clauses in alphabetical order. Each statement is given with its syntax and an explanation. Optional clauses and flags are shown in square brackets. Particular components, such as a database or table name, are shown in italic. The vertical bar is used to separate alternative choices and is not part of the statement syntax.

Some statements have alternative structures to their syntax. Those alternatives are usually shown in complete form. The curly braces indicate that one of the choices is required. Examples are provided to show how a statement and the various clauses may be used for almost all statements. The examples involve a fictitious database for a computer consulting firm that maintains work requests for computer maintenance. Some examples involve a fictitious database of a vendor.

To save space, almost all of the examples are shown without their results. To be able to focus on the particulars of the statements and clauses, the statements are fairly straightforward and do not make much use of the many built-in functions available with MySQL. Explanations of any functions used, though, can be found in other chapters.

ALTER DATABASE

ALTER DATABASE *database*

> [DEFAULT] CHARACTER SET character_set |

> [DEFAULT] COLLATE collation

Use this statement to alter settings for a database. Version 4.1.1 introduced this function and added a file named *db.opt* containing the database settings to the database directory. Currently, two options are available: CHARACTER SET and COLLATE. Here are the contents of a typical *db.opt* file:

```
default-character-set=latin1
default-collation=latin1_swedish_ci
```

The CHARACTER SET option sets the first line, which specifies the default database character set that will be used. The COLLATE option sets the second line, which specifies the default database collation. Here's an example of how you can use this statement:

```
ALTER DATABASE human_resources
    CHARACTER SET latin2_bin
    COLLATE latin2_bin;
```

Notice that both options may be given in one SQL statement. The DEFAULT keyword is unnecessary, but is offered for compatibility with other database systems. Beginning with Version 4.1.8 of MySQL, if the name of the database is omitted from this SQL statement, the current database will be assumed.

ALTER TABLE

ALTER [IGNORE] TABLE *table changes*[, ...]

Use this statement to change an existing table's structure and other properties. Alterations to a table can include adding a new column (see the ADD clauses that follow), changing an existing column (see the ALTER, CHANGE, and MODIFY clauses), deleting a column or index (see the DROP clauses), and miscellaneous other tablewide settings. The IGNORE flag applies to all clauses and instructs MySQL to ignore any error messages regarding duplicate rows that may occur as a result of a column change. It will keep the first unique row found and drop any duplicate rows. Otherwise, the statement will be terminated and changes rolled back.

The following are the syntax and explanations of each clause, with examples, grouped by type of clause. Multiple alterations may be combined in a single ALTER TABLE statement. They must be separated by commas and each clause must include the minimally required elements.

ADD clauses for columns and indexes

```
ALTER [IGNORE] TABLE table
ADD [COLUMN] column definition [FIRST|AFTER column]
ADD INDEX [index] [USING type] (column,...)
ADD [FULLTEXT|SPATIAL] [index] (column,...)
```

These clauses add columns and indexes to a table. The first syntax adds a new column to a table. The same column definition that would be used in a CREATE TABLE statement is used in this syntax and in several others found with the ALTER TABLE statement. Basically, the name of the column is given, followed by the column datatype and the default value or other relevant components of a column desired. The COLUMN keyword is shown but is not necessary.

By default, a column that is added is appended to the end of the table definition. To insert a new column at the beginning of a table, use the FIRST keyword at the end of the ADD COLUMN clause. To insert it after a particular existing column, use the AFTER keyword followed by the name of the column after which the new column is to be inserted:

```
ALTER TABLE workreq
    ADD COLUMN req_type CHAR(4) AFTER req_date,
    ADD COLUMN priority CHAR(4) AFTER req_date;
```

In this example, two columns are to be added after the existing *req_date* column. When *req_type* is added, it will be placed after *req_date*. When the column called *priority* is added, it will be added after *req_date* and before *req_type*.

To add an index to a table, you can use the ADD INDEX clause. The name of the index may be given with this clause. If it's not given, though, the first column name on which the index is based will be used for the index name, as well. The type of index may be stated, but usually it's not necessary, because there's usually only one choice for most table types. The names of one or more columns for indexing must be given within parentheses, separated by commas. Here is an example of how you can add an index using the ALTER TABLE statement:

```
ALTER TABLE clients
    ADD INDEX client_index
    USING BTREE (client_name(10), city(5));
```

This index is to be added to the table clients and is to be called *client_index*. The index is based on two columns: the first 10 characters of the *client_name* column and the first five characters of the *city* column. Limiting the number of characters used in the index makes for a smaller index, which will be faster and probably just as accurate as using the complete column widths. This table is a MyISAM table, so the only index type currently allowed is a BTREE index. However, starting in Version 5 of MySQL, MyISAM tables allow RTREE types of indexes in addition to BTREE.

The third syntax structure shown previously is used for adding either FULLTEXT or SPATIAL indexes to an existing MyISAM table. A FULLTEXT index can index only CHAR, TEXT, or VARCHAR types of columns. A SPATIAL index can only index spatial columns. Note that the INDEX keyword is omitted from this syntax structure.

ADD clauses for foreign keys

```
ALTER [IGNORE] TABLE table
ADD [CONSTRAINT [symbol]] PRIMARY KEY [type] (column,...)
ADD [CONSTRAINT [symbol]] UNIQUE [index] [type] (column,...)
ADD [CONSTRAINT [symbol]] FOREIGN KEY [index] (column,...)
```

```
REFERENCES table (column, ...)
[ON DELETE {RESTRICT|CASCADE|SET NULL|NO ACTION|SET DEFAULT}]
[ON UPDATE {RESTRICT|CASCADE|SET NULL|NO ACTION|SET DEFAULT}]
```

These three ADD clauses are for use in InnoDB tables and are for adding foreign keys and references. A foreign key is an index to a key or index in another table. See the explanation of the CREATE TABLE statement in this chapter for more information and an example of an SQL statement involving the creation of foreign keys in a table. The various flags shown are also explained under the CREATE TABLE statement.

CHANGE clauses

```
ALTER [IGNORE] TABLE table
ALTER [COLUMN] column {SET DEFAULT value|DROP DEFAULT}
CHANGE [COLUMN] column column definition [FIRST|AFTER column]
MODIFY [COLUMN] column definition [FIRST|AFTER column]
```

These three clauses are used to alter an existing column. The first syntax structure is used either to set the default value of a column or to reset it back to its default value. The other two syntax structures are roughly synonymous. They follow the standards of different SQL systems for the sake of compatibility (e.g., MODIFY is used with Oracle). In all three syntax methods, the COLUMN keyword is not necessary. Here's an example of the first clause:

```
ALTER TABLE clients
    ALTER COLUMN city SET DEFAULT 'New Orleans';
```

This statement sets the default value of the *city* column in the *clients* table to a value of *New Orleans*, because that's where most of the clients are located.

The other two clauses are used primarily to change the column definitions. They can also be used to relocate the column in the table schema with the FIRST or the AFTER keywords, just as the ADD clause does. In the CHANGE clause, the current column name must be specified first, followed by either the same column name or a new column name if the name is to be changed. The column definition for the column is to be given, as well, even if it's not to be changed. The MODIFY clause cannot be used to change a column's name, so the column name is listed only once. The following SQL statement uses both of these clauses to change two columns:

```
ALTER TABLE clients
    CHANGE COLUMN city client_city VARCHAR(100),
    MODIFY COLUMN client_state CHAR(4) AFTER client_city;
```

The first clause changes the name of the *city* column, and potentially its column type and size. The second clause changes the column type and size and relocates the *client_state* column to a position after the *client_city* column. Incidentally, when a column is changed, MySQL will attempt to preserve the data. If a column size is reduced, the data won't be completely deleted, but may be truncated.

DROP clauses

```
ALTER [IGNORE] TABLE table
DROP [COLUMN] column
DROP PRIMARY KEY
DROP INDEX index
DROP FOREIGN KEY foreign_key_symbol
```

The DROP clauses of the ALTER TABLE statement remove columns or indexes. These clauses delete the data contained within the columns dropped. Here is an example of the first syntax for deleting a column:

```
ALTER TABLE clients
    DROP COLUMN miscellaneous,
    DROP COLUMN comments;
```

This statement deletes two columns. To delete the primary key index of a table, you'd the second syntax structure shown at the beginning of this subsection. If the primary key is based on a column with an AUTO_INCREMENT type, you may need to change the column definition in the same statement like so:

```
ALTER TABLE clients
    CHANGE client_id client_id INT,
    DROP PRIMARY KEY;
```

The CHANGE clause here changes the *client_id* column from its original type of INT AUTO_INCREMENT to INT. After the AUTO_INCREMENT is removed, the PRIMARY KEY may be dropped.

To drop an index, the third syntax structure is used. To delete a foreign key, the fourth syntax is used. Here is an example of deleting an index:

```
ALTER TABLE client
    DROP INDEX client_name;
```

In this example, the name of the index is not the name of any of the columns. It's an index that was created by combining two columns and was given a unique name. To get a list of indexes for a table, use the SHOW INDEX statement.

Miscellaneous clauses

```
ALTER [IGNORE] TABLE table
ENABLE|DISABLE KEYS
RENAME [TO] table
ORDER BY column
CONVERT TO CHARACTER SET charset [COLLATE collation]
[DEFAULT] CHARACTER SET charset [COLLATE collation]
DISCARD|IMPORT TABLESPACE
```

You can use these miscellaneous clauses with the ALTER TABLE statement. You can use the first clause to enable or disable the updating of nonunique indexes. When running a large number of row inserts, it can be useful to disable indexing afterward. You can use the next clause syntax to change the name of an existing table. Here is an example of this clause:

```
ALTER TABLE client RENAME TO clients;
```

This statement renames the *client* table to *clients*. The TO keyword, incidentally, is not required. It's a matter of style preference and compatibility.

You can use the next clause syntax structure, the ORDER BY clause, to permanently reorder the rows in a given table. Note that after an ALTER TABLE statement any new rows inserted will be added to the end of the table and the table will not be reordered automatically. The ALTER TABLE statement will need to be run again with this clause. Therefore, the ORDER BY clause with SELECT statements is recommended. Here's an example of this clause:

```
ALTER TABLE programmers
    ORDER BY programmer_name;
```

You can use the next two syntaxes to change the character set and collation for tables. When a table is first created with the `CREATE TABLE` statement, unless specified otherwise, a default character set and collation are used. To see the character set and collation for a particular table, use the `SHOW TABLE STATUS` statement. The following example shows how to convert a table's character set:

```
ALTER TABLE clients
    CONVERT TO CHARACTER SET latin2 COLLATE latin2_bin,
    DEFAULT CHARACTER SET latin2 COLLATE latin2_bin;
```

The first clause in this example converts the data in the *clients* table from its default of *latin1* to *latin2*. The second clause sets the new default for the table to *latin2*, as well. The `CONVERT` clause may cause problems with the data. Be sure to make a backup copy before experimenting with this clause.

InnoDB tables use table-spaces instead of individual files for each table. A table-space can involve multiple files and can allow a table to exceed the filesystem file limit as a result. You can use the last clause shown for the `ALTER TABLE` statement to delete or to import a table-space.

```
ALTER TABLE workreq
    IMPORT TABLESPACE;
```

This statement will import the *.idb* file if it's in the database's directory. Replacing the `IMPORT` keyword with `DISCARD` will delete the *.idb* file.

Table options

```
ALTER TABLE table options
```

This clause sets the same table options as those set by the `CREATE TABLE` statement. You can find a list of them under the explanation for that statement. As an example of their use with this statement, to change the starting point for an `AUTO_INCREMENT` column, you can enter the following statement:

```
ALTER TABLE clients
    AUTO_INCREMENT=1000;
```

This statement will set the value of the key column to 1,000 for the next row inserted. You can add more options to this statement in a comma-separated list.

ALTER VIEW

```
ALTER VIEW view [(column, ...)] AS SELECT...
```

Use this statement to change a view. It's used primarily to change the `SELECT` statement that determines the view. The new `SELECT` statement for the view is simply given after the `AS` keyword. You can change the associated column names for the view by providing the new column names in a comma-separated list within the parentheses following the view's name. Neither the old `SELECT` statement nor the old column names are to be given. To change a view's name, use the `DROP VIEW` statement, and then create a new view with the `CREATE VIEW` statement. View statements are available as of Version 5.0.1 of MySQL.

ANALYZE TABLE

```
ANALYZE [LOCAL|NO_WRITE_TO_BINLOG] TABLE table[, ...]
```

Use this statement to analyze and store the key distribution of a table. It works on BDB, InnoDB, and MyISAM tables. Unless the NO_WRITE_TO_BINLOG option is given, the statement is written to the binary log file. The LOCAL option is synonymous.

```
ANALYZE TABLE workreq;
```

```
+----------------------+---------+----------+----------+
| Table                | Op      | Msg_type | Msg_text |
+----------------------+---------+----------+----------+
| workrequests.workreq | analyze | status   | OK       |
+----------------------+---------+----------+----------+
```

The message type results can be *status*, *error*, *info*, or *warning*. If the table hasn't changed since it was last analyzed, the message text will read *"Table is already up to date"* and the table won't be analyzed. This statement is equivalent to using myisamchk -a at the command line for MyISAM tables.

BACKUP TABLE

```
BACKUP TABLE table[, ...] TO '/path'
```

Use this statement to make a backup copy of a table. You can specify additional tables in a comma-separated list. The absolute path to the directory to which MySQL is to copy files is given in quotes after the TO keyword. Only MyISAM tables work with this statement. This statement has been deprecated. It's recommended that *mysqlhotcopy* (see Chapter 11) be used until this statement is replaced.

The statement copies the *.frm* file and the *.MYD* file, which contain the table structure and the table data, respectively. The *.MYI* file containing the index is not copied, but will be rebuilt with the RESTORE TABLE statement when restoring the table.

```
BACKUP TABLE clients TO '/tmp/backup';
```

```
+----------------------+--------+----------+----------+
| Table                | Op     | Msg_type | Msg_text |
+----------------------+--------+----------+----------+
| workrequests.clients | backup | status   | OK       |
+----------------------+--------+----------+----------+
```

If the backup succeeds, the results will look like the preceding results and two files will be created for each table backed up: a *.frm* file and a *.MYD* file. If MySQL does not have the filesystem privileges necessary to write to the backup directory, or if a file with the same name is already in the directory, the backup will fail. The results set will include one row with an error message type and another with a status type and the message text stating "Operation failed."

CACHE INDEX

```
CACHE INDEX table[[INDEX|KEY] (index, ...), ...] IN cache
```

This statement tells MySQL to cache the given indexes to a specific index cache, which can be created with a SET GLOBAL statement. This statement is used only on MyISAM tables. Multiple tables may be listed in a comma-separated list. To specify only certain indexes of a table, they may be given in a comma-separated list in parentheses after the table name. The INDEX or KEY keyword may be given for clarity and compatibility. Note that the naming of specific indexes for a table is ignored in the current versions of MySQL. This option is for a future release. For now, all indexes are assigned to the named cache, which is the same as specifying no indexes.

To create an additional cache, issue a SET GLOBAL statement with the key_buffer_size variable like this:

```
SET GLOBAL my_cache.key_buffer_size = 100*1024;
CACHE INDEX workreq, clients IN my_cache\G

*************************** 1. row ***************************
    Table: workrequests.workreq
       Op: assign_to_keycache
 Msg_type: status
 Msg_text: OK
*************************** 2. row ***************************
    Table: workrequests.clients
       Op: assign_to_keycache
 Msg_type: status
 Msg_text: OK
```

In this example, a cache called *my_cache* is created in the first line with a buffer size of 100 megabytes. The second line assigns the indexes for the two tables named to *my_cache*. As long as this cache exists, all queries by all users will use this cache. If the key cache is eliminated for any reason, the indexes will be assigned back to the default key cache for the server.

CHANGE MASTER TO

```
CHANGE MASTER TO option[, ...]
          MASTER_HOST = 'host'
          MASTER_USER = 'user'
          MASTER_PASSWORD = 'password'
          MASTER_PORT = port
          MASTER_CONNECT_RETRY = count
          MASTER_LOG_FILE = 'filename'
          MASTER_LOG_POS = position
          RELAY_LOG_FILE = 'filename'
          RELAY_LOG_POS = position
          MASTER_SSL = {0|1}
          MASTER_SSL_CA = 'filename'
          MASTER_SSL_CAPATH = 'path'
          MASTER_SSL_CERT = 'filename'
          MASTER_SSL_KEY = 'filename'
          MASTER_SSL_CIPHER = 'list'
```

Use this statement to change several properties regarding connections to the master MySQL server. Some of the variables relate to connecting to the server and some relate to master log files and the current position in the logfiles. This statement is run from the slave. If the slave is running, it may be necessary to use the STOP SLAVE statement before using this statement, and the START SLAVE statement afterward.

The following SQL statement sets several properties for this slave:

```
CHANGE MASTER TO
    MASTER_HOST='mysql.company.com',
    MASTER_PORT=3306,
    MASTER_USER='slave_server',
    MASTER_PASSWORD='password',
    MASTER_CONNECT_RETRY=5;
```

The log clauses for this statement are used to name the master logfiles and to provide the slave with the current position of the master logfiles. This may be necessary when first setting up a new slave or when a slave has been disabled for awhile. Use the SHOW MASTER STATUS statement to determine the current position of the master logfiles. Use the SHOW SLAVE STATUS statement to confirm a slave's position for the related files. Here is an example using these clauses:

```
CHANGE MASTER TO
    MASTER_LOG_FILE= 'log-bin.000153',
    MASTER_LOG_POS = 79,
    RELAY_LOG_FILE = 'log-relay.000153',
    RELAY_LOG_POS = 112;
```

The remaining clauses set various secure socket layer (SSL) variables. These values are saved to the *master.info* file. To see the current values for these options, use the SHOW SLAVE STATUS statement. Relay log options are available as of Version 4.1.1 of MySQL. The MASTER_SSL variable is set to 0 if the master does not allow SSL connections, and 1 if it does. The MASTER_SSL_CA variable holds the name of the file that contains a list of trusted CAs. MASTER_SSL_CAPATH contains the absolute path to that file. The MASTER_SSL_CERT variable specifies the name of the SSL certificate file for secure connections, and MASTER_SSL_KEY specifies the SSL key file used to negotiate secure connections. Finally, MASTER_SSL_CIPHER provides a list of acceptable cipher methods for encryption.

CHECK TABLE

CHECK TABLE *table*[, ...] [CHANGED|QUICK|FAST|MEDIUM|EXTENDED|]

Use this statement to check MyISAM and InnoDB tables for errors. If errors are discovered, you should run the REPAIR TABLE statement to repair the table. Multiple tables may be given in a comma-separated list. There are several methods of checking. The CHANGED method checks only tables that have been changed since the last check. The QUICK option will check tables for errors, but won't scan individual rows for linking problems. The FAST option instructs MySQL to check only tables that have not been closed properly. The MEDIUM option determines the key checksum for the rows and compares the results against the checksum for the keys. It also checks rows to ensure that links were deleted properly. The EXTENDED method thoroughly checks each row for errors. Here is an example of how you can use this statement.

```
CHECK TABLE workreq MEDIUM;
```

```
+----------------------+-------+----------+----------+
| Table                | Op    | Msg_type | Msg_text |
+----------------------+-------+----------+----------+
| workrequests.workreq | check | status   | OK       |
+----------------------+-------+----------+----------+
```

CHECKSUM TABLE

CHECKSUM TABLE *table*[, ...] [QUICK|EXTENDED]

Use this statement to determine a table's checksum value. Multiple tables may be given in a comma-separated list. If the QUICK option is employed, the live table checksum will be returned, if available. If not, NULL will be returned. You would tend to use QUICK when the table is probably fine. To enable live checksum for a table, use the ALTER TABLE statement with a table option of CHECKSUM=1. The EXTENDED option instructs the server to check each row. You should use this option only as a last resort. If no option is specified, the QUICK option is the default, if available. Otherwise, the EXTENDED option is the default. Here is an example of this statement's use and its results:

```
CHECKSUM TABLE workreq;
```

```
+----------------------+-----------+
| Table                | Checksum  |
+----------------------+-----------+
| workrequests.workreq | 195953487 |
+----------------------+-----------+
```

COMMIT

COMMIT

Use this statement to commit transactions in an InnoDB or a BDB table. If AUTOCOMMIT is enabled, it must be disabled for this statement to be meaningful. To do this, set the value of AUTOCOMMIT to 0 with the SET statement. AUTOCOMMIT will also be disabled with the use of the START TRANSACTION statement and reinstated with the COMMIT statement. Here is an example of this statement:

```
START TRANSACTION;
LOCK TABLES orders WRITE;
INSERT DATA INFILE '/tmp/customer_orders.sql'
  INTO TABLE orders;
SELECT ...;
COMMIT;
UNLOCK TABLES;
```

In this example, after inserting a batch of orders into the *orders* table, an administrator enters a series of SELECT statements to check the integrity of the data. They are omitted here to save space. If there is a problem, the ROLLBACK statement could be issued rather than the COMMIT statement shown here. ROLLBACK would remove the data imported by the INSERT DATA INFILE statement. The ROLLBACK statement works only with InnoDB and BDB tables. If everything seems alright, the COMMIT statement would be issued to commit the transactions.

CREATE DATABASE

```
CREATE DATABASE [IF NOT EXISTS] database [options]
```

This statement creates a new database with the name given. You can use the IF NOT EXISTS flag to suppress an error message when the statement fails if a database with the same name already exists. As of Version 4.1.1, a *db.opt* file is added to the filesystem subdirectory created for the database in the MySQL server's data directory. This file contains a couple of settings for the database. You can specify these settings as options to this SQL statement in a comma-separated list.

Currently, two options are available: CHARACTER SET and COLLATE. Here is an example of how you can create a database with both of these options:

```
CREATE DATABASE db1
    CHARACTER SET latin1
    COLLATE latin1_bin;
```

Unlike most lists of options, there is no comma between the first option and the second option. Below is the contents of the *db.opt* file created for this statement:

```
default-character-set=latin1
default-collation=latin1_bin
```

For a list of character sets, use the SHOW CHARACTER SET statement. For a list of collation possibilities, use the SHOW COLLATION statement.

CREATE INDEX

```
CREATE [UNIQUE|FULLTEXT|SPATIAL] INDEX index

    [USING type|TYPE type]

    ON table (column [(length)] [ASC|DESC], ...)
```

Use this statement to add an index to a table after it has been created. This is an alias of the ALTER TABLE statement that adds an index. You can add indexes only to MyISAM, InnoDB, and BDB types of tables. You can also create these tables with indexes, as shown under the CREATE TABLE statement.

To prevent duplicates, add the UNIQUE flag between the CREATE keyword and INDEX. Only columns with CHAR, TEXT, and VARCHAR datatypes of MyISAM tables can be indexed with FULLTEXT indexes. SPATIAL indexes can index spatial columns only in MyISAM tables. This is available starting with Version 4.1 of MySQL.

After the INDEX keyword, the name of the index or key is given. This name can be the same as one of the columns indexed, or a totally new name.

You can specify the type of index with the USING keyword. For MyISAM and InnoDB tables, BTREE is the default and only choice currently. The RTREE type will be available as of Version 5 of MySQL. The TYPE keyword is an alias for USING.

For wide columns, it may be advantageous to specify a maximum number of characters to use from a column for indexing. This can speed up indexing and reduce the size of index files on the filesystem.

Although there is an ASC option for sorting indexes in ascending order and a DESC option for sorting in descending order, these are for a future release of MySQL. All indexes are currently sorted in ascending order. Additional columns for indexing may be given within the parentheses.

```
CREATE UNIQUE INDEX client_name
    ON clients (client_lastname, client_firstname(4), rec_date);
```

In this example, an index is created called *client_name*. It is based on the last names of clients, the first four letters of their first names, and the dates that the records were created. This index is based on it being unlikely that a record would be created on the same day for two people with the same last name and a first name starting with the same four letters.

To see the indexes that have been created for a table, use the SHOW INDEX statement. To remove an index, use the DROP INDEX statement.

CREATE TABLE

```
CREATE [TEMPORARY] TABLE [IF NOT EXISTS] table
```

```
{[(definition)][options]|[[AS] SELECT...]|[LIKE table]}
```

Use this statement to create a new table within a database. This statement has many clauses and options. However, when creating a basic table, you can omit many of them. You can use the TEMPORARY keyword to create a temporary table that is used only for the current connection thread and not accessible by other users. You can use the IF NOT EXISTS flag to suppress error messages caused by attempting to create a table by the same name as an existing one. After the table name is given, either the table definition is given (i.e., a list of columns and their datatypes) along with table options or properties, or a table can be created based on another table. You create a table based on the schema of another table with a SELECT statement or with a LIKE clause. These two possibilities are covered at the end of this statement's explanation. Here is a simple example of how you can use this statement:

```
CREATE TABLE clients
    (client_id INT AUTO_INCREMENT PRIMARY KEY,
     client_name VARCHAR(75), telephone CHAR(15));
```

This creates a table with three columns. The first column is called *client_id* and may contain integers. It will be incremented automatically as records are created. It will also be the primary key field for records, which means that no duplicates are allowed and that the rows will be indexed off of this column. The second column, *client_name*, is a variable-width, character-type column with a maximum width of 75 characters. The third column is called *telephone* and is a fixed-width, character-type column with a minimum and maximum width of 15 characters. To see the results of this statement, you can use a DESCRIBE statement. Many column datatypes are available. They are described in Appendix A.

Column flags

```
CREATE [TEMPORARY] TABLE [IF NOT EXISTS] table
(column type[(width)] [ASC|DESC] [NOT NULL|NULL] [DEFAULT value]
    [AUTO_INCREMENT] [[PRIMARY] KEY] [COMMENT 'string']
[,...]) [options]
```

This is the syntax for the CREATE TABLE statement again, but detailing the column flags portion of the column definition. For some column types, you may need to specify the size of the column within parentheses after the column name and column type.

If a column is indexed, the keyword ASC or DESC may be given next to indicate whether indexes should be stored in ascending or descending order, respectively. By default, they are stored in ascending order. For the current and past versions of MySQL, these flags are ignored. Adding the NOT NULL flag indicates the column may not be NULL. The NULL flag may be given to state that a NULL value is allowed. To set a default value for a column, you can use the DEFAULT keyword. The AUTO_INCREMENT option has MySQL assign a unique identification number automatically to a column. If a column is to be the basis of an index, either PRIMARY KEY or just KEY can be given.

As a reference for an administrator or a developer, a comment regarding a column may be given. It won't be displayed in the results of a SELECT statement, but it will be revealed with a SHOW FULL COLUMNS statement. To add a comment, use the COMMENT keyword followed by a string within quotes. Here is an example using some of the flags and clauses mentioned here:

```
CREATE TABLE clients
    (client_id INT NOT NULL AUTO_INCREMENT PRIMARY KEY,
    client_name VARCHAR(75),
    client_city VARCHAR(50) DEFAULT 'New Orleans',
    telephone CHAR(15) COMMENT 'Format: ###-###-####');
```

In this example, the *client_id* column is a primary key. The NOT NULL option is included for completeness, even though it's not necessary, because a primary key must be unique and non-NULL. For the *client_city* column, the DEFAULT clause is used to provide the default value of the column. It will be used when no value is given, although you can override it by specifying an explicit blank value for the column. This statement also includes a comment regarding the typical format for entering telephone numbers in the *telephone* column. Again, this will be displayed only with the SHOW FULL COLUMNS statement.

Index and key definitions

```
CREATE [TEMPORARY] TABLE [IF NOT EXISTS] table
(column, ..., index type[(width)] [ASC|DESC]

|[CONSTRAINT [symbol]] PRIMARY KEY [type] (column,...)
|INDEX|[PRIMARY] KEY [index] [type] (column,...)
|[CONSTRAINT [symbol]] UNIQUE [INDEX] [index] [type] (column,...)
|[FULLTEXT|SPATIAL] [INDEX] [index] (column,...)
|[CONSTRAINT [symbol]] FOREIGN KEY [index] (column,...)
    [reference_definition]
|CHECK (expression)]

[,...]) [options]
```

You can use one or more columns for an index, and a table can contain multiple indexes. Indexes can greatly increase the speed of data retrieval from a table. You can define an index involving multiple columns with this statement, or later with the ALTER TABLE statement or the CREATE INDEX statement. With the CREATE TABLE statement, though, indexes can be given after the definition of the columns they index.

A key (also called a primary key) is a particular kind of index obeying certain constraints: it must be unique, for instance. It often is combined in MySQL with the AUTO_INCREMENT keyword, and it is often used for identifiers that appear as columns in tables. The general format is to specify the type of index, such as KEY, INDEX, or UNIQUE. This is followed by the index name. Optionally, the index type may be specified with the USING keyword. For most tables there is only one type of index, so this is unnecessary. Before Version 5 of MySQL, BTREE is the only type for MyISAM tables. Beginning with Version 5, the RTREE index type also will be available, so you may want to specify the index type. After the index type, one or more columns for which the index is based are listed within parentheses, separated by commas. Before explaining the various possibilities, let's look at an example:

```
CREATE TABLE clients
    (client_id INT AUTO_INCREMENT KEY,
    name_last VARCHAR(50), name_first VARCHAR(50),
    telephone CHAR(15),
    INDEX names USING BTREE (name_last(5), name_first(5) DESC));
```

In this example, the *client_id* column is a PRIMARY KEY, although it has been abbreviated to just KEY. This abbreviation is available as of Version 4.1 of MySQL. There can be only one PRIMARY KEY, but several other indexes. The table contains a second index using the first five characters of the two name columns. To do a combination, the index definition is generally given at the end of the table's column definitions with the INDEX keyword. The index is named *names* in the example. After the index name, the type of index to be used is specified with the USING clause. Currently, this is unnecessary because BTREE is the default type for a MyISAM table. Next, the two columns to index are named in parentheses. The name columns are variable-width columns and 50 characters in length, so to speed up indexing only the first five characters of each column are to be used. The *name_first* column is supposed to be used in descending order per the DESC flag. However, this will be ignored for the current version of MySQL.

The syntax structures for the index clauses listed here vary depending on the type of table index to be created: PRIMARY KEY, INDEX, UNIQUE, FULLTEXT (or BLOB column types), or SPATIAL.

For creating constraints on tables based on columns in another table, you would use the FOREIGN KEY index syntax structures. Foreign keys are used only between InnoDB tables. The CHECK clause is not used in MySQL but is available for porting to applications for other database systems. Here is an example of how you can use foreign keys to create a table:

```
CREATE TABLE employees
    (rec_id INT NOT NULL PRIMARY KEY,
     name_last VARCHAR(25), name_first VARCHAR(25))
TYPE = INNODB;

CREATE TABLE programmers
    (rec_id INT, emp_id INT,
     INDEX (emp_id),
     FOREIGN KEY (emp_id) REFERENCES employees(rec_id)
     ON DELETE CASCADE)
TYPE=INNODB;
```

The first SQL statement creates a table for basic information on employees. The second table creates a simple table of programmers. In the *employees* table, the key column *rec_id* will be used to identify employees and will be the foreign key for the *programmers* table. The *programmers* table sets up an index based on *emp_id*, which will be tied to the *rec_id* column in the *employees* table. The FOREIGN KEY clause establishes this connection using the REFERENCES keyword to indicate the *employees* table and the key column in that table to use in that table. Additionally, the ON DELETE CASCADE clause instructs MySQL to delete the row in the *programmers* table for a programmer that is deleted from the *employees* table. The next subsection gives the syntax for references to foreign keys and the meaning of each component. At the end of both of these SQL statements, the table type is set to InnoDB with the TYPE clause. The ENGINE keyword could have been used instead.

References

```
CREATE [TEMPORARY] TABLE [IF NOT EXISTS] table
(column, ..., index type[(width)] [ASC|DESC]

[CONSTRAINT [symbol]] FOREIGN KEY [index] (column,...)
REFERENCES table [(column,...)]
    [MATCH FULL|MATCH PARTIAL]
    [ON DELETE [RESTRICT|CASCADE|SET NULL|NO ACTION|SET DEFAULT]]
    [ON UPDATE [RESTRICT|CASCADE|SET NULL|NO ACTION|SET DEFAULT]]

[,...]) [options]
```

This subsection describes the FOREIGN KEY clause, which creates a relationship between an index and another table. The MATCH FULL clause requires that the reference match on the full width of each column indexed. MATCH PARTIAL allows for partial columns to be used. Partial columns can accelerate indexing only when the first few characters of a column are necessary for determining the uniqueness of a row. The ON DELETE clause instructs MySQL to react to deletions of matching rows from the foreign table according to the option that follows. The ON UPDATE clause has MySQL respond to updates made to the referenced table according to the options that follow it. You can use both clauses in the same CREATE TABLE statement.

The RESTRICT keyword option instructs MySQL not to allow the deletion or updating (depending on the clause in which it's used) of the rows in the foreign table if rows in the current table are linked to them. The CASCADE keyword says that when deleting or updating the rows that are referenced in the parent table, delete or update the related rows in the child table accordingly (as in the last example). SET NULL has MySQL change the data contained in the related columns to a NULL value. For this to work, the column in the child table must allow NULL values. The NO ACTION setting has MySQL not react to deletions or updates with regard to the referencing table. The SET DEFAULT option would seem to suggest that the referencing column's value would be set to the column's default, but at this time, it does nothing.

Table options

```
CREATE [TEMPORARY] TABLE [IF NOT EXISTS] table
(column, ..., index type[(width)] [ASC|DESC]

{ENGINE|TYPE} = {BDB|HEAP|ISAM|InnoDB|MERGE|MRG_MYISAM|MYISAM}
AUTO_INCREMENT = value
AVG_ROW_LENGTH = value
CHECKSUM = {0|1}
COMMENT = 'string'
MAX_ROWS = value
MIN_ROWS = value
PACK_KEYS = {0|1|DEFAULT}
PASSWORD = 'string'
DELAY_KEY_WRITE = {0|1}
ROW_FORMAT = {DEFAULT|DYNAMIC|FIXED|COMPRESSED}
```

```
    RAID_TYPE = {1|STRIPED|RAID0}
        RAID_CHUNKS = value
        RAID_CHUNKSIZE = value
    UNION = (table[,...])
    INSERT_METHOD = {NO|FIRST|LAST }
    DATA DIRECTORY = '/path'
    INDEX DIRECTORY = '/path'
    [DEFAULT] CHARACTER SET characterset [COLLATE collation]

[,...]) [options]
```

When creating a table, in addition to defining the columns and indexes, you can also set various table properties. You set the type of table—also known as the storage engine—with a TYPE or ENGINE clause, which are synonymous. By default, if the TYPE clause isn't used, a table will be a MyISAM table type. You can set the default to a different table type with the --default-table-type option when starting the *mysqld* daemon. See Chapter 10 for more information on this option. The different table types are listed in the syntax for the preceding clause. To see the values for an existing table, use the SHOW TABLE STATUS statement. See the explanation of that statement for the meaning of each variable. To set or change any of these values after a table has been created, use the ALTER TABLE statement.

Create a table based on an existing table

```
CREATE [TEMPORARY] TABLE [IF NOT EXISTS] table
LIKE table
|[IGNORE|REPLACE] [AS] SELECT...
```

These two structural syntax choices for the CREATE TABLE statement allow a new table to be created based on an existing table. With the LIKE clause, a table is created based on the structure of the existing table given. For example, suppose a database has a table called *employees* that contains information on full-time and part-time employees. Suppose further that it has been decided that information on part-time employees should be stored in a separate table. You could execute the following statement to create a new table for part-time employees with the same structure as the existing *employees* table:

```
CREATE TABLE part_time_employees
    LIKE employees;
```

This statement results in a new table with the same structure, but without any data. If the table that was copied has a primary key or any indexing, they won't be copied. You can use the CREATE INDEX statement to create an index.

To create a new table based on the structure of an existing table and to copy the data from the old table to the new one, you can enter something like the following statement:

```
CREATE TABLE part_time_employees
    AS SELECT *
        FROM employees
        WHERE part_time='Y';
```

In this example, the table structure is copied and the data is copied for rows where the *part_time* column has a value of 'Y', as in *yes*. (A WHERE clause is optional.) Then you could issue a DELETE statement to delete the rows for part-time employees from the *employees* table.

You can use the IGNORE keyword before the SELECT statement to instruct MySQL to ignore any error messages regarding duplicate rows, to not insert them, and to proceed with the remaining rows of the SELECT statement. Use the REPLACE keyword instead if duplicate rows are to be replaced in the new table.

CREATE VIEW

```
CREATE [OR REPLACE] [ALGORITHM = {MERGE|TEMPTABLE}]

VIEW view [(column, ...)] AS SELECT...

[WITH [CASCADED|LOCAL] CHECK OPTION]
```

Use this statement to create a view, which is a preset result set in a database. It's available as Version 5.0.1 of MySQL. A view is created based on a given SELECT statement. The view is displayed with a SELECT statement naming the view instead of a table. The OR REPLACE clause may be given to overwrite an existing view with the same name. The name of the view is given immediately after the VIEW keyword and cannot be the same as a table in the database, because they share the same tablespace. To label the column headings for the view's results set, column names may be given in a comma-separated list in parentheses after the view name. The WITH CHECK [CASCADED|LOCAL] OPTION clause is available as of Version 5.0.2 of MySQL. Here is an example of how you can use this statement:

```
CREATE VIEW employee_directory(ID, Name, Ext.) AS
  SELECT emp_id, CONCAT(emp_first, ' ', emp_last), tel_extension
  FROM employees;
```

This SQL statement will create a view that will contain each employee's identification number, the employee's first and last name concatenated together with a space in between, and the employee's office telephone extension. To retrieve this data, enter the following SQL statement:

```
SELECT * FROM employee_directory LIMIT 1;
```

```
+------+------------+------+
| ID   | Name       | Ext. |
+------+------------+------+
| 1000 | Marie Dyer | 1207 |
+------+------------+------+
```

Notice that the column names are the ones named by the CREATE VIEW statement. This view will be available for all users that have SELECT privileges for the database in which it was created. By default, a view is created in the default database at the time that the CREATE VIEW statement is entered. To create a view in a different database from the default, simply add the database name and a dot as a separator in front of the view name in the CREATE VIEW statement. To delete a view from a database, use the DROP VIEW statement.

DELETE

```
DELETE [LOW_PRIORITY] [QUICK] [IGNORE] FROM table

    [WHERE condition]

    [ORDER BY column [ASC|DESC][, ...]] [LIMIT row_count]


DELETE [LOW_PRIORITY] [QUICK] [IGNORE] table[, table]

    FROM table[, ...] [WHERE condition]


DELETE [LOW_PRIORITY] [QUICK] [IGNORE] FROM table[, table]

    USING table[, ...] [WHERE condition]
```

Use this statement to delete rows of data from a given table. Three basic syntax structures are allowed. The first one shown here is for one table only. The other two are for
multiple tables. For all three, the LOW_PRIORITY flag instructs the server to wait until
there are no queries on the table named before deleting rows. The QUICK flag is used
with MyISAM tables to make deletions faster by not merging index leaves. The IGNORE
flag instructs MySQL to continue even if it encounters errors. You can retrieve error
messages afterward with the SHOW WARNINGS statement. You can use the WHERE clause to
specify which rows are to be deleted based on a given condition. You can use the
DELETE statement in conjunction with the JOIN clause, which is explained later in this
chapter.

Here is a simple example of this statement:

```
DELETE LOW_PRIORITY FROM workreq
    WHERE client_id = '1076'
        AND status <> 'DONE';
```

In this example, the client 1076 has closed its account, and management has decided
just to delete all of their incomplete work requests. If a WHERE clause is not given, all the
rows for the table would be deleted permanently. Row deletions are performed one
row at a time with the DELETE statement, so using this statement to delete all rows is
slower than when using the TRUNCATE TABLE statement. However, the TRUNCATE TABLE
statement doesn't return the number of rows deleted.

To delete only a certain number of rows in a table, use the ORDER BY clause along with
the LIMIT clause. For example, suppose an account executive informed the database
administrator that the last four work requests she entered for a particular client (1023)
need to be deleted. The database administrator can enter the following to delete those
rows:

```
DELETE FROM workreq
    WHERE client_id = '1023'
    ORDER BY request_date
    LIMIT 4;
```

In this example, the rows are first ordered by the date of the work request. Additional
columns may be given in a comma-separated list for the ordering. The LIMIT clause is
used to limit the number of deletions to the first four rows of the results of the WHERE
clause and the ORDER BY clause.

The second syntax structure shown earlier for this statement allows other tables to be referenced. In the first example shown here, the rows from the work request table were being deleted based on the client account number. However, if that number wasn't known, but the database administrator knows the client's name begins with *Cole*, the following could be entered to delete the records instead:

```
DELETE workreq FROM workreq, clients
    WHERE workreq.client_id = clients.client_id
    AND client_name LIKE 'Cole%';
```

In this example, the table in which rows will be deleted is given after the DELETE keyword. It's also given in the list of tables in the FROM clause, which specifies the table from which information will be obtained to determine the rows to delete. The two tables are joined in the WHERE clause on the client identification number column in each. Using the LIKE keyword, the selection of rows is limited to clients with a name beginning with the name *Cole*. Incidentally, if more than one client has a name beginning with *Cole*, the rows for both will be deleted from the work request table. You can delete rows in more than one table with a single statement by listing the tables in a comma-separated list after the DELETE keyword. For example, suppose that it has been decided to delete not only the work requests for the client, but also the row for the client in the *clients* table:

```
DELETE workreq, clients FROM workreq, clients
    WHERE workreq.clientid = clients.clientid
    AND client_name LIKE 'Cole%';
```

Notice that the only syntactical difference between this statement and the one for the previous example is that in this statement both tables for which rows are to be deleted are listed after the DELETE keyword and before the FROM clause. Deletions are permanent, so care should be taken as to which tables are listed for deletion.

The third syntax structure operates in the same way as the second one, but offers a couple of keywords that may be preferred for clarity. If the second-to-last statement example were entered with this third syntax structure, it would look like this:

```
DELETE FROM workreq USING workreq, clients
    WHERE workreq.clientid = clients.clientid
    AND client_name LIKE 'Cole%';
```

Notice that the table for which rows will be deleted is listed in the FROM clause. The tables that the statement will search to obtain information for determining which rows to delete are listed in the USING clause. The results of statements using this syntax structure and the previous one are the same. It's just a matter of style preference and compatibility with other database systems.

DESCRIBE

{DESCRIBE|DESC} *table* [*column*]

This statement displays information about the columns of a given table. The DESCRIBE keyword can be abbreviated to DESC. For information on a specific column, give the column name or a naming pattern within quotes to include multiple columns. For instance, to display a list of columns in the *workreq* table that begin with the characters *client_*, enter the following:

```
DESCRIBE workreq 'client_%';
```

```
+-------------+------------+------+-----+---------+-------+
| Field       | Type       | Null | Key | Default | Extra |
+-------------+------------+------+-----+---------+-------+
| client_id   | varchar(4) | YES  |     | NULL    |       |
| client_type | char(1)    | YES  |     | NULL    |       |
+-------------+------------+------+-----+---------+-------+
```

DO

DO *expression*[, ...] | (*statement*)

This statement suppresses the results of an expression. Multiple expressions may be given in a comma-separated list. As of Version 4.1 of MySQL, subqueries may be given:

```
DO  (SET @company = 'Van de Lay Industries' );
```

This statement creates the @company variable with the value given, but without displaying any results.

DROP DATABASE

DROP DATABASE [IF EXISTS] *database*

Use this statement to delete a given database along with all its tables and data. The addition of the IF EXISTS flag suppresses an error message if the database does not already exist:

```
DROP DATABASE IF EXISTS test;
Query OK, 6 rows affected (0.42 sec)
```

Notice that the number of tables deleted is returned in the *rows affected* count. If the database doesn't exist or if there are other files in the database's filesystem directory, an error message will be displayed. The tables will be deleted if other files exist, but the foreign file and the directory won't be removed. They will have to be deleted manually at the command line using a filesystem command such as *rm* in Unix or *del* in Windows.

DROP INDEX

DROP INDEX *index* ON *table*

This statement deletes a given index from a table. To determine the name of a particular index, use the SHOW INDEX statement. The key name for the index found in the results of that statement is used with this statement.

```
DROP INDEX client_name ON contacts;
```

This statement drops the index with the key name of *client_name* from the *contacts* table.

DROP TABLE

```
DROP [TEMPORARY] TABLE [IF EXISTS] table[, ...]
```

>   [RESTRICT|CASCADE]

Use this statement to delete a table from a database, including its data. You can delete additional tables in the same statement by naming them in a comma-separated list. The addition of the IF EXISTS flag prevents error messages from being displayed if the table doesn't already exist. If the TEMPORARY flag is given, only temporary tables matching the table names given will be deleted. DROP privileges won't be checked with this flag, because temporary tables are visible and usable only by the user of the current session who created the temporary tables. The RESTRICT and CASCADE flags are for future versions and are related to compatibility with other systems.

```
DROP TABLE IF EXISTS repairs, clientss_old;
Query OK, 0 rows affected (0.00 sec)

SHOW WARNINGS;
+-------+------+-----------------------------+
| Level | Code | Message                     |
+-------+------+-----------------------------+
| Note  | 1051 | Unknown table 'clientss_old' |
+-------+------+-----------------------------+
```

In this example, the user tried to instruct MySQL to delete both the *repairs* and the *clients_old* tables, but misspelled *clients_old*. Because the IF EXISTS flag was included, the statement doesn't give an error message. Starting with Version 4.1 of MySQL, a note is created that you can retrieve by issuing a SHOW WARNINGS statement, as shown in this example. Notice that the number of tables deleted is not returned.

DROP USER

```
DROP USER 'user'@'host'
```

Use this statement to delete privileges for a user by deleting the row for that user and host, given the *user* table of the *mysql* database. This statement won't delete a user that has any privileges set to 'Y', though. To be assured that the user has no privileges, issue a REVOKE statement. You will have to issue a separate statement for each host for which the user has privileges.

```
REVOKE ALL ON *.* FROM 'rstringer'@'localhost';
DROP USER 'rstringer'@'localhost';
```

The ALL option is used to assure revocation of all privileges. The *.* covers all tables in all databases. Prior to Version 4.1.1 of MySQL, you would have to issue the following instead of a DROP USER statement:

```
DELETE FROM mysql.user
    WHERE User='rstringer' AND Host='localhost';

FLUSH PRIVILEGES;
```

Notice that the FLUSH PRIVILEGES statement is necessary so that the preceding DELETE statement takes effect immediately. It's not necessary after the DROP USER statement, though.

DROP VIEW

```
DROP VIEW [IF EXISTS] view[, ...] [RESTRICT|CASCADE]
```

Use this statement to delete a view. The IF EXISTS flag prevents error messages if the view doesn't exist before attempting to delete it. To retrieve the error message when this flag is added, use the SHOW WARNINGS statement. The RESTRICT or CASCADE options are for a future release of MySQL. This statement is available as of Version 5.0.1 of MySQL.

EXPLAIN

```
EXPLAIN {table|SELECT...}
```

You can use this statement to display information about the columns of a given table, or to display information about the results set of a given SELECT statement without displaying the rows of data. For this latter use, it will show which index the statement will use and, when multiple tables are queried, the order in which the tables are used. This can be helpful in determining the cause of a slow query.

FLUSH

```
FLUSH [LOCAL|NO_WRITE_TO_BINLOG] option[, ...]
```

Options:

```
DES_KEY_FILE, HOSTS, LOGS, PRIVILEGES, QUERY_CACHE,
STATUS, TABLE, TABLES, TABLES WITHOUT READ LOCK, USER_RESOURCES
```

Use this statement to clear temporary caches in MySQL. It requires RELOAD privileges. To prevent this statement from writing to the binary log file, the NO_WRITE_TO_BINLOG flag or its LOCAL alias may be given. The cache may be given as an option to the statement to be flushed. Multiple options may be given in a comma-separated list:

DES_KEY_FILE
: Reloads the DES encryption file.

HOSTS
: Clears the hosts cache, which is used to minimize host/IP address lookups. The hosts cache may need to be flushed if a host has been blocked from accessing the server.

LOGS
: Used to close all of the logfiles and reopen them.

PRIVILEGES
: Reloads the grant table for users. This is necessary if the *user* table in the *mysql* database is modified manually, without a GRANT statement.

QUERY CACHE
: Instructs the server to defragment the query cache.

STATUS
: Resets the various status variables.

TABLE
: Followed by one or more table names, forces the given tables to be closed. This will terminate any active queries on the given tables.

TABLES
> Causes all tables to be closed, all queries to be terminated, and the query cache will be flushed, as well. This is the same as TABLE with no table name.

TABLES WITH READ LOCK
> Closes all tables and locks them with a read lock. This will allow users to view the data, but not to update it or to insert records. The lock will remain in place until the UNLOCK TABLES statement is executed.

USER_RESOURCES
> Resets all user resources. You can use this when users have been locked out due to exceeding usage limits.

GRANT

```
GRANT privileges [(columns)][, ...] ON database.table

TO 'user'*'host' [IDENTIFIED BY [PASSWORD] 'password'][, ...]

[REQUIRE NONE|[{SSL|X509}]

[CIPHER 'cipher' [AND]]

[ISSUER 'issuer' [AND]]

[SUBJECT 'subject']]

[WITH [GRANT OPTION | MAX_QUERIES_PER_HOUR count |

                      MAX_UPDATES_PER_HOUR count |

                      MAX_CONNECTIONS_PER_HOUR count]]
```

Use this statement to create new MySQL users and to grant user privileges. Privileges can be global (apply to all databases on the server), database-specific, table-specific, or column-specific. User information is stored in the grant tables in the *mysql* database on the server. Global privileges are stored in the *user* table. Database-specific privileges are stored in the *db* table. Table privileges are in the *tables_priv* table and column privileges are in the *columns_priv* table. You can edit these tables directly with SQL statements, such as INSERT, UPDATE, and DROP, followed by a FLUSH PRIVILEGES statement to update the server's cache. However, it's recommended that you use the GRANT statement to create users and to grant privileges, and the REVOKE statement to revoke privileges.

In the syntax, the privileges to grant to a user are listed immediately after the GRANT keyword in a comma-separated list. Several privileges may be granted to a user. To give a user all simple user privileges, you can use the ALL keyword. Here is an example of how you can grant privileges to a user:

```
GRANT ALL PRIVILEGES ON *.*
   TO 'tina'@'localhost'
   IDENTIFIED BY 'muller'
   WITH GRANT OPTION;
```

In this example, the user *tina* is created and granted all basic privileges because of the ALL keyword. This does not include GRANT privilege, the ability to use the GRANT statement. To do that, the WITH GRANT OPTION clause is given, as shown here, to explicitly give that privilege to the user. It's not a good idea to give users this privilege unless they are MySQL server administrators. Table 4-1 lists and describes each privilege.

Table 4-1. Privileges in GRANT and REVOKE

Privilege	Description
ALL [PRIVILEGES]	Grants all of the basic privileges. Does not include GRANT OPTION.
ALTER	Allows use of the ALTER TABLE statement.
CREATE	Grants CREATE TABLE statement privileges.
CREATE TEMPORARY TABLES	Allows the CREATE TEMPORARY TABLES statement to be used.
CREATE VIEW	Permits the CREATE VIEW statement. This is for Version 5.0.1 of MySQL.
DELETE	Allows the DELETE statement to be used.
DROP	Permits the user to execute DROP TABLE and TRUNCATE statements.
EXECUTE	Allows the execution of stored procedures. This is available as of Version 5 of MySQL.
FILE	Allows the use of SELECT . . . INTO OUTFILE and LOAD DATA INFILE statements to export and import to and from a filesystem.
GRANT OPTION	Permits the use of the GRANT statement to grant privileges to users.
INDEX	Grants the use of CREATE INDEX and DROP INDEX statements.
INSERT	Permits the use of INSERT statements.
LOCK TABLES	Allows the use of LOCK TABLES statements for tables for which the user has SELECT privileges.
PROCESS	Allows the use of SHOW FULL PROCESSLIST statements.
REFERENCES	This is not used. It's for future releases.
RELOAD	Allows the FLUSH statement to be used.
REPLICATION CLIENT	Allows the user to query master and slave servers for status information.
REPLICATION SLAVE	Required for replication slave servers. Allows binary log events to be read from the master server.
SELECT	Allows the use of the SELECT statement.
SHOW DATABASES	Permits the use of the SHOW DATABASES statement for all databases, not just the ones for which the user has privileges.
SHOW VIEW	Allows the use of the SHOW CREATE VIEW statement. This is for MySQL Version 5.0.1 and above.
SHUTDOWN	Allows the use of the shutdown option with the *mysqladmin* utility.
SUPER	Grants use of CHANGE MASTER, KILL, PURGE MASTER LOGS, and SET GLOBAL statements, and the debug option with the command-line utility *mysqladmin*.
UPDATE	Allows the UPDATE statement to be used.
USAGE	Used to create a user without privileges.

A user's privileges can be refined to specific SQL statements and specific databases. A GRANT statement can also restrict a user only to certain tables and columns. Here is an example of a statement that leaves the user fairly limited:

```
GRANT SELECT ON workrequests.*
    TO 'jerry'@'localhost' IDENTIFIED BY 'neumeyer3186';
GRANT SELECT,INSERT,UPDATE ON workrequests.workreq
    TO 'jerry'@'localhost' IDENTIFIED BY 'neumeyer3186';
```

Assuming the user *jerry* does not already exist, the first statement here creates the user and gives him SELECT privileges only for the *workrequests* database for all of its tables. This will allow him to read from the various tables but not edit the data. The second

SQL statement grants *jerry* the right to add and to change data in the *workreq* table of the *workrequests* database. This will allow him to enter work requests and to make changes to them. The first statement makes an entry in the *db* table in the *mysql* database. The second one makes an entry in the *tables_priv* table. An entry is also made to the *user* table showing the user *jerry* but with no global privileges. This is the equivalent of granting just the USAGE privilege.

A user can also be required to communicate through an SSL connection. Various clauses specify the cipher method and other aspects of an encrypted connection.

You can use the WITH clause to grant the GRANT OPTION privilege to a user, as mentioned earlier. You also can use this clause to specify the maximum number of queries that a user may execute per hour (MAX_QUERIES_PER_HOUR), the maximum number of UPDATE statements that may be issued per hour (MAX_UPDATES_PER_HOUR), or the maximum number of connections to the server per hour (MAX_CONNECTIONS_PER_HOUR). Here is an example of how a user might be limited in such a way:

```
GRANT SELECT ON catalogs.*
  TO 'webuser'@'%'
  WITH MAX_QUERIES_PER_HOUR 1000
  MAX_CONNECTIONS_PER_HOUR 100;
```

This account is designed for large numbers of users running queries through a web server. The *webuser* user is created, and is allowed to read tables from the *catalogs* database. The user may not run more than 1,000 queries in an hour and may establish only 100 connections in an hour.

HANDLER

HANDLER *table* OPEN [AS *handle*]

HANDLER *handle* READ *index operator* (*value*,...)

  [WHERE *condition*] [LIMIT ...]

HANDLER *handle* READ *index* {FIRST|NEXT|PREV|LAST}

  [WHERE *condition*] [LIMIT ...]

HANDLER *handle* READ {FIRST|NEXT}

  [WHERE *condition*] [LIMIT ...]

HANDLER *handle* CLOSE

Use this statement as a faster alternative to the SELECT statement. The HANDLER statement establishes a handle for reading a MyISAM or an InnoDB table, much like a file handle in a programming language such as Perl. You must issue the HANDLER *table* OPEN method first to establish a table handle and assign it the name in the AS clause. The AS clause and handle name are optional, though. If an alias is not set up, the table name is used for subsequent HANDLER statements. A handle provides direct access to the table, as opposed to working from a results set. The handle is usable only by the current connection thread that established it. The table is still accessible by others, though, and is not locked by this statement. Because of this and because the method provides direct table access, the data read can change and even be incomplete on an active database while running subsequent read statements.

You can use the three HANDLER *handle* READ... formats shown here to read data from a table. The HANDLER *handle* CLOSE method is used to close a table handle. Here are a couple of basic examples of the HANDLER statement:

```
HANDLER clients OPEN AS clients_handle;
HANDLER clients_handle READ FIRST;
```

The first line creates the table handle called *clients_handle*, based on the *clients* table. The next SQL statement retrieves the first row of data from the table. The result of this statement is the same as a SELECT for all columns of the table.

If the second SQL statement in this example was run again, but with the FIRST keyword replaced with NEXT, the next row of data would be displayed. Every time the statement is run with the NEXT flag, the pointer is advanced and the next row in the table is displayed until the end of the table is reached. To retrieve more than one row, you can use the LIMIT clause like this:

```
HANDLER client_handle READ NEXT LIMIT 3;
```

This statement will display the next three rows from the table. The WHERE clause may be used with a HANDLER...READ statement in the same way as with the SELECT statement. Here is an example of this:

```
HANDLER clients_handle READ FIRST
    WHERE state = 'MA' LIMIT 5;
```

This statement will display the first five rows in which the client is located in the state of Massachusetts. Note that no ORDER BY clause is available for HANDLER...READ statements. Therefore, the first five rows are based on the order in which they are stored in the table.

To extract data based on an index, use the two HANDLER *handle* READ...*index* syntax structures. Here is example like the previous one, but with the addition of an index:

```
HANDLER clients_handle READ cid PREV
    WHERE state = 'MA' LIMIT 2;
```

In this example, two rows matching the condition of the WHERE clause, from the previous batch of rows displayed (due to the PREV flag), will be retrieved. The cid index was created when the table was created and is based on a couple of columns for uniqueness and quick retrieval of data. To retrieve the next set of rows using this syntax structure, the PREV flag would be replaced with the NEXT flag. The LAST flag searches and retrieves rows starting from the last row of the table. Here is another example using an index and not a WHERE clause:

```
HANDLER clients_handle READ name = ('NeumeyerGera');
```

The name index is a combination of the *name_last* and the *name_first* column, but only the first four characters of the first name are used by the index. Given the sample database used for this book, this statement displays the row for the client Gerard Neumeyer. The values for each column may be given with commas (e.g., *'Neumeyer'*, *'Gera'*) in between, or spliced together as shown. This feature of being able to provide a condition for a multicolumn index would be a difficult contortion with a SELECT statement.

INSERT

```
INSERT [LOW_PRIORITY|DELAYED|HIGH_PRIORITY] [IGNORE]
    [INTO] table
    SET column={expression|DEFAULT}, ...
    [ON DUPLICATE KEY UPDATE column=expression, ... ]

INSERT [LOW_PRIORITY|DELAYED|HIGH_PRIORITY] [IGNORE]
    [INTO] table [(column, ...)]
    VALUES ({expression|DEFAULT},...),(...),...
    [ON DUPLICATE KEY UPDATE column=expression, ... ]

INSERT [LOW_PRIORITY|DELAYED|HIGH_PRIORITY] [IGNORE]
    [INTO] table [(column, ...)]
    SELECT...
```

Use this statement to add rows of data to a table. Three statement structures are available. The first syntax format, the INSERT...table SET... method, can insert only one row of data per statement. The second syntax structure shown, the INSERT...table (columns) VALUES(values) method, can handle one or more rows in one statement. The columns and their order are specified once, but values for multiple rows may be given. Each row of values is to be contained in its own set of parentheses, separated by commas. The third syntax structure for this statement, the INSERT...table...SELECT... method, allows columns from rows in other tables to be inserted. Explanations of each type of statement, their various clauses and flags, and examples of their use follow.

Single-row insertion with SET clause

```
INSERT [LOW_PRIORITY|DELAYED|HIGH_PRIORITY] [IGNORE]
    [INTO] table
    SET column={expression|DEFAULT}, ...
    [ON DUPLICATE KEY UPDATE column=expression, ... ]
```

This method of the INSERT statement allows only one row of data to be inserted into a table at a time. Each column name and the value to which it's to be set is given in the SET clause, with the use of the equals-sign operator. The value given can be a static value or an expression. The DEFAULT keyword can be given instead to instruct the server to use the default value for the column. You can set the default either with the CREATE TABLE statement when the table is created or with the ALTER TABLE statement for existing tables.

You can use the LOW_PRIORITY flag to instruct the server to wait until all other queries related to the table in which data is to be added are finished before running the INSERT statement. When the table is free, the table is locked for the INSERT statement and will prevent concurrent inserts.

The DELAYED flag indicates the same priority status, but releases the client so that other queries may be run and so that the connection may be terminated. It does not confirm the success of the DELAYED query; it confirms only that the query is to be processed. If the server crashes, the data additions may not be executed when the server restarts and the user won't be informed of the failure. To confirm a DELAYED insert, the user must check the table later for the inserted content with a SELECT statement. The DELAYED option works only with MyISAM, InnoDB, and ISAM tables. It's also not applicable when the ON DUPLICATE KEY UPDATE clause is used. See the explanation for the next syntax structure of this method for more on this clause.

Use the HIGH_PRIORITY flag to override the default setting of --low-priority-updates and to disable concurrent inserts.

Here is an example of the INSERT statement using this particular syntax structure:

```
INSERT INTO clients
  SET client_name = 'Geoffrey & Company',
      city = 'Boston', state = 'MA';
```

This example lists three columns along with the values set in a row entry in the *clients* table. Other columns in that table will be handled in a default manner—for instance, an AUTO_INCREMENT column, *client_id*, that will receive the next number in sequence.

The ON DUPLICATE KEY UPDATE clause allows an INSERT statement to handle the case where an entry exists already for the data to be inserted. The clause's operation is illustrated in the following example:

```
CREATE UNIQUE INDEX client_name
  ON clients(client_name);

INSERT INTO clients
  SET client_name = 'Marie & Associates',
    telephone = '504-486-1234'
ON DUPLICATE KEY UPDATE
    telephone=VALUES(telephone);
```

This example starts by creating an index on the *client_name* column in the *clients* table. The index type is UNIQUE, which means that duplicate values for the *client_name* column are not allowed. The INSERT statement tries to insert the specified client name and telephone number. But it indicates that if there is already a row in the table for the client, a new row is not to be added. Instead, the existing row is to be updated per the UPDATE clause, setting the original entry's *telephone* column to the value given in the SET clause of the same INSERT statement. The assumption is that the new data being inserted either is for a new client or is an update to the existing client's telephone number. Instead of using a column value after the equals sign, a literal value or an expression may be given.

Multiple-row insertions

```
INSERT [LOW_PRIORITY|DELAYED|HIGH_PRIORITY] [IGNORE]
    [INTO] table [(column,...)]
    VALUES ({expression|DEFAULT},...),(...)
    [ON DUPLICATE KEY UPDATE column=expression,...]
```

This method of the INSERT statement allows for multiple rows to be inserted in one SQL statement. The columns in which data is to be inserted may be given in parentheses in a comma-separated list. If no columns are specified, the statement must include a value for each column in each row, in the order that they appear in the table. The VALUES clause lists the values of each row to be inserted into the table. The values for each row are enclosed in parentheses; each row is separated by a comma. Here is an example of this syntax structure:

```
INSERT INTO clients (client_name, telephone)
  VALUES('Marie & Associates', '504-486-1234'),
        ('Geoffrey & Company', '617-522-1234'),
        ('Kenneth & Partners', '617-523-1234');
```

In this example, three rows are inserted into the *clients* table with one SQL statement. Although the table has several columns, only two columns are inserted for each row here. The other columns are set to their default or to NULL. The order of the values for each row corresponds with the order that the columns are listed.

Normally, if a multiple INSERT statement is entered and one of the rows to be inserted is a duplicate, an error is triggered and an error message is displayed. The statement is terminated and no rows are inserted. The IGNORE flag, however, instructs the server to ignore any errors encountered, suppress the error messages, and insert only the non-duplicate rows. The INTO keyword is optional and only for compatibility. The results of this statement display like so:

```
Query OK, 120 row affected (4.20 sec)
Records: 125  Duplicates: 5  Warnings: 0
```

These results indicate that 125 records were to be inserted, but only 120 rows were affected or successfully inserted. There were five duplicates in the SQL statement, but there were no warnings because of the IGNORE flag.

Inserting rows based on a SELECT

```
INSERT [LOW_PRIORITY|DELAYED|HIGH_PRIORITY] [IGNORE]
    [INTO] table [(column,...)]
    SELECT...
```

This method of the INSERT statement allows for multiple rows to be inserted in one SQL statement, based on data retrieved from another table by way of a SELECT statement. If a list of columns is given, those columns in the new table are filled with values returned by the SELECT statement from the other table, on a one-by-one basis in the order listed. If no columns are listed, the SELECT must return values for all columns in the order in which they appear in the new table.

For the following example, suppose that the *employees* table contains a column called *softball* to indicate whether an employee is a member of the company's softball team. Suppose further that it is decided that a new table should be created to store information about members of the softball team and that the team's captain will have privileges to this new table (*softball_team*), but no other tables. The employee names and telephone numbers need to be copied into the new table, because the team's captain will not be allowed to do a query on the *employees* table to extract that information. Here are the SQL statements to set up the new table with its initial data:

```
CREATE TABLE softball_team
    (rec_id INT AUTO_INCREMENT PRIMARY KEY,
    name VARCHAR(50),  position VARCHAR(20),
    emp_id INT, telephone CHAR(8));

INSERT INTO softball_team
    (emp_id, name, telephone)
    SELECT rec_id, CONCAT(name_first, ' ', name_last),
        RIGHT(telephone_home, 8)
      FROM employees
      WHERE softball = 'Y';
```

The first SQL statement creates the new table. The columns are very simple: one column for both the first and last name of the player, and one column for the player's home telephone number. There's also a column for a record identification number and another for the player's position, to be filled in later by the team's captain. In the second SQL statement, the INSERT statement uses an embedded SELECT statement to retrieve data from the *employees* table where the *softball* column for the row is set to 'Y'. The CONCAT( ) function is used to put together the first and last name, separated by a space. This will go into the *name* column in the new table. The RIGHT( ) function is used to extract only the last eight characters of the *telephone_home* column, because all of the employees on the softball team are from the same telephone dialing area. See Chapter 5 for more information on these functions.

JOIN

SELECT... | UPDATE... | DELETE...

table [INNER|CROSS] JOIN *table* [ON *condition*|USING (*column*,...)]

table STRAIGHT_JOIN *table*

table LEFT [OUTER] JOIN *table* [ON *condition*|USING (*column*,...)]

table NATURAL [LEFT [OUTER]] JOIN *table*

   [OJ *table* LEFT OUTER JOIN *table* ON *condition*]

table RIGHT [OUTER] JOIN *table* [ON *condition*|USING (*column*,...)]

table NATURAL [RIGHT [OUTER]] JOIN *table*

The JOIN clause is common to several SQL statements (SELECT, UPDATE, DELETE) and is complex: therefore, it is listed here as its own entry in the chapter. You use JOIN to link tables together based on columns with common data for purposes of selecting, updating, or deleting data. The JOIN clause is entered at the place in the relevant statement that specifies the tables to be referenced. This precludes the need to join the tables based on key columns in the WHERE clause. The ON keyword is used to indicate the condition by which the tables will be joined.

As an alternative method, the USING keyword may be given along with a comma-separated list of columns within parentheses. The columns must be contained in each table that is joined. Here is an example of a JOIN:

```
SELECT CONCAT(name_first, SPACE(1), name_last) AS Name
    FROM employees
    JOIN branches ON branch_id = branches.rec_id
    WHERE location = 'New Orleans';
```

This statement will display a list of employees from the *employees* table who are located in the New Orleans branch office. The problem being solved with the JOIN is that the *employees* table doesn't indicate New Orleans by name as the branch; that table just has a numeric identifier. The *branches* table is used to retrieve the branch name for the WHERE clause. The *location* column is a column in the *branches* table. Nothing is actually displayed from the *branches* table here.

If the record identification column for *branches* was named *branch_id* rather than *rec_id*, the USING keyword and associated method could be used for the same JOIN. Here is an example of this method for the same statement:

```
SELECT CONCAT(name_first, SPACE(1), name_last) AS Name
    FROM employees
    JOIN branches USING (branch_id)
    WHERE location = 'New Orleans';
```

This will join the two tables on the *branch_id* column in each table. These tables have only one row in common, so it's not necessary to specify that row; instead, you can use the NATURAL keyword. Here is the same statement with this change:

```
SELECT CONCAT(name_first, SPACE(1), name_last) AS Name
    FROM employees
    NATURAL JOIN branches
    WHERE location = 'New Orleans';
```

Notice that the USING keyword and the column for linking were omitted. The results of this SQL statement will be the same as for the previous one.

When joining two tables in a simple join, as shown in the previous example, if no rows in the second table match rows from the first table, no row will be displayed for the unmatched data. Sometimes, though, it can be useful to display a record regardless. The LEFT keyword may be given in front of the JOIN keyword to indicate that records from the first table listed on the left are to be displayed regardless of whether there is a matching row in the table on the right:

```
SELECT CONCAT(name_first, SPACE(1), name_last) AS Name,
        location AS Branch
    FROM employees
    LEFT JOIN branches USING (branch_id);
```

This SQL statement will list a row for each employee along with the employee's location. If a row for an employee has either a NULL value for the *branch_id*, or a branch number that is not in the *branches* table, the employee name will still be displayed but with the branch name reading as NULL. This can be useful for spotting errors or inconsistencies in the data between related tables.

In contrast to LEFT JOIN, the RIGHT JOIN clause includes all matching entries from the table on the right even if there are no matches from the table on the left. Here is an example using a RIGHT JOIN:

```
SELECT CONCAT(name_first, SPACE(1), name_last) AS 'Sales Rep',
        SUM(total_order) AS Sales
    FROM orders
    RIGHT JOIN employees ON sales_rep = employees.rec_id
    WHERE dept = 'sales'
    GROUP BY sales_rep;
```

This example displays a list of employees who are members of the sales department, with the sum of their orders. If a sales representative does not have any orders, a row will still be presented because of the RIGHT JOIN. For both the LEFT and RIGHT JOIN methods, the OUTER keyword may be included, but it's not necessary and has no effect on the results. It's just a matter of preference and compatibility. NATURAL may also be combined with LEFT JOIN and RIGHT JOIN clauses.

The JOIN clause has a few other options. The STRAIGHT_JOIN flag explicitly instructs MySQL to read the tables as listed, from left to right. The keywords INNER and CROSS have no effect on the results, as of recent versions of MySQL. They cannot be used in conjunction with the keywords LEFT, RIGHT, or NATURAL. The syntax starting with the OJ keyword is for compatibility with ODBC.

Table flags and indexing options

You can use the AS keyword to introduce aliases for tables. Several examples of aliasing were provided earlier in the explanation of this clause.

When tables are joined and data is searched by MySQL, use indexes to increase the speed of SQL statements. To indicate to MySQL which index or key it should look to first for queries, you can provide the USE INDEX option along with the names of the keys to use in a comma-separated list, within parentheses. To instruct MySQL not to use certain keys, list them with the IGNORE INDEX option in the same manner. The FORCE INDEX option instructs MySQL to attempt to limit its search to the specified index; others, however, will be used if the requested columns make it necessary.

KILL

KILL [CONNECTION|QUERY] *thread*

Use this statement to terminate a client connection to MySQL. You can use the SHOW PROCESSLIST statement to obtain a connection thread identifier. As of Version 5, you can use CONNECTION or QUERY flags to distinguish between terminating a connection or terminating just the query associated with the connection for the given thread. Some processes cannot be terminated immediately. Instead, this statement flags the process for termination. The system may not check the flag until the process is completed. This will occur with statements such as REPAIR TABLE.

Here is an example of this statement:

    KILL 22;

This simple example terminates the connection for the client associated with the thread identifier 22. If that client attempts to issue another SQL statement, it will receive an error 2006 message stating that the MySQL server has gone away. Then it typically will try to reconnect to the server, establish a new thread, and run the requested query.

LOAD DATA FROM MASTER

LOAD DATA FROM MASTER

This statement makes a copy of all the databases on the master server (except the *mysql* database) and then copies them to the slave servers. This statement will get a global read lock on all tables while it takes a snapshot of the databases. It will release the lock before copying them to the slaves. The MASTER_LOG_FILE and the MASTER_LOG_POS variables will be updated so that the slave knows where to begin logging. This statement currently works only with MyISAM tables, but will eventually work with InnoDB tables in future releases. The user for the connection must have RELOAD, SELECT, and SUPER privileges on the master server. The user must also have CREATE and DROP privileges on the slave server.

For large databases, increase the values of the net_read_timeout and net_write_timeout variables with the SET statement. To load a specific table from the master server, use the LOAD TABLE...FROM MASTER statement.

LOAD DATA INFILE

```
LOAD DATA [LOW_PRIORITY|CONCURRENT] [LOCAL] INFILE 'filename'

    [REPLACE|IGNORE] INTO TABLE table

    [FIELDS [TERMINATED BY 'C']

        [[OPTIONALLY] ENCLOSED BY 'C']

        [ESCAPED BY 'C']]

    [LINES [STARTING BY 'C'] [TERMINATED BY 'C']]

    [IGNORE count LINES]

    [(column,...)]
```

You can use this statement to import organized data properly from a text file into a table on the server. The data text file must be located either in the directory of the database into which the data is to be imported or in a directory on the server's file-system with the file permission set to read for all filesystem users. If the text file is on the client's filesystem, the LOCAL flag must be given. This feature must be enabled on both the client and the server with --local-infile=1. See Chapter 10 for more information on these settings. Here is a basic example of how you can use this statement:

```
LOAD DATA INFILE '/tmp/catalog.txt'
    INTO TABLE catalog
    FIELDS TERMINATED BY '|'
    LINES TERMINATED BY '\n';
```

In this example, the file to be loaded is in the */tmp* directory and is called *catalog.txt*. The data contained in the file is to be inserted into the *catalog* table in the current database in use. Each field in the text file is terminated with a vertical bar character. The rows of data in the text file are on separate lines. They are separated by a newline character (\n). This is the default for a Unix text file. For DOS or Windows systems, lines are usually terminated with a \n\r, signifying a newline and a return character. If the rows start with a special character, you can identify that character with the LINES STARTED BY clause.

If a data text file contains rows of data that are duplicates of some of the rows in the table into which it's being imported, an error will occur and the import may end without importing the remaining data. Duplicate rows are those that have the same values for key columns. To instruct the server to ignore any errors encountered and to proceed with the import, you should use the IGNORE flag. Use the SHOW WARNINGS statement to retrieve the error messages that would have been displayed. To instruct the server to replace any duplicate rows with the ones being imported, use the REPLACE flag with the statement. This will completely replace the values of all columns, even when the new record contains no data for a column and the existing one does.

This statement also offers the ENCLOSED BY clause to specify a character that can start and terminate a field, such as a quotation mark. You can use the OPTIONALLY flag to indicate that the character is an optional one. The character which is used to escape special characters may be given with the ESCAPED BY clause. The backslash is the default value.

Some data text files contain one or more lines of column headings that should not be imported. To omit these initial lines from the import, use the IGNORE *count* LINES clause, where *count* is the number of lines to ignore.

For some data text files, the fields of data are not in the same order as the columns of the receiving table. Sometimes there are fewer fields in the text file than in the table. For both of these situations, to change the order and number of columns, add a list of columns and their order in the text file to the end of the statement within parentheses. Here is an example of such a scenario:

```
LOAD DATA LOW_PRIORITY INFILE '/tmp/catalog.txt' IGNORE
    INTO TABLE catalog
    FIELDS TERMINATED BY '|'
    LINES TERMINATED BY '\n'
    IGNORE 1 LINES
    (cat_id, description, price);
```

The first line of the text file contains column headings describing the data, but that line will not be imported because of the IGNORE 1 LINES clause here. The *catalog* table has several more columns than the three that are being imported and they are in a different order. This import is not critical. Therefore, the LOW_PRIORITY flag near the beginning of the statement instructs the server to handle other queries on the *catalog* table before running this statement. If this was replaced with CONCURRENT, the import would be performed even if other clients are querying the same table.

LOAD INDEX INTO CACHE

LOAD INDEX INTO CACHE

  table [[INDEX|KEY] (*index*[, ...)] [IGNORE LEAVES]

  [, ...]

Use this statement to preload a table's index into a given key cache for a MyISAM table. Although one or more indexes may be specified in a comma-separated list in parentheses, all indexes for the table will be loaded into the cache. This will change in future versions of MySQL. The keywords INDEX and KEY are interchangeable and are not necessary. The IGNORE LEAVES clause instructs MySQL not to preload leaf nodes of the index. Here is an example of how you can use this statement:

```
LOAD INDEX INTO CACHE workreq;
```

```
+----------------------+--------------+----------+----------+
| Table                | Op           | Msg_type | Msg_text |
+----------------------+--------------+----------+----------+
| workrequests.workreq | preload_keys | status   | OK       |
+----------------------+--------------+----------+----------+
```

LOAD TABLE...FROM MASTER

LOAD TABLE *table* FROM MASTER

Use this statement to copy a MyISAM table from the master server to a slave server. The user for the connection must have RELOAD and SUPER privileges as well as SELECT privileges for the table on the master server. The user must also have CREATE and DROP privileges on the slave server.

LOCK TABLES

LOCK TABLES *table* [AS *alias*]

    {READ [LOCAL]|[LOW_PRIORITY] WRITE]} [, ...]

Use this statement to lock given tables for exclusive use of the current connection thread. A READ lock will allow the locked tables to be read, but will not allow writes to them even by the thread which locked them. A READ LOCAL lock will allow all threads to read the tables that are locked while the locking connection can execute INSERT statements. Until the lock is released, though, direct data manipulation by command-line utilities should be avoided. A WRITE lock will not allow other threads to read or write to tables locked, but will permit reads and writes by the locking thread. SQL statements for tables that are locked with the WRITE option have priority over statements involving tables with a READ lock. However, the LOW_PRIORITY flag may be given before the WRITE to instruct the server to wait until there are no queries on the tables being locked.

Only locked tables may be accessed by a locking thread. So, all tables to be used must be locked. To illustrate this, assume a new programmer has been hired. The programmer's information will need to be added to the *programmers* table. The *wk_schedule* table that contains the records for scheduling work will also need to be adjusted to assign work to the new programmer and away from others. Here is how you might lock the relevant tables:

    LOCK TABLES workreq READ, programmers READ LOCAL,
      wk_schedule AS work LOW_PRIORITY WRITE;

In this example, the *workreq* table is locked with a READ flag so that no new work requests may be added while the table for the programmers' work schedules is being updated, but the work requests may still be viewed by other users. The *programmers* table is locked for writing with the READ LOCAL flag, because one record needs to be inserted for the new programmer's personal information. The *wk_schedule* table is locked for exclusive use by the current thread.

For convenience, you can give a table an alias with the AS keyword. In the previous example, the *wk_schedule* table is referred to as *work* for subsequent SQL statements until the tables are unlocked. During this time, the thread can refer to the table only by this name in all other SQL statements.

You can release locks with the UNLOCK TABLES statements. Issuing a START TRANSACTION statement will also cause tables to unlock. Executing another TABLE LOCKS statement will also release table locks. Therefore, all tables to be locked should be named in one statement. Additional tables can be added to the end of the TABLE LOCKS statement in a comma-separated list.

You can lock all tables with a FLUSH TABLES WITH READ LOCK statement. You can use the GET_LOCK( ) and RELEASE_LOCK( ) functions as alternatives to LOCK TABLES and UNLOCK TABLES. See Chapter 9.

OPTIMIZE TABLE

OPTIMIZE [LOCAL|NO_WRITE_TO_BINLOG] TABLE *table*[, ...]

Use this statement to optimize the data contained in a table. Optimization is useful when many rows have been deleted from a table. It's also useful to run this statement periodically with a table that contains several variable-character-width columns (i.e., VARCHAR, BLOB, and TEXT columns). This statement generally works only with MyISAM, BDB, and InnoDB tables. It may work on other tables, however, if the *mysqld* daemon is started with the `--skip-new` option or the `--safe-mode` option. See Chapter 10 for more information on setting server startup options.

This statement will repair some row problems and sort indexes. It will temporarily lock the tables involved while optimizing. Multiple tables can be listed for optimization in a comma-separated list. To prevent the activities of this statement from being recorded in the binary log file, use the `NO_WRITE_TO_BINLOG` flag or its alias, `LOCAL`. Here is an example of its use:

```
OPTIMIZE LOCAL TABLE workreq, clients;
```

```
+----------------------+----------+----------+----------+
| Table                | Op       | Msg_type | Msg_text |
+----------------------+----------+----------+----------+
| workrequests.workreq | optimize | status   | OK       |
| workrequests.clients | optimize | status   | OK       |
+----------------------+----------+----------+----------+
```

Here two tables were optimized successfully and the activity was not written to the binary log file.

PURGE MASTER LOGS

`PURGE {MASTER|BINARY} LOGS {TO 'filename'|BEFORE 'date'}`

Use this statement to delete the binary logs from a master server. The keywords `MASTER` and `BINARY` are synonymous and one is required for the statement. Log files are deleted sequentially from the starting logfile to the one named with the `TO` clause, or up until (but not including) the date named with the `BEFORE` clause. Here is an example of each method:

```
PURGE MASTER LOGS TO 'log-bin.00110';
PURGE MASTER LOGS BEFORE '2004-11-03 07:00:00';
```

Use the `SHOW MASTER LOGS` statement to obtain a list of logfiles before purging. When using slave servers, run the `SHOW SLAVE LOGS` statement on each slave to determine the oldest log that is still in use before deciding which logfiles to delete. It would also be prudent to make a backup of the logs before running this statement.

RENAME TABLE

`RENAME TABLE table TO table[,...]`

Use this statement to rename a given table to the name given after the `TO` keyword. Additional tables may be specified for renaming in a comma-separated list. Multiple renames are performed left to right, and if any errors are encountered, all of the table name changes are reversed from right to left. While tables are being renamed, no other client can interact with the tables involved. Tables that are currently locked or tables that are part of a transaction in progress cannot be renamed.

Tables can be renamed and moved to databases on the same filesystem. As an example, suppose that users add data to a particular table during the course of the day and that each day the contents of the table are to be preserved. Suppose further that you want to reset the table back to no data. Here's how to do that:

```
CREATE TABLE survey_new LIKE survey_bak;
RENAME TABLE survey TO survey_bak,
             survey_new TO survey;
```

In this example, a new table called *survey_new* is created based on the table structure of the old table called *survey*, but without the data. In the second SQL statement, the old table is renamed to *survey_bak* and the blank table, *survey_new*, is renamed to *survey*. If issued from a program, the new name could be generated based upon the date so that each day's data could be preserved.

REPAIR TABLE

REPAIR [LOCAL|NO_WRITE_TO_BINLOG] TABLE

    table[, ...] [QUICK] [EXTENDED] [USE_FRM]

Use this statement to repair corrupted MyISAM tables. Multiple tables may be given in a comma-separated list. To prevent this statement from recording its activities in the binary log file, the NO_WRITE_TO_BINLOG flag or its LOCAL alias may be given. The QUICK flag instructs MySQL to repair the table indexes only. The EXTENDED flag is for rebuilding the indexes one row at a time. This option takes longer, but can be more effective, especially with rows containing duplicate keys. Before running this statement, make a backup of the table. If a table continues to have problems, there may be other problems (e.g., filesystem problems) that you should consider. Here is an example of this statement:

```
REPAIR TABLE systems QUICK EXTENDED;
```

```
+---------------------+--------+----------+----------+
| Table               | Op     | Msg_type | Msg_text |
+---------------------+--------+----------+----------+
| workrequests.systems | repair | status   | OK       |
+---------------------+--------+----------+----------+
```

In this example, the repair was successful. This is indicated by the OK in the *Msg_text* field. If it were unsuccessful, you could try the USE_FRM option with this statement. This option will create a new index file (*.MYI*) using the table schema file (*.frm*). It won't be able to determine the current value for AUTO_INCREMENT columns or for DELETE LINK, so it shouldn't be used unless the original *.MYI* file is lost. Incidentally, if the MySQL server dies while the REPAIR TABLE statement is running, you should run the statement again as soon as the server is back up, before running any other SQL statements.

REPLACE

```
REPLACE [LOW_PRIORITY|DELAYED] [INTO] table [(column,...)]

    VALUES ({expression|DEFAULT},...)[, (...)]

REPLACE [LOW_PRIORITY|DELAYED] [INTO] table

    SET column={expression|DEFAULT}, ...

REPLACE [LOW_PRIORITY|DELAYED] [INTO] table [(column,...)]

    SELECT...
```

Use this statement to insert new rows of data and to replace existing rows where the PRIMARY KEY or UNIQUE index key is the same as the new record being inserted. The LOW_ PRIORITY flag instructs the server to wait until there are no queries on the table named, including reads, and then to lock the table for exclusive use by the thread so that data may be inserted and replaced. When the statement is finished, the lock is released automatically. For busy servers, a client may be waiting for quite a while. The DELAYED flag will free the client by storing the statement in a buffer for processing when the table is not busy. The client won't be given notice of the success of the statement, just that it's buffered. If the server crashes before the changes to the data are processed, the client will not be informed and the buffer contents will be lost. The INTO keyword is optional, and is a matter of style preference and compatibility. This statement requires INSERT and DELETE privileges, because it is potentially a combination of both.

Three basic statement structures may be used to insert and replace data. For the syntax of the first one shown, the values for each row are placed in parentheses after the VALUES keyword. If the number of values and their order do not match the columns of the table named, the columns will have to be listed in parentheses after the table name in the order in which the values are arranged. Here is an example of the REPLACE statement using this syntax structure:

```
REPLACE INTO workreq (wr_id, client_id, description)
VALUES('5768','1000','Network Access Problem'),
      ('5770','1000','Network Access Problem');
```

Notice that this statement is able to insert two rows without the column names being listed twice. In this example, the first row already existed before this statement was to be executed. Once it's run, the row represented by work request identifier 5768 is completely replaced with this data. Columns that are not included in the list of columns here are reset to their default values or to NULL, depending on the column.

The second syntax structure for the REPLACE statement shown does not allow for multiple rows. Instead of grouping the column names in one part of the statement and the values in another part, column names and values are given in a *column=value* pair. To enter the REPLACE statement from the preceding example in the format of the second syntax structure, you would have to enter the following two statements:

```
REPLACE INTO workreq
    SET wr_id = '5768', client_id = '1000',
        description = 'Network Access Problem';
REPLACE INTO workreq
    SET wr_id = '5770', client_id = '1000',
        description = 'Network Access Problem';
```

The third syntax structure for the REPLACE statement involves a subquery, which is available as of Version 4.1 of MySQL. With a subquery, data can be retrieved from another table and inserted into the table referenced in the main query for the statement. Here is an example of this:

```
REPLACE INTO workreq (wr_id, client_id, status)
SELECT wr_id, client_id, 'HOLD'
   FROM wk_schedule
   WHERE programmer_id = '1000';
```

In this example, work requests assigned to a particular programmer are being changed to a temporarily on-hold status. The values for two of the columns are taken from the work schedule table and the fixed string of HOLD is inserted as the value of the third column. Currently, the table for which replacement data is being inserted cannot be used in the subquery.

RESET

RESET option[, ...]

Use this statement to reset certain server settings and files. Currently, you can reset the MASTER, QUERY CACHE, and SLAVE options. See the RESET MASTER statement and the RESET SLAVE statement for detailed explanations of each option. The QUERY CACHE option will clear the cache containing SQL query results.

RESET MASTER

RESET MASTER

Use this statement to delete all the binary log files on the master server. Binary logfiles are located in the directory indicated by the value of the --bin-log option of *mysqld* (see Chapter 10). The logfiles are typically named *log-bin.n*, where *n* is a six-digit numbering index. Use the SHOW MASTER LOGS statement to get a list of log files to be sure.

This statement will delete all of the master logfiles and begin the numbering of the new file at 000001. To get the slave servers in line with the reset master, run the RESET SLAVE statement. You can run the MASTER and SLAVE options together in a comma-separated list like so:

```
RESET MASTER, SLAVE;
```

This is a recommended method for ensuring consistency.

RESET SLAVE

RESET SLAVE

Use this statement within or after the RESET MASTER statement that sets the binary logging index back to 1. This statement will delete the *master.info* file, the *relay-log. info* file, and all of the relay logfiles on the slave server. A new *.info* file will be created with the default, start-up values.

RESTORE TABLE

RESTORE TABLE *table*[, ...] FROM '*/path*'

Use this statement to restore a table that was saved to the filesystem by the BACKUP TABLE statement. Multiple tables may be given in a comma-separated list. The absolute path to the directory containing the backup files is given within quotes. If the tables already exist in the database, an error message will be generated and the restore will fail. If it's successful, the table indexes will be built automatically. This is necessary because the BACKUP TABLE statement doesn't back up the index files.

    RESTORE TABLE clients, programmers FROM '/tmp/backup';

```
+-------------------------+---------+----------+----------+
| Table                   | Op      | Msg_type | Msg_text |
+-------------------------+---------+----------+----------+
| workrequests.clients    | restore | status   | OK       |
+-------------------------+---------+----------+----------+
| workrequests.programmers | restore | status  | OK       |
+-------------------------+---------+----------+----------+
```

In this example, the statement was successful in restoring the *.frm* and *.MYD* files located in the backup directory. The *.MYI* files were generated automatically after they were restored.

REVOKE

REVOKE ALL PRIVILEGES, GRANT OPTION FROM *user*[, ...]

REVOKE *privileges* [(*column*, ...)]

   ON *table.database*

   FROM *user*[, ...]

Use this statement to revoke all or certain privileges that were granted to a user with the GRANT statement. The first syntax structure is used to revoke all privileges from a user. Multiple users may be given in a comma-separated list. A list of users and their privileges are stored in the *mysql* database, in particular in the *user* table.

To revoke only some privileges, you can use the second syntax structure. The specific privileges are to be given in a comma-separated list after the keyword REVOKE. To revoke privileges for specific columns, those columns may be listed within parentheses in a comma-separated list. Privileges that are granted based on columns are stored in the *columns_priv* table of the *mysql* database. Privileges may be revoked on a specific table for a specific database. To revoke privileges on all tables of a database, the table name should be substituted with an asterisk as a wildcard. You can do the same for the database name for the statement to apply to all databases. Table-specific privileges are stored in the *tables_priv* table, and database privileges are stored in the *db* table.

ROLLBACK

ROLLBACK

Use this statement with an InnoDB or BDB table to reverse transactions that have not yet been committed. If AUTOCOMMIT is enabled, it must be disabled for this statement to be meaningful. To do this, set the value of AUTOCOMMIT to 0 with the SET statement. You can also disable AUTOCOMMIT with the START TRANSACTION statement and reinstate it with the COMMIT statement.

Here is an example of this statement's use:

```
START TRANSACTION;
LOCK TABLES orders WRITE;
INSERT DATA INFILE '/tmp/customer_orders.sql'
  INTO TABLE orders;
SELECT ...;
ROLLBACK;
UNLOCK TABLES;
```

In this example, after the batch of orders was inserted into the *orders* table, the administrator manually enters a series of SELECT statements (not shown) to check the integrity of the data. If everything seems alright, the COMMIT statement would be issued instead of the ROLLBACK statement shown here, to commit the transactions. If there is a problem, though, the ROLLBACK statement could be issued as shown here. It would remove the data imported by the INSERT DATA INFILE statement.

The ROLLBACK statement works only with InnoDB and BDB tables. A rollback will not undo the creation or deletion of databases. It also cannot be performed on changes to table schema (i.e., ALTER TABLE, CREATE TABLE, or DROP TABLE statements).

Transactions cannot be reversed with the ROLLBACK statement if they have been committed. Commits are caused by the COMMIT statement, as well as with the following statements: ALTER TABLE, BEGIN, CREATE INDEX, DROP DATABASE, DROP INDEX, DROP TABLE, LOAD MASTER DATA, LOCK TABLES, RENAME TABLE, SET AUTOCOMMIT=1, START TRANSACTION, TRUNCATE TABLE, and UNLOCK TABLES.

ROLLBACK TO SAVEPOINT

ROLLBACK TO SAVEPOINT *identifier*

This statement instructs the server to reverse SQL statements for the current transaction back to a saved point in the transaction identified by the SAVEPOINT statement. See the SAVEPOINT statement for an example of its use. It works only on InnoDB and BDB tables.

SAVEPOINT

SAVEPOINT *identifier*

Use this statement in conjunction with the ROLLBACK TO SAVEPOINT statement to identify a point in a transaction to which SQL statements may potentially be undone later. You can use any unreserved word to identify a save point and create several save points during a transaction. If an additional SAVEPOINT statement is issued with the same name, the previous point will be replaced with the new point for the name given.

```
START TRANSACTION;
LOCK TABLES orders WRITE;
INSERT DATA INFILE '/tmp/customer_info.sql'
  INTO TABLE orders;
SAVEPOINT orders_import;
INSERT DATA INFILE '/tmp/customer_orders.sql'
  INTO TABLE orders;
```

At this point in this example, the administrator can check the results of the orders imported before committing the transactions. If the administrator decides that the orders imported have problems, but not the client information that was first imported, the following statement could be entered:

```
ROLLBACK TO SAVEPOINT orders_import;
```

If the administrator also decides that the customer information that was imported also has problems, the ROLLBACK statement can be issued to undo the entire transaction.

SELECT

SELECT [*flags*] {*column,* ... |*expressions*}[, ...]

  FROM *table*[, ...]

  [WHERE *condition*]

  [GROUP BY {*column*|*expression*|*position*}[ASC|DESC], ...

     [WITH ROLLUP]]

  [HAVING *condition*]

  [ORDER BY {*column*|*expression*|*position*}[ASC|DESC] , ...]

  [LIMIT {[*offset,*] *count*|*count* OFFSET *offset*}]

  [PROCEDURE *procedure*(*arguments*)]

   options

Use this statement to retrieve and display data from tables within a database. It has many clauses and options. However, for simple data retrieval many of them can be omitted. The basic syntax for the statement is shown. After the SELECT keyword, some flags may be given. Next, a list of columns to retrieve and/or expressions may be given, separated by commas. For the tables, all that is required is one or more table names from which to retrieve data in a comma-separated list. The remaining clauses may be called on to refine the data to be retrieved, to order it, and so forth. These various flags, options, and clauses are detailed in subsections to this statement explanation. Here is a simple example of how you can use this statement:

```
SELECT name_first, name_last, telephone_home,
       DATEDIFF(now( ), last_review)
       AS 'Days Since Last Review'
    FROM employees;
```

In this example, three columns and the results of an expression based on a fourth column are to be displayed. The first and last name of each employee, each employee's home telephone number, and the difference between the date of the employee's last employment review and the date now are listed. This last field has the addition of the

AS keyword to set the column heading of the results set, and to name an alias for the field. An alias may be referenced in subsequent clauses of the same statement (e.g., the ORDER BY clause). To select all columns in the table, the wildcard * can be given instead of the column names.

SELECT statement flags

```
SELECT
    [ALL|DISTINCT|DISTINCTROW]
    [HIGH_PRIORITY] [STRAIGHT_JOIN]
    [SQL_SMALL_RESULT] [SQL_BIG_RESULT] [SQL_BUFFER_RESULT]
    [SQL_CACHE|SQL_NO_CACHE] [SQL_CALC_FOUND_ROWS]
  {column|expression}[, ...]
  FROM table[, ...]
    [WHERE condition] [other clauses] [options]
```

After the SELECT keyword and before the columns and expressions are listed in the SELECT statement, several flags may be given. They are shown in the preceding syntax, with the other components of the statement abbreviated.

When a WHERE clause is used with the statement, sometimes rows contain duplicate data. If you want all rows that meet the selection conditions to be displayed, you may include the ALL flag. This is the default, so it's not necessary to give this flag. If only the first occurrence of a row should be displayed and the duplicates should not be displayed, you should include the DISTINCT flag. The DISTINCTROW flag is a synonym for DISTINCT.

Any UPDATE statements that are issued have priority over SELECT statements; they will be run first. To give a particular SELECT statement higher priority than any UPDATE statements, you will need to use the HIGH_PRIORITY flag.

Multiple tables may be selected in this statement. The column on which they should be joined is given with the WHERE clause, the JOIN clause, or the UNION clause. The JOIN clause and the UNION (or SELECT...UNION) clause are described separately in this chapter. For optimization, MySQL might not join tables in the order that they are listed in the SQL statement. To insist on joining in the order given, you must use the STRAIGHT_JOIN flag.

When you know that the results of a SELECT statement using the DISTINCT flag or the GROUP BY clause will be small, you can use the SQL_SMALL_RESULT flag. This will cause MySQL to use temporary tables, with a key based on the GROUP BY clause elements, to sort the results and will possibly make for faster data retrieval. If you expect the results to be large, you can use the SQL_BIG_RESULT flag. This will cause MySQL to use temporary tables on the filesystem. Regardless of whether you use DISTINCT or GROUP BY, the SQL_BUFFER_RESULT flag may be given for any SELECT statement to have MySQL use a temporary table to buffer the results. You can use only one of the three flags mentioned in this paragraph in each statement.

If the MySQL server does not use the query cache by default, it can be overridden for a particular SELECT statement. To do this, include the SQL_CACHE flag. If the server does use the query cache by default, you can use the SQL_NO_CACHE to instruct MySQL not to use the cache for a particular SELECT statement. To determine if the server uses query cache by default, use the SHOW VARIABLES statement and look for the query_cache_type variable in the results.

The last flag available is SQL_CALC_FOUND_ROWS. With this flag, the number of rows that meet the conditions of the statement are counted. This is not affected by a LIMIT clause. The results of this count must be retrieved in a separate SELECT statement with the FOUND_ROWS( ) function. See Chapter 9 for information on this function.

Exporting SELECT results

```
SELECT [flags] columns|expressions
    [INTO OUTFILE 'filename'
        [FIELDS TERMINATED BY 'C']
        [FIELDS ENCLOSED BY 'C']
        [ESCAPED BY 'C' ]]
        [LINES [STARTING BY 'C'] [TERMINATED BY 'C']]

    |INTO DUMPFILE 'filename']
    FROM table[, ...]
    [WHERE condition]
    [other clauses] [options]
```

The INTO clause is used to export data selected to an external text file. The column names and other information will not be exported. To set the character used to terminate fields, use the FIELDS TERMINATED BY option. Use the FIELDS ENCLOSED BY option to specify the character to be placed around each field. You can set the character which is to be used to escape special characters with the ESCAPED BY option. By default, the backslash is used. You can use the LINES STARTING BY option to set the character that will signify the beginning of a row. Use the LINES TERMINATED BY option to identify the character that indicates the end of a line. Here is an example of this clause and these options:

```
SELECT * FROM employees
    INTO OUTFILE '/tmp/employees.txt'
    FIELDS TERMINATED BY '|'
    LINES TERMINATED BY '\n'
    ESCAPED BY '\\';
```

The text file that's created by this SQL statement will contain a separate line for each row selected. Each field will end with a vertical bar. Any special characters (e.g., an apostrophe) will be preceded by a backslash. Because a backslash is an escape character within an SQL statement, two are needed in the ESCAPE BY clause, because the first escapes the second. To import such a data text file, use the INSERT...LOAD DATA INFILE statement.

The second syntax structure uses the clause INTO DUMPFILE. This clause is used to export only one row into an external text file. It does not allow for any field or line terminator like the INTO OUTFILE clause. Here is an example of its use:

```
SELECT photograph
    INTO DUMPFILE '/tmp/bobs_picture.jpeg'
    FROM employees
    WHERE emp_id = '1827';
```

This statement will export the contents of the photograph column for an employee's record. It's a BLOB type column and contains an image file. The result of the exported file is a complete and usable image file.

Grouping SELECT results

```
SELECT [flags] column|expression[, ...]
    FROM table[, ...]
        [WHERE condition]
        [GROUP BY {column|expression|position}[ASC|DESC], ...
            [WITH ROLLUP]]
        [other clauses] [options]
```

When running a SELECT statement, sometimes it's more meaningful to group together those rows containing the same value for a particular column. The GROUP BY clause specifies one or more columns by which MySQL is to group the data retrieved. This is used with aggregate functions so that the values of numeric columns for the rows grouped will be aggregated. For instance, suppose that a SELECT statement is to list the sales representatives for a business and their orders for the month. Without a GROUP BY clause, one line would be displayed for each sales representative for each order. Here's an example of how this might be resolved:

```
SELECT CONCAT(name_first, ' ', name_last) AS 'Sales Rep.',
       SUM(total_order) AS 'Sales for Month'
  FROM orders, employees
  WHERE employees.rec_id = sales_rep
    AND MONTH(order_date) = MONTH(CURDATE())
  GROUP BY sales_rep;
```

This statement will concatenate the first and last name of each sales representative who placed an order for a customer during the current month. The GROUP BY clause will group together the rows found for each sales representative. The SUM( ) function will add the values of the *total_order* column for each row within each group. See Chapter 7 for more information on the SUM( ) function and other aggregate functions.

You can specify multiple columns in the GROUP BY clause. Instead of stating a column's name, you can state its position in the table. A value of 1 would represent the first column in the table. Expressions may be given, as well.

The GROUP BY clause does its own sorting and cannot be used with the ORDER BY clause. To set the sorting to ascending order explicitly for a column, enter the ASC keyword after the column in the clause which is to be set. This is not necessary, though, since it is the default setting. To set sorting to descending, add DESC after each column that is to be sorted in reverse.

When grouping rows by one column, it may be desirable not only to have a total of the values for certain columns, but also to display a total for all of the grouped rows at the end of the results set. To do this, use the WITH ROLLUP flag. Here is an example with this flag:

```
SELECT location AS Branch,
       CONCAT(name_first, ' ', name_last) AS 'Sales Rep.',
       SUM(total_order) AS 'Sales for Month'
  FROM orders, employees, branches
  WHERE sales_rep = employees.rec_id
    AND MONTH(order_date) = MONTH(CURDATE())
    AND branch_id = branches.rec_id
  GROUP BY Branch, sales_rep WITH ROLLUP;
```

Branch	Sales Rep.	Sales for Month
Boston	Sean Wilson	2472
Boston	Morgan Miller	1600
Boston	Morgan Miller	**4072**
New Orleans	Marie Dyer	1750
New Orleans	Tom Smith	6407
New Orleans	Sean Johnson	5722
New Orleans	Sean Johnson	**13879**
San Francisco	Geoffrey Dyer	500
San Francisco	Kenneth Dyer	500
San Francisco	Kenneth Dyer	**1000**
NULL	Kenneth Dyer	18951

The total for each sales representative is grouped and summed. When there aren't any more sales representatives for a branch, a row in the display for the subtotal is generated. It displays the branch name and the name of the last representative. When there are no more branches, a row for the grand total of sales is generated. The branch shows NULL. For clarity, I've boldfaced the subtotals and the grand total in the results set.

Having SELECT results

```
SELECT [flags] column|expression[, ...]
    FROM table[, ...]
        [WHERE condition]
        [GROUP BY condition]
        [HAVING condition]
        [other clauses] [options]
```

The HAVING clause is similar to the WHERE clause, but it is used for conditions returned by aggregate functions (e.g., AVG( ), MIN( ), and MAX( )). For older versions of MySQL, you must use aliases for aggregate functions in the main clause of the SELECT statement. Here is an example of how you can use this clause:

```
SELECT CONCAT(name_first, ' ', name_last) AS 'Sales Rep',
        total_order
    FROM orders, employees
    WHERE sales_rep = employees.rec_id
    GROUP BY sales_rep
    HAVING MAX(total_order);
```

This SQL statement will retrieve a list of employee names from the *employees* table where the employee is located in the New Orleans branch office. From this list, it will refine the results by grouping the data for each representative together and determine the sum of each one's *total_order* column. Because of the MAX( ) function, it will display data only for the row with the maximum number.

Ordering SELECT results

```
SELECT [flags] column|expression[, ...]
    FROM table[, ...]
        [WHERE condition]
        [ORDER BY {column|expression|position}[ASC|DESC], ...]
        [other clauses] [options]
```

The results of a SELECT statement will be displayed in the order in which the rows of data are found in the table, which may be the order in which they were entered into the table. To change the order of a results set, use the ORDER BY clause. As a basis for ordering the results, one or more columns may be named, separated by commas. The order in which columns are listed is the order in which sorts will be conducted. You can also use aliases for columns, column combinations, or expressions that were established earlier in the same SELECT statement. Instead of stating a column's name, you can state its position. A value of 1 would represent the first column in the table. Here is an example of a SELECT statement using the ORDER BY clause:

```
SELECT CONCAT(name_first, ' ', name_last) AS Name,
        MONTH(birth_date) AS 'Birth Month', email_address
    FROM employees
    ORDER BY 'Birth Month' ASC, Name ASC;
```

Here a list of employees, the month in which they were born, and their email addresses are to be extracted. For the name, the CONCAT( ) function is used to put the first and last name together, separated by a space. The AS clause establishes an alias of *Name*. The MONTH( ) function is used to extract the month from the *birth_date* column and the AS clause sets up the alias *Birth Date*. In the ORDER BY clause, the alias for the birth date is used for the initial sort and the name for the secondary sort. The results will be that all of the employees who have a birth date in the same month will be listed together and in alphabetical order by name. Both aliases are followed by the ASC flag to indicate that the results should be sorted in ascending order. This is unnecessary, as ascending order is the default. However, to change an ordering method to descending, use the DESC flag.

You can also use expressions for ordering results. The expressions may, of course, be based on columns or aliases. Here is an example of a SELECT statement using an expression for ordering:

```
SELECT CONCAT(name_first, ' ', name_last) AS name,
       pay_rate, hours
   FROM employees
   ORDER BY pay_rate * hours DESC;
```

In this example, the first and last names are selected and concatenated together under the *name* column heading in the results set. The *pay_rate* column lists the hourly dollar rate an employee is paid and the *hours* column contains the typical number of hours a week that an employee works. In the ORDER BY clause, the product of the hourly pay rate multiplied by the number of hours is determined for the ordering of the results set. The rows are to be listed in descending order per the DESC flag based on the expression.

Limiting SELECT results

```
SELECT [flags] column|expression[, ...]
   FROM table[, ...]
     [WHERE condition]
      other clauses]
     [LIMIT {[offset,] count|count OFFSET offset}]
       [PROCEDURE procedure(arguments)]
       [FOR UPDATE|LOCK IN SHARE MODE]]
     [other clauses] [options]
```

The LIMIT clause is used to limit the number of rows displayed by the SELECT statement. The most straightforward method of limiting the number of rows is to specify the maximum row count to be displayed, like this:

```
SELECT * FROM employees
   LIMIT 5;
```

To begin listing rows after a specific number of records, an offset may be given. The offset for the first row is 0. Two syntax structures accomplish this. One is to give the amount of the offset, followed by a comma and then the maximum count of rows to display. The other syntax structure is to specify the count followed by the OFFSET keyword, followed by the amount of the offset. Here is an example of the first structure, which is preferred:

```
SELECT * FROM employees
   LIMIT 10, 5;
```

In this example, after the 10th record is reached, the next 5 records will be displayed— in other words, results 11 through 15 are returned. The offset and count for the LIMIT clause are based on the rows in the results set, not necessarily on the rows in the tables. So, the amount of the offset is related to the order of the rows retrieved from the tables based on clauses, such as the WHERE clause and the ORDER BY clause.

Other SELECT clauses and options

```
SELECT [flags] column|expression[, ...]
    FROM table[, ...]
      [WHERE condition]
      [other clauses]
      [PROCEDURE procedure(arguments)]
      [LOCK IN SHARE MODE|FOR UPDATE]
```

To send the results of a SELECT statement as standard input to an external script, use the PROCEDURE clause. The syntax for this clause is the PROCEDURE keyword, followed by the name of the path and filename of the external script. Any parameters or arguments to be passed to the script may be given after the script name within parentheses. Here is an example of this clause:

```
SELECT * FROM employees
    PROCEDURE /scripts/script.plx(250, 225);
```

In this statement, the results of the SELECT statement are sent to the script.plx script, located in the *scripts* directory. Two numeric parameters are sent to the script.

To lock the rows that are being selected from a table by a SELECT statement, the LOCK IN SHARE MODE flag may be given at the end of the statement. This will stop other clients from changing the data while the SELECT statement is running. The FOR UPDATE option will instruct MySQL to invoke a temporary write lock on the rows being selected. Both of these locks will be terminated when the statement is finished running.

SET

```
SET [GLOBAL|@@global.|SESSION|@@session.] variable = expression
```

Use this statement to set a system or user variable for global or session use. Global variables relate to all users. Session variables are available only to the connection thread that creates the variable. For system variables to be recognized as global, the GLOBAL flag is used. Alternatively, the variable can be preceded by @@global. to signify that it is global. For system variables that are limited to the current session, use the SESSION flag, or place @@session. or just @@ immediately in front of the variable name. The default for variables is to limit them to the session, to make them local. LOCAL and @@local. are aliases for SESSION and @@session., respectively. For a user variable, a single @ is placed in front of the variable name. Here is an example of creating a user variable:

```
SET @current_quarter = QUARTER(CURDATE());
```

This statement uses the CURDATE() function to determine the current date. It's wrapped in the QUARTER() function, which determines the quarter for the date given. The result is a number from one to four depending on the date. The number is stored in the user variable, @current_quarter. Here are a couple of examples involving system variables—one using the flag method and the other using the variable prefix method:

```
SET GLOBAL concurrent_insert = 1;
SET @@session.interactive_timeout=40000;
```

The first statement disables concurrent inserts without having to restart the server. The second statement changes the interactive timeout to a higher value than normal. This setting is for the current client connection only. For other clients, this variable will still contain the default value. To see a list of system variables and their values, use the SHOW VARIABLES statement. For a description of these variables, see Appendix C.

SET PASSWORD

```
SET PASSWORD [FOR 'user'@'host'] = PASSWORD('password')
```

Use this statement to change the password for a user. If the FOR clause is not given, the current user is assumed. The PASSWORD( ) function will encrypt the password given. This statement does not require the use of the FLUSH PRIVILEGES statement. It will automatically update the privileges cache for the new password.

```
SET PASSWORD FOR 'kenneth'@'localhost' = PASSWORD('password');
```

SET SQL_LOG_BIN

```
SET SQL_LOG_BIN = {0|1}
```

Use this statement to enable or disable binary logging of SQL statements for the current connection. It does not affect logging for the activities of other threads and is reset to the default value when the connection is closed. This statement requires SUPER privileges. A value of 0 disables binary logging; 1 enables it.

```
SET SQL_LOG_BIN = 0;
```

SET TRANSACTION

```
SET [GLOBAL|SESSION] TRANSACTION ISOLATION LEVEL
```

```
{READ UNCOMMITTED|READ COMMITTED|REPEATABLE READ|SERIALIZABLE}
```

Use this statement to set an isolation level for a transaction that's about to be started, globally or only for the current session. This statement applies only to InnoDB and BDB tables.

The GLOBAL flag indicates that the isolation level should be applied to all transactions on the server that have not yet started. The SESSION flag limits the isolation level setting to just the current session.

The READ UNCOMMITTED isolation level allows SELECT statements to read tables without locking them and to read changes to rows that are not yet committed. The READ COMMITTED option is used to ensure consistent reading of data and to avoid any outside inserts while reading a table. The REPEATABLE READ option is used to ensure consistent SELECT statements during a transaction. The SERIALIZABLE option is used to ensure consistent reads; all simple SELECT statements are converted to SELECT...LOCK IN SHARE MODE statements.

Here is an example of how you can use this statement:

```
SET SESSION TRANSACTION ISOLATION LEVEL READ COMMITTED;
START TRANSACTION;
...
```

SHOW BINLOG EVENTS

```
SHOW BINLOG EVENTS [IN 'filename']
  [FROM position] [LIMIT [offset,] count]
```

Use this statement to display the events in a binary logfile. Use the IN clause to specify a particular logfile. If the IN clause is omitted, the current file is used. To obtain a list of binary logfiles, use the SHOW MASTER LOGS statement. Here is an example of how you can use this statement with the results following the SQL statement:

```
SHOW BINLOG EVENTS IN 'log-bin.000161'\G

*************************** 1. row ***************************
   Log_name: log-bin.000161
        Pos: 4
 Event_type: Start
  Server_id: 1
Orig_log_pos: 4
       Info: Server ver: 4.1.7-standard-log, Binlog ver: 3
1 row in set (0.00 sec)
```

This logfile has only one row of data, because the SQL statement was run shortly after the server was started. For a larger logfile with many rows of events recorded, you can focus and limit the results with the FROM and LIMIT clauses. In the results, notice the *Pos* label with a value of 4. In a large logfile, that number might be higher, in the thousands. The results displayed could be focused only to rows starting from a particular position in the log with the FROM clause. You can limit the number of rows of events displayed with the LIMIT clause. In the LIMIT clause, you can set the starting point of the output based on the number of rows in the results set and limit them to a certain number of rows. Here is an example of both of these clauses:

```
SHOW BINLOG EVENTS IN 'log-bin.000160'
FROM 3869 LIMIT 2,1\G

*************************** 1. row ***************************
   Log_name: log-bin.000160
        Pos: 4002
 Event_type: Intvar
  Server_id: 1
Orig_log_pos: 4002
       Info: INSERT_ID=5
```

In this example, the retrieval of log events is to begin from position 3869 because of the FROM clause. The results set contains several rows, although only one is shown here. The display is limited to one row, starting from the third one in the results set per the LIMIT clause.

SHOW CHARACTER SET

```
SHOW CHARACTER SET [LIKE 'pattern']
```

This statement will show all of the character sets installed on the server. To be more selective, use a pattern with the LIKE clause. For instance, to list all of the character sets beginning with the name *latin*, enter the following:

```
SHOW CHARACTER SET LIKE 'latin%'\G

*************************** 1. row ***************************
          Charset: latin1
      Description: ISO 8859-1 West European
Default collation: latin1_swedish_ci
           Maxlen: 1
*************************** 2. row ***************************
          Charset: latin2
      Description: ISO 8859-2 Central European
Default collation: latin2_general_ci
           Maxlen: 1
*************************** 3. row ***************************
          Charset: latin5
      Description: ISO 8859-9 Turkish
Default collation: latin5_turkish_ci
           Maxlen: 1
*************************** 4. row ***************************
          Charset: latin7
      Description: ISO 8859-13 Baltic
Default collation: latin7_general_ci
           Maxlen: 1
```

To see the default character set, use the SHOW VARIABLES statement. To change the client's character set, use the SET CHARACTER SET statement.

SHOW COLLATION

SHOW COLLATION [LIKE '*pattern*']

Use this statement to list all of the collation character sets. You can use the LIKE clause to list character sets based on a naming pattern. This statement is available as of Version 4.1 of MySQL. Here is an example:

```
SHOW COLLATION LIKE '%bin%';
```

In this example, character sets that contain the letters *bin* in their name will be listed. These are binary character sets.

SHOW COLUMNS

SHOW [FULL] COLUMNS FROM *table* [FROM *database*] [LIKE '*pattern*']

Use this statement to display the columns for a given table. If the table is not in the current default database, the FROM *database* clause may be given to name another database. You can use the LIKE clause to list only columns that match a naming pattern given in quotes.

```
SHOW COLUMNS FROM clients FROM workrequests LIKE 'client%';
```

Field	Type	Null	Key	Default	Extra
client_id	varchar(4)		PRI		
client_name	varchar(50)	YES		NULL	

In this example, only information for columns beginning with the name *client* are retrieved. The following example is for just the *client_id* column and uses the FULL flag along with the alternate display method (\G):

```
SHOW FULL COLUMNS FROM clients FROM workrequests
LIKE 'client_id'\G

*************************** 1. row ***************************
      Field: client_id
       Type: varchar(4)
  Collation: latin1_swedish_ci
       Null:
        Key: PRI
    Default:
      Extra:
 Privileges: select,insert,update,references
    Comment:
```

Notice that information on collation and the user's privileges with regard to the column is provided.

SHOW CREATE DATABASE

SHOW CREATE DATABASE *database*

Use this statement to display an SQL statement that can be used to create a database like the one given. This statement is mostly useful for determining the default character set. It's available as of Version 4.1 of MySQL.

```
SHOW CREATE DATABASE richard_stringer\G

*************************** 1. row ***************************
Database: richard_stringer
Create Database: CREATE DATABASE `richard_stringer`
                 /*!40100 DEFAULT CHARACTER SET latin2 */
```

SHOW CREATE TABLE

SHOW CREATE TABLE *table*

Use this statement to display an SQL statement that can be used to create a table like the one named. The results may be copied and used with another database. They also could be copied and the name of the table modified so that the statement may be used on the same database.

```
SHOW CREATE TABLE programmers\G

*************************** 1. row ***************************
Table: programmers
Create Table: CREATE TABLE `programmers` (
                `prog_id` varchar(4) NOT NULL default '',
                `prog_name` varchar(50) NOT NULL default '',
                PRIMARY KEY (`prog_id`)
                ) ENGINE=MyISAM DEFAULT CHARSET=latin1
```

Notice that the results include the table type and other default options.

SHOW CREATE VIEW

```
SHOW CREATE VIEW view
```

Use this statement to display an SQL statement that can be used to create a view like the one named. The results may be copied and used with another database. They also could be copied and the name of the view modified so that the statement may be used on the same database. This statement is available as of Version 5.0.1 of MySQL.

```
SHOW CREATE VIEW employee_directory\G
```

```
*************************** 1. row ***************************
Table: employees
Create Table: CREATE VIEW `employee_directory`.`personnel`
        (`ID`, `Name` `Ext.`,)
        AS SELECT emp_id,
        CONCAT(emp_first, ` `, emp_last),
        tel_extension
        FROM employees;
```

This view is the same one that is created in the example given for the CREATE VIEW statement earlier. Notice that the database name (*personnel*) has been added to the end of the view name (*employee_directory*).

SHOW DATABASES

```
SHOW DATABASES [LIKE 'pattern']
```

This statement displays a list of databases for the server. Using the LIKE clause, a naming pattern may be given. For example, suppose that a server has a separate database for each customer of the organization and that the pattern for the names of the databases is *cust_number*, where the number is the customer account number. You could enter the following SQL statement to obtain a list of databases based on this pattern:

```
SHOW DATABASES LIKE 'cust_%';
```

SHOW ENGINES

```
SHOW [STORAGE] ENGINES
```

This statement will list the table types or storage engines available for the version of MySQL running on the server. It will state which are disabled on the server and which are enabled, as well as which is the default type. It will also provide comments on each type. The STORAGE keyword is optional and has no effect on the results. This SQL statement replaces SHOW TABLE TYPES, which produced the same results, but is deprecated.

SHOW ERRORS

```
SHOW [COUNT(*)] ERRORS [LIMIT [offset,] count]
```

Use this statement to display error messages for previous SQL statements for the current session. To get a total number of error messages, use the COUNT(*) clause. This cannot be used with the LIMIT clause, though. The LIMIT clause is used to limit the number of errors displayed. An offset can be given along with the count to specify a starting point for displaying error messages.

This statement is available as of Version 4.1 of MySQL. It will not display warnings or notes—just error messages. Use the SHOW WARNINGS statement to get all three.

Here are a couple of examples of how you can use this statement:

```
SHOW ERRORS;
SHOW COUNT(*) ERRORS;
```

The first line displays all error messages in an ASCII-formatted table. The second line returns the number of error messages.

SHOW GRANTS

```
SHOW GRANTS FOR user
```

This SQL statement displays the GRANTS statement for a given user. This is useful in duplicating an existing user's privileges for another. If the username is given without reference to a particular host, the wildcard % is assumed. Otherwise, the username should be stated with the related host as shown here:

```
SHOW GRANTS FOR 'russell'@'localhost'\G

*************************** 1. row ***************************
Grants for russell@localhost: GRANT ALL PRIVILEGES ON *.* TO
'russell'@'localhost' IDENTIFIED BY PASSWORD '1ajk6f3845a1bbca' WITH GRANT
OPTION
```

To reduce clutter, this example is issued with \G instead of a semicolon to omit table formatting of the results. Notice that with the exception of the encrypted password in single quotes, the resulting statement is what would be entered to create the user *russell* for the host *localhost*, with the given privileges including the WITH GRANT OPTION flag.

SHOW INDEX

```
SHOW INDEX FROM table [FROM database]
```

This SQL statement will display information on the indexes for a given table. A table from a different database can be specified by either naming it with the table (e.g., *database.table*) or adding the FROM clause.

```
SHOW INDEX FROM contacts FROM sales_dept\G

*************************** 1. row ***************************
        Table: contacts
   Non_unique: 0
     Key_name: PRIMARY
 Seq_in_index: 1
  Column_name: rec_id
    Collation: A
  Cardinality: 5
     Sub_part: NULL
       Packed: NULL
         Null:
   Index_type: BTREE
      Comment:
```

In this example, instead of ending the statement with a semicolon, which would insert extra table formatting, a \G is used to alter the display to the format shown. This table has only one index, so only one is listed here. For each index, the table name is given. This is followed by a field indicating whether the index is nonunique. A unique index is indicated by 0. The name of the index or key (e.g., PRIMARY) is shown next. For indexes that use only one column, the key name and the column name are often the same. For indexes that use more than one column, a row will be listed for each column, each row having the same table name and the same key name. The sequence of the column in the table is given, where 1 is the first column. The name of the column or columns indexed is given next. Then the collation, how the column is sorted in the index, is specified. A value of A is given for ascending, D for descending. If the index is not sorted, the value would be NULL. The cardinality is based on the number of unique indexes contained in the column. This is used for determining whether an index is used with a JOIN. The higher the cardinality, the more likely it will be used. The *Sub_part* field indicates the number of characters of the column that are indexed for partially indexed columns (see the CREATE INDEX statement). This is NULL if all of the column is indexed. The *Packed* field indicates the method by which the key is packed. This index isn't packed, so the value for the field in this example is NULL. If the column may contain NULL, the NULL field will read NULL. Otherwise, it will be blank, as shown in the example. *Index_type* is the type of method used. The possibilities are BTREE, FULLTEXT, and HASH. Starting with Version 5.0.1 of MySQL, RTREE will be another possibility. The *Comments* field contains any comments associated with the index.

SHOW INNODB STATUS

SHOW INNODB STATUS

Use this statement to display details on the status of the InnoDB storage engine. This statement provides information on table and record locks for transactions, waiting locks, pending requests, buffer statistics and activity, and logs related to the engine.

SHOW LOGS

SHOW [BDB] LOGS

Use this statement to show information on logs for MySQL server. The type of log may be given as a qualifier to the statement. However, currently information only on logs for BDB tables is provided. The statement returns a results set containing the path and name of the logfile, the type of log (e.g., BDB), and the status of the log. The status possibilities are FREE if the file isn't being used at the moment and IN USE if it is.

SHOW MASTER LOGS

SHOW MASTER LOGS

This statement displays a list of binary logs created by the master MySQL server in the filesystem directory. To delete logs, use the PURGE MASTER LOGS statement. For information on enabling logs, see Chapter 10.

SHOW MASTER STATUS

SHOW MASTER STATUS

This statement displays information on the status of the binary logfile that is being used currently on the master MySQL server.

```
SHOW MASTER STATUS;
```

```
+----------------+----------+--------------+------------------+
| File           | Position | Binlog_Do_DB | Binlog_Ignore_DB |
+----------------+----------+--------------+------------------+
| log-bin.000141 |    1123  |              |                  |
+----------------+----------+--------------+------------------+
```

SHOW PRIVILEGES

SHOW PRIVILEGES

This statement provides a list of privileges available, the context of each (e.g., server administration), and a description of each. It is not based on the user. Instead, it's a complete listing of the privileges that may be assigned to a user. This statement is available as of Version 4.1 of MySQL.

SHOW PROCESSLIST

SHOW [FULL] PROCESSLIST

This statement displays a list of connection threads running on the MySQL server. This statement requires SUPER privileges to be able to see all threads. Otherwise, only threads related to the current connection are shown. The FULL keyword shows the full text of the information field.

```
SHOW PROCESSLIST\G
```

```
*************************** 1. row ***************************
     Id: 1
   User: root
   Host: localhost
     db: workrequests
Command: Query
   Time: 0
  State: NULL
   Info: SHOW PROCESSLIST
```

You can use this statement to determine a thread identification number to be used with the KILL statement.

SHOW SLAVE HOSTS

```
SHOW SLAVE HOSTS
```

This statement displays a list of slave servers for the master server. Slaves must be started with the --report-host=*slave* option to be shown.

SHOW SLAVE STATUS

```
SHOW SLAVE STATUS
```

This statement displays information on the slave thread. Here is an example of this statement and its results:

```
SHOW SLAVE STATUS\G

*************************** 1. row ***************************
               Slave_IO_State: Waiting for master to send event
                  Master_Host: localhost
                  Master_User: root
                  Master_Port: 3306
                Connect_Retry: 5
              Master_Log_File: log-bin.000154
          Read_Master_Log_Pos: 159
               Relay_Log_File: log-relay-bin.154
                Relay_Log_Pos: 694
        Relay_Master_Log_File: log-bin.154
             Slave_IO_Running: Yes
            Slave_SQL_Running: Yes
              Replicate_Do_DB:
          Replicate_Ignore_DB:
                   Last_Errno: 0
                   Last_Error:
                 Skip_Counter: 0
          Exec_Master_Log_Pos: 159
              Relay_Log_Space: 694
              Until_Condition: None
               Until_Log_File:
                Until_Log_Pos: 0
            Master_SSL_Allowed: Yes
            Master_SSL_CA_File: ssl_ca.dat
            Master_SSL_CA_Path: /data/mysql/ssl_ca
               Master_SSL_Cert: ssl_cert.dat
             Master_SSL_Cipher:
                Master_SSL_Key:
        Seconds_Behind_Master: 3
```

You can set some of these values at startup with the MySQL server daemon (*mysqld*). See Chapter 10 for more information on setting server variables at startup. You can set some of these variables with the SET statement. You can adjust others for particular tables with the ALTER TABLE statement. You can reset some of the logfile variables with the RESET MASTER and RESET SLAVE statements.

SHOW STATUS

```
SHOW STATUS [LIKE 'pattern']
```

This statement displays status information and variables from the server. You can reduce the number of variables with the LIKE clause, based on a naming pattern for the variable name. Here is an example of how you can use this statement:

```
SHOW STATUS LIKE '%log%';
```

```
+------------------------+-------+
| Variable_name          | Value |
+------------------------+-------+
| Binlog_cache_disk_use  | 0     |
| Binlog_cache_use       | 3     |
| Com_show_binlog_events | 0     |
| Com_show_binlogs       | 0     |
| Com_show_logs          | 0     |
+------------------------+-------+
```

In this example, the results are limited only to variables that contain the word *log* in their names. You can change these variables at startup with certain options for the MySQL server daemon. See Chapter 10. You can change some of them while the daemon is running with the SET statement, without having to restart the server.

SHOW TABLE STATUS

```
SHOW TABLE STATUS [FROM database] [LIKE 'pattern']
```

This statement displays status information on a set of tables from a database. To obtain the status of tables from a database other than the current default one, use the FROM clause. The results will include information on all of the tables of the database unless the LIKE clause is used to limit the tables displayed by a naming pattern.

```
SHOW TABLE STATUS FROM workrequests LIKE 'workreq'\G
```

```
*************************** 1. row ***************************
           Name: workreq
         Engine: MyISAM
        Version: 7
     Row_format: Dynamic
           Rows: 543
 Avg_row_length: 983
    Data_length: 534216
Max_data_length: 4294967295
   Index_length: 6144
      Data_free: 120
 Auto_increment: 5772
    Create_time: 2002-04-23 14:41:58
    Update_time: 2004-11-26 16:01:46
     Check_time: 2004-11-28 17:21:20
      Collation: latin1_swedish_ci
       Checksum: NULL
 Create_options:
        Comment:
```

In this example, the number of tables is limited to one, because a specific table name is given in the LIKE clause without the % wildcard. Incidentally, the display here is not in the typical ASCII table format, because the statement ends with a \G instead of the usual semicolon. You can change some of these variables or table options using the ALTER TABLE statement.

SHOW TABLES

SHOW [OPEN] TABLES [FROM *database*] [LIKE '*pattern*']

This statement displays a list of tables. For a listing of tables that is currently being used by queries, add the OPEN flag. The tables shown will not include temporary tables and will be from the current default database. To list tables from another database, add the FROM clause along with the name of the database. You can reduce the list of tables to ones with a name meeting a given naming pattern. As of Version 5.0.1 of MySQL, the results set will include tables and views for the database. It will also include a second column to specify whether a row is for a table or a view. This is indicated by the values of BASE TABLE and VIEW, respectively.

SHOW TABLES FROM workrequests LIKE 'work%';

This statement will list all of the tables and views (if the server is running Version 5.0.1 or higher) with a name that begins with the word "work," for the database *workrequests*. Incidentally, by default, only tables for which the user has privileges will be listed.

SHOW VARIABLES

SHOW [GLOBAL|SESSION] VARIABLES [LIKE '*pattern*']

This statement displays the system variables for the MySQL server. The SESSION flag will display values for current sessions or connections. This is the default and is synonymous with LOCAL. The GLOBAL flag will provide variables that will relate to new connections. You can limit the variables with the LIKE clause and a naming pattern for the variables. Here is an example of this statement:

SHOW VARIABLES LIKE 'version%';

```
+-------------------------+--------------------+
| Variable_name           | Value              |
+-------------------------+--------------------+
| version                 | 4.1.7-standard-log |
| version_comment         | Official MySQL RPM |
| version_compile_machine | i686               |
| version_compile_os      | pc-linux           |
+-------------------------+--------------------+
```

In this example, the variables shown are limited to variable names beginning with the word "version."

SHOW WARNINGS

SHOW [COUNT(*)] WARNINGS [LIMIT [*offset*,] *count*]

Use this statement to display warning messages, error messages, and notes for previous SQL statements for the current session. To get a count of the number of such messages, use the COUNT(*) clause. You cannot use this with the LIMIT clause. The LIMIT clause is used to limit the number of messages displayed. An offset can be given along with the limit to specify a starting point for displaying messages. This statement is available as of Version 4.1 of MySQL. Here are a couple of examples of how you can use this statement:

```
SHOW WARNINGS;
SHOW COUNT(*) WARNINGS;
```

The first line displays all messages in an ASCII-formatted table. The second line returns the number of messages. Here's another example, but with the LIMIT clause:

```
SHOW WARNINGS LIMIT 3,2;
```

START SLAVE

START SLAVE [IO_THREAD|SQL_THREAD]

START SLAVE [SQL_THREAD]

   UNTIL MASTER_LOG_FILE = '*filename*', MASTER_LOG_POS = *position*

START SLAVE [SQL_THREAD]

   UNTIL RELAY_LOG_FILE = '*filename*', RELAY_LOG_POS = *position*

Use this statement to start a slave server. In the first syntax structure shown, you can start the slave with the I/O thread or just with the SQL thread by using the respective keyword. You can start both by listing both keywords, separated by a comma. The default is to start both. The I/O thread will cause the slave to read SQL queries from the master server and to record them in the relay logfile. The SQL thread will read the relay logfile and then execute the SQL statements.

The second syntax structure is used to limit the reading of the threads to a specific point (given with MASTER_LOG_POS) in the master logfile (named with the MASTER_LOG_FILE parameter). With the UNTIL clause, processing of the logfiles given will stop when the position given is reached. The third syntax structure is used to specify the relay log file and to limit the reading of it. If the SQL_THREAD keyword is given in either of these latter two syntax structures, the reading will be limited to the SQL thread.

The starting of a slave thread isn't always dependable. Run the SHOW SLAVE STATUS statement to confirm that the thread began and remained running.

START TRANSACTION

START TRANSACTION

Use this statement to start a transaction, or a set of SQL statements for an InnoDB or a BDB table. Transaction statements are ignored when you use them with MyISAM tables. The purpose of a transaction is to be able to undo SQL statements if need be.

You can reverse a transaction if the transaction has not yet been committed either with a COMMIT statement, implicitly by starting another transaction, or by terminating the connection. In earlier versions of MySQL, BEGIN or BEGIN WORK were used instead of START TRANSACTION. See the explanation of the COMMIT statement and the ROLLBACK statement for more information on transactions. The SAVEPOINT statement and the ROLLBACK TO SAVEPOINT statements may also be useful.

Here is an example of this statement's use:

```
START TRANSACTION;
INSERT DATA INFILE '/tmp/customer_orders.sql'
  INTO TABLE orders;
COMMIT;
```

In this example, after the batch of orders was inserted into the *orders* table, if there was a problem the ROLLBACK statement could be issued instead of the COMMIT statement shown here. It would remove the data imported by the INSERT DATA INFILE statement. The ROLLBACK statement works only with InnoDB and BDB tables. If everything seems alright, the COMMIT statement would be issued to commit the entries and to end the transaction started with the START TRANSACTION statement.

STOP SLAVE

STOP SLAVE [IO_THREAD|SQL_THREAD]

Use this statement to stop slave server threads. To stop a specific type of slave thread, one or both of the thread types may be given. Both may be given in a comma-separated list. The default is to stop both. You can start slave threads with the START SLAVE statement.

TRUNCATE TABLE

TRUNCATE TABLE *table*

Use this statement to delete the contents of a table rapidly. This statement is similar to the DELETE statement in that it will delete all of the data contained in a given table. Its method is to delete the table and then to re-create the table, but without data. As a result, this statement is faster than using DELETE. However, the TRUNCATE statement does not report the number of rows deleted. Another minor drawback to this statement is that the value for an AUTO_INCREMENT column will be lost along with the data.

UNION

SELECT ... UNION [ALL|DISTINCT] [SELECT ...]

The UNION keyword unites the results of multiple SELECT statements into one results set. The SELECT statements can retrieve data from the same table or from different tables. If different tables are used, the results set generated by each SQL statement should match in column count and in the order of column types. The column names do not need to be the same, but the data sent to the respective fields in the results set needs to match. Here is an example of a UNION used to merge the results of two SELECT statements:

```
SELECT CONCAT(name_first, SPACE(1), name_last) AS Name,
       telephone_work AS Telephone
  FROM employees
UNION
SELECT location, telephone FROM branches
ORDER BY Name;
```

This statement will present a list of employees and branch office locations in one column, with the telephone number for each in the second. The column headings used for the results set will be the ones used for the first SELECT statement. Because of the ORDER BY clause, the results will be sorted by the values for the alias *Name*. Otherwise, the names of employees would be listed before the names of offices.

The example shown merges the results of only two SELECT statements. You can merge several SELECT statements, entering the UNION keyword between each one.

UNLOCK TABLES

UNLOCK TABLES

Use this statement to unlock tables that were locked by the current connection thread with the LOCK TABLES statement. See the description of the ROLLBACK statement for an example of its use.

USE

USE *database*

This statement sets the default database MySQL is to use for the current session. This allows the name of the default database to be omitted from statements. For instance, *db1.table1* can be written as just *table1*, and *db1* is assumed.

5

String Functions

MySQL has several built-in functions for formatting, manipulating, and analyzing strings, both user-specified and within columns of data. This chapter lists these string functions, provides the syntax of each, and gives examples of their use. For the examples in this chapter, a fictitious database for a university is used.

String Functions Grouped by Type

The list of string functions is quite long, but many perform similar roles. The following list groups the functions by these roles.

Converting

ASCII( ), BIN( ), BINARY( ), CHAR( ), COMPRESS( ), CONV( ), EXPORT_SET( ), HEX( ), INET_ATON( ), INET_NTOA( ), MAKE_SET( ), OCT( ), ORD( ), SOUNDEX( ), UNCOMPRESS( ), UNHEX( )

Formatting

CONCAT( ), CONCAT_WS( ), LCASE( ), LENGTH( ), LOWER( ), LPAD( ), LTRIM( ), OCTET_LENGTH( ), QUOTE( ), RPAD( ), RTRIM( ), SPACE( ), TRIM( ), UCASE( ), UPPER( )

Expressions

BIT_LENGTH( ), CHAR_LENGTH( ), CHARACTER_LENGTH( ), ELT( ), FIELD( ), FIND_IN( ), INSTR( ), LOCATE( ), MATCH( ), AGAINST( ), POSITION( ), STRCMP( ), SUBSTRING_INDEX( ), UNCOMPRES_LENGTH( )

Extracting

LEFT( ), LOAD_FILE( ), MID( ), RIGHT( ), SUBSTRING( )

Manipulating

INSERT( ), REPEAT( ), REPLACE( ), REVERSE( )

Security

DECODE( ), ENCODE( ), ENCRYPT( ), MD5( ), PASSWORD( )

String Functions in Alphabetical Order

The rest of this chapter lists the string functions in alphabetical order.

AES_DECRYPT( )

AES_DECRYPT(*string, password*)

This function decrypts text that was encrypted using the AES algorithm with a 128-bit key length, and it returns NULL if one of the given parameters is NULL. This function reverses the AES_ENCRYPT( ) function. This function is available as of Version 4.0.2 of MySQL.

```
SELECT AES_DECRYPT(personal, 'my_password') AS Personal
    FROM teachers
    WHERE teacher_id='730522';
```

```
+----------+
| Personal |
+----------+
| text     |
+----------+
```

In this example, the value for the *personal* column is decrypted using the password given. The result is just the plain text.

AES_ENCRYPT( )

AES_ENCRYPT(*string, password*)

This function returns encrypted text using the AES algorithm with a 128-bit key length and returns NULL if one of the given parameters is NULL. The results of this function can be reversed with AES_DECRYPT( ). This function is available as of Version 4.0.2 of MySQL.

```
UPDATE teachers
    SET personal = AES_ENCRYPT('text', 'my_password')
    WHERE teacher_id = '730522';
```

ASCII( )

ASCII(*string*)

This function returns the ASCII code for the first character of a given string. If you're entering raw text, you must enclose *string* within quotes. If the argument is a column, do not enclose it in quotes. If *string* is empty, 0 is returned.

```
SELECT ASCII('A') AS A, ASCII(name_last) AS Professor
FROM teachers WHERE name_last = 'McAllister';
```

```
+----+-----------+
| A  | Professor |
+----+-----------+
| 65 |        77 |
+----+-----------+
```

Only the M in the professor's name is converted to its ASCII equivalent. It displays the ASCII value for A and the first letter of the name.

BIN( )

BIN(*number*)

This function returns a binary number for a given integer. It returns NULL if the string is NULL.

```
SELECT BIN(1), BIN(2), BIN(3);
+--------+--------+--------+
| BIN(1) | BIN(2) | BIN(3) |
+--------+--------+--------+
| 1      | 10     | 11     |
+--------+--------+--------+
```

For the number 1 in a base 10 system, the first position in a binary system is *on* or 1. For the number 2, the first position from the right is *off* and the second is *on*. For 3, the first and the second positions are *on*.

BINARY

BINARY *string*

Use this function to treat strings in their binary state. This function is useful for making SQL statements case-sensitive. Notice that the syntax does not call for parentheses:

```
SELECT student_id, name_last
FROM students
WHERE BINARY LEFT(UCASE(name_last), 1) <>
    LEFT(name_last, 1);
```

```
+------------+-----------+
| student_id | name_last |
+------------+-----------+
|  433302000 | dyer      |
|  434016005 | de Vitto  |
+------------+-----------+
```

This SQL statement checks for any students whose last name starts with a lowercase letter. To do this, each student's last name is converted to uppercase letters and then the first letter starting from the left is extracted to compare it to the first letter of the last name without case conversion. The results show one record that is probably a typing error and another (the second one) that is probably correct. Notice that the BINARY keyword is specified before the comparison is made between the strings and is applied to both strings.

BIT_LENGTH( )

BIT_LENGTH(*string*)

This function returns the number of bits in a given string. The following example uses the default character set, where one character requires 8 bits.

```
SELECT BIT_LENGTH('a') AS 'One Character',
BIT_LENGTH('ab') AS 'Two Characters';
```

```
+---------------+----------------+
| One Character | Two Characters |
+---------------+----------------+
|             8 |             16 |
+---------------+----------------+
```

CHAR( )

CHAR(*ascii*[, ...])

This function returns a string or text for ASCII code. This is the reverse of ASCII( ). This statement returns NULL values.

```
SELECT ASCII('A'), CHAR('65');
```

```
+------------+------------+
| ASCII('A') | CHAR('65') |
+------------+------------+
|         65 | A          |
+------------+------------+
```

CHAR_LENGTH( )

CHAR_LENGTH(*string*)

This function returns the number of characters of a given string. A multiple-byte character is treated as one character. This is synonymous with CHARACTER_LENGTH( ).

```
SELECT course_id,
    CASE
    WHEN CHAR_LENGTH(course_desc) > 30
    THEN CONCAT(SUBSTRING(course_desc, 1, 27), '...')
    ELSE course_desc
    END AS Description
FROM courses;
```

In this example, a CASE control statement is used to specify different display results based on a condition. Using the CHAR_LENGTH( ) function MySQL determines if the content of course_desc is longer than 30 characters. If it is, the SUBSTRING( ) function extracts the first 27 characters and the CONCAT( ) function adds ellipsis points to the end of the truncated data to indicate that there is more text. Otherwise, the full contents of course_desc are displayed.

CHARACTER_LENGTH( )

CHARACTER_LENGTH(*string*)

This function returns the number of characters of a given string. A multiple-byte character is treated as one character. This is synonymous with CHAR_LENGTH( ).

COMPRESS( )

COMPRESS(*string*)

This function returns a given string compressed. It requires MySQL to have been compiled with a compression library (i.e., zlib). This statement is available as of Version 4.1 of MySQL.

```
SELECT COMPRESS(essay)
FROM applications
WHERE applicant_id = '7382';
```

CONCAT( )

CONCAT(*string*, ...)

With this function, strings of text and strings from columns can be concatenated or pasted together under one resulting column. If any of the strings are NULL, a NULL value is returned for the selected row.

```
SELECT CONCAT(name_first, ' ', name_last) AS Student
FROM students WHERE name_last = 'Dyer';
```

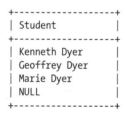

```
+-------------------+
| Student           |
+-------------------+
| Kenneth Dyer      |
| Geoffrey Dyer     |
| Marie Dyer        |
| NULL              |
+-------------------+
```

In this example, the database contained four students with the last name *Dyer*, but for one of them there was a NULL value in the *name_first* column. Within the parentheses of the function, notice that a space is given within quotes as the second element so that the display shows a space between each student's first and last name.

CONCAT_WS( )

CONCAT_WS(*separator, string, ...*)

This function combines strings of text and columns together with a separator specified in the first argument. Any number of strings may be specified after the first argument, with each argument separated by a comma. Null values are ignored.

```
SELECT CONCAT_WS('|', student_id, name_last, name_first)
AS 'student_record'
FROM students LIMIT 3;
```

```
+---------------------------+
| student_record            |
+---------------------------+
| 433342000|Dyer|Russell    |
| 434892001|Dyer|Marie      |
| 433892002|Zabalaoui|Michael |
+---------------------------+
```

Here the vertical bar is used to separate the columns. This function can be useful for exporting data to formats acceptable to other software. However, you will require some programming to export the data to an external file using an SQL statement such as this one.

CONV( )

CONV(*number, from_base, to_base*)

This function converts a number from one numeric base system to another. The number to convert is given in the first argument, the base from which to convert the number in the second argument, and the base to which to convert the number in the third argument. The minimum base allowed is 2 and the maximum is 36.

```
SELECT CONV(4, 10, 2) AS 'Base-10 4 Converted',
CONV(100, 2, 10) AS 'Binary 100 Converted';
```

```
+---------------------+----------------------+
| Base-10 4 Converted | Binary 100 Converted |
+---------------------+----------------------+
| 100                 | 4                    |
+---------------------+----------------------+
```

Here the number 4 under the base 10 system is converted to the base-two or binary equivalent and back again.

DECODE( )

DECODE(*encrypted, password*)

This function decrypts a given string that was encrypted with a given password.

```
SELECT ENCODE(pwd, 'oreilly')
FROM teachers
WHERE teacher_id = '730522';
```

This function decrypts the contents of the *pwd* column and unlocks it using the *oreilly* password, which was used to encrypt it originally using ENCODE( ).

DES_DECRYPT( )

DES_DECRYPT(*string*, [*key*])

This function decrypts text that was encrypted using the triple DES algorithm with a 128-bit key length. It returns NULL if an error occurs. This function will work only if MySQL has been configured for secure sockets layer (SSL) support. It reverses the DES_ENCRYPT( ) function. This function is available as of Version 4.0.1 of MySQL.

```
SELECT DES_DECRYPT(credit_card_nbr, 0)
    FROM orders
    WHERE order_nbr = '8347';
```

In this example, the value for the *credit_card_nbr* column is decrypted using the first key string in the key file. See the description of DES_ENCRYPT( ) for more information on key files.

DES_ENCRYPT( )

DES_ENCRYPT(*string*, [*key*])

This function returns encrypted text using the triple DES algorithm with a 128-bit key length. It returns NULL if an error occurs. This function will work only if MySQL has been configured for SSL support. To use this function, a key file must be created and specified with the --des-key-file option when starting the *mysqld* daemon. To encrypt a given string, either a key string must be given as the second argument of the function, or it can be retrieved from a file containing key strings.

A key file should be set up with a separate key string on each line. Each line should begin with a single-digit number (0–9) as an index, followed by a space before the key string (e.g., key_number des_string).

To reference key strings in the key file, the number of the line to retrieve may be given as the key to the function. If a key number is not given with this function, the first key in the key file is used for encryption.

The results of this function can be reversed with DES_DECRYPT( ). This function is available as of Version 4.0.1 of MySQL.

```
UPDATE orders
    SET credit_card_nbr = DES_ENCRYPT('4011-7839-1234-4321')
    WHERE order_nbr = '8347';
```

ELT( )

ELT(*number*, *string*, ...)

This function returns the *number* element from the list of remaining arguments given. If the number given is less than one or if the number of elements is less than the number given, this statement will return NULL.

```
SELECT ELT(2, 'one','two','three')
AS 'ELT() Test';

+------------+
| ELT() Test |
+------------+
| two        |
+------------+
```

ENCODE( )

ENCODE(*string*, *password*)

This function encrypts a given string in binary format and locks it with the *password*. You should not use this function for the *password* column in the *user* table of the *mysql* database. Use PASSWORD( ) instead.

```
UPDATE teachers
SET pwd = ENCODE('test', 'oreilly')
WHERE teacher_id = '730522';
```

The function here encrypts the word "test" and locks it with the *oreilly* password. The results are stored in the *pwd* column for the teacher chosen. To unlock the results, you can use the DECODE( ) function with the password.

ENCRYPT( )

ENCRYPT(*string*[, *seed*])

This function returns encrypted text using the C function crypt. A two-character string may be given in the second argument to increase the randomness of encryption. Encryption cannot be decrypted in MySQL. You should not use this function for the *password* column in the *user* table of the *mysql* database. Use PASSWORD( ) instead.

```
UPDATE teachers
    SET pwd = ENCRYPT('test', 'JT')
    WHERE teacher_id = '730522';
```

EXPORT_SET( )

EXPORT_SET(*number*, *on*, *off*[, *separator*,[*count*]])

This function returns a series of strings in order that represent each bit of a given *number*. The equivalent of 1 (an *on* bit) is given in the second argument and the equivalent of 0 (an *off* bit) is given in the third. A separator may be specified in the fourth argument, and a number of bit equivalents to display for the last argument. The default is a comma.

```
SELECT BIN(4) AS 'Binary Number',
        EXPORT_SET(4, 'on', 'off', '-', 8)
            AS 'Verbal Equivalent';

+---------------+--------------------------------+
| Binary Number | Verbal Equivalent              |
+---------------+--------------------------------+
| 100           | off-off-on-off-off-off-off-off |
+---------------+--------------------------------+
```

Notice that the conversion of the binary equivalent of 4 is displayed by EXPORT_SET( ) in what one might consider reverse order, from right to left: not 100, but 001 (or rather, 00100000) instead.

FIELD( )

FIELD(*string*, *string*[, ...])

This function searches for the first string given in the list of other strings and returns the numeric position of the first argument that matches. The first element is 1 among the arguments being searched. If the search string is not found or is NULL, 0 is returned.

```
SELECT FIELD('test', 'test','one','two','three')
       AS 'FIELD( ) Test';
```

```
+--------------+
| FIELD( ) Test |
+--------------+
|            1 |
+--------------+
```

Notice that each string is a separate argument. To provide one string containing a comma-separated list instead, use FIND_IN_SET( ).

FIND_IN_SET( )

FIND_IN_SET(*string*, *string_list*)

This function returns the location of a string given in the first argument of the function, in a comma-separated list in a string given in the second argument. The first element of the list is 1. A 0 is returned if the string is not found in the set. It returns NULL if either argument is NULL.

```
SELECT FIND_IN_SET('test', 'test,one,two,three')
       AS 'FIND_IN_SET( ) Test';
```

```
+---------------------+
| FIELD_IN_SET( ) Test |
+---------------------+
|                   1 |
+---------------------+
```

HEX( )

HEX(*number*)

This function returns the hexadecimal value of *number*.

```
SELECT CONCAT('#', HEX(255), HEX(255), HEX(255))
       AS White;
```

```
+---------+
| White   |
+---------+
| #FFFFFF |
+---------+
```

This SQL statement converts the RGB (red, green, and blue) values given to their hexadecimal equivalent for the color white.

INET_ATON( )

INET_ATON(*IP_address*)

This function converts an Internet Protocol (IP) address in dot-quad notation to its numeric equivalent. The function INET_NTOA( ) can be used to reverse the results.

```
SELECT INET_ATON('12.127.17.72')
        AS 'AT&T';
```

```
+-----------+
| AT&T      |
+-----------+
| 209654088 |
+-----------+
```

This function is useful in sorting IP addresses that lexically might not sort properly. For instance, an address of 10.0.11.1 would come after 10.0.1.1 and before 10.0.2.1 under normal sort conditions in an ORDER BY clause.

INET_NTOA( )

INET_NTOA(*IP_address*)

This function converts numeric equivalent of an IP address to an IP address equivalent. The function INET_ATON( ) can be used to reverse the results.

```
SELECT INET_NTOA('209654088')
        AS 'AT&T';
```

```
+--------------+
| AT&T         |
+--------------+
| 12.127.17.72 |
+--------------+
```

INSERT( )

INSERT(*string, position, length, new_string*)

This function inserts a *string* into another string at the specified position, optionally overwriting the *new_string* provided for a specified *length*. It returns NULL if any of the arguments are NULL. The first position is 1. To prevent overwriting, give a length of 0 for the third argument, which specifies how many characters to overwrite before inserting. Don't confuse this function with the INSERT statement.

```
UPDATE courses
SET course_name =
    INSERT(course_name, LOCATE('Eng.', course_name), 4, 'English')
WHERE course_name LIKE "%Eng.%";
```

In this example, it was discovered that some course names have the word "English" abbreviated as "Eng." This SQL statement overwrites any such occurrences with the word "English." It uses the LOCATE( ) function to find the starting point of the abbreviation. This number is used as the position argument for the INSERT( ) function. If it's not found, the course name will not be changed.

INSTR( )

INSTR(*string*, *substring*)

This function returns the starting position of the first occurrence of the *substring*. The index of the first position is 1. This function is case-insensitive unless the argument is a binary string.

```
SELECT INSTR('Where are you?', 'you')
       AS 'INSTR( ) Test';
```

```
+--------------+
| INSTR( ) Test |
+--------------+
|           11 |
+--------------+
```

LCASE( )

LCASE(*string*)

This function converts a string of text or a string from a column given to all lowercase letters. An alias to LOWER( ).

```
SELECT teacher_id AS 'Teacher ID',
       CONCAT(LEFT(UCASE(name_last), 1),
       SUBSTRING(LCASE(name_last), 2))
           AS Teacher
FROM teachers;
```

To ensure that the first letter of the teacher's name is displayed in uppercase and the rest of the name is in lowercase letters, a combination of the LEFT( ) function and the SUBSTRING( ) function is used in conjunction with the UCASE( ) function and the LCASE( ) function.

LEFT( )

LEFT(*string*, *length*)

This function returns characters from a string given in the first argument for the length specified in the second argument, starting from the left end of the string.

```
SELECT LEFT(home_telephone, 3) AS 'Area Code'
FROM students GROUP BY 'Area Code';
```

This SQL statement extracts the first three digits of the telephone number of each student, which is the telephone area code, and then groups the results by the *Area Code* alias to determine the telephone area codes in which students reside.

LENGTH( )

LENGTH(*string*)

This function returns the number of bytes contained in a given string. Note that there are eight bits to a byte and there is one byte to a letter. OCTET_LENGTH( ) is an alias.

```
SELECT LENGTH('test') AS 'Number of Bytes';
```

```
+-----------------+
| Number of Bytes |
+-----------------+
|               4 |
+-----------------+
```

There are four letters in the word "test," so the string examined is composed of four bytes.

LOAD_FILE( )

LOAD_FILE(*filename*)

This function reads the contents of a file. The user must have file privileges in MySQL, and the file must be readable by all users on the filesystem. It returns NULL if the file doesn't exist, if the user doesn't have proper permissions, or if the file is otherwise unreadable.

```
UPDATE applications
SET essay = LOAD_FILE('/tmp/smith_john.txt')
WHERE applicant_id = '7382';
```

In this example, an essay written by someone who is applying for admission to the university is loaded into the *essay* column (which is a BLOB datatype) of the row for the applicant in the *applications* table. The entire contents of the file, including any binary data such as hard returns and photographs, are loaded from the file into the table.

LOCATE( )

LOCATE(*string, string[, start_position]*)

This function returns the numeric starting point of the first occurrence of a string given in the first argument, of the function found in the string given in the second argument. MySQL does not search beyond this point. A starting position for searching may be specified as a third argument.

```
SELECT name_last AS 'Name',
LOCATE('n', name_last) AS 'First n',
LOCATE('n', name_last, 5) AS 'After 5th Char'
FROM teachers
WHERE teacher_id = '730522';
```

```
+--------+---------+----------------+
| Name   | First n | After 5th Char |
+--------+---------+----------------+
| Vernon |       4 |              6 |
+--------+---------+----------------+
```

In this SQL statement, the last name of the teacher selected contains the letter "n" twice. However, the first use of the LOCATE( ) function makes note only of the position of the first occurrence. The second use of LOCATE( ) gives a starting point for MySQL to search name_last that is beyond the first occurrence, so the position of the next one is returned.

LOWER( )

LOWER(*string*)

This function converts a string of text or a column given to all lowercase letters. It is synonymous with LCASE( ).

```
SELECT course_id AS 'Course ID',
LOWER(course_name) AS Course
FROM courses;
```

This statement displays the name of each course in all lowercase letters.

LPAD( )

LPAD(*string, length, padding*)

This function adds padding specified in the third argument of the function to the left end of the string given, until the result reaches the maximum length (second argument) of the string contents and padding combined.

```
SELECT LPAD(course_name, 25, '.') AS Courses
FROM courses LIMIT 3;
```

```
+-------------------------+
| Courses                 |
+-------------------------+
| .........Creative Writing |
| .....Professional Writing |
| ......American Literature |
+-------------------------+
```

In this example, a list of three courses is retrieved and the results are padded with dots to the left of the course names.

LTRIM( )

LTRIM(*string*)

The function returns a string given with any leading spaces removed.

```
UPDATE students
SET name_last = LTRIM(name_last);
```

In this example, the last names of several students have been entered inadvertently with a space in front of the names. This SQL statement removes any leading spaces from each name retrieved and then writes the trimmed text over the existing data.

MAKE_SET( )

MAKE_SET(*bits, string1, string2, ...*)

This function returns a comma-separated list of values that coincide with bits of a base 10 number converted to its binary equivalent.

```
SELECT BIN(9) AS 'Binary 9',
       MAKE_SET(100, 'A','B','C','D')
          AS Set;
```

```
+----------+------+
| Binary 9 | Set  |
+----------+------+
| 1001     | A,D  |
+----------+------+
```

Notice that the binary equivalent of 9 is 1001. The first bit starting from the right of the binary number shown is 1 (or *on*), so the first string starting from the right of the list of strings is put into the set. The second and third bits of the binary number are 0, so the second and third strings (i.e., B and C) are not added to the set. The fourth bit counting from the right is 1, so the fourth string of the list of strings is added to the set.

MATCH ( ) AGAINST( )

MATCH(*column[, ...]*) AGAINST (*string*)

Use this function in WHERE clauses as a condition to search table columns for a given string. Text in the string delimited by spaces or quotes is parsed into separate words. Small words (three characters or less) are ignored. Then the words are used for searching columns. It requires a FULLTEXT index for columns searched.

```
SELECT applicant_id
FROM applications
WHERE MATCH (essay) AGAINST ('English');
```

This SQL statement searches the table containing data on people applying for admission to the university. The *essay* column contains a copy of the applicant's admission essay. The column is searched for applicants who mention the word "English" so that a list of applicants that have voiced an interest in the English program will be displayed.

MD5( )

MD5(*string*)

This function returns 32-character hash value of *string* from the RFC 1321 standard.

```
SELECT MD5('Test') AS 'MD5( ) Test';
```

```
+----------------------------------+
| MD5( ) Test                      |
+----------------------------------+
| 0cbc6611f5540bd0809a388dc95a615b |
+----------------------------------+
```

MID( )

MID(*string, position[, length]*)

This function returns the characters of a given string, starting from the left position specified in the second argument. The first character is numbered 1. You can limit the length of the string retrieved by specifying a limit in the third argument. This function is similar to SUBSTRING( ).

```
SELECT CONCAT(name_first, ' ', name_last) AS Teacher,
       CONCAT('(', LEFT(home_telephone, 3), ') ',
       MID(home_telephone, 4, 3), '-',
       MID(home_telephone, 7)) AS Telephone
FROM teachers LIMIT 1;
```

```
+----------------+----------------+
| Teacher        | Telephone      |
+----------------+----------------+
| Olympia Vernon | (504) 230-1748 |
+----------------+----------------+
```

This convoluted SQL statement produces the output shown by concatenating the extracted components of the selected teacher's telephone number with opening and closing parentheses, a dash, and a space.

OCT( )

OCT(*number*)

This function returns the octal or base 8 numeric system value of the given number. It returns NULL if the argument is NULL.

```
SELECT OCT(1), OCT(9), OCT(16);
+--------+--------+---------+
| OCT(8) | OCT(9) | OCT(16) |
+--------+--------+---------+
| 10     | 11     | 20      |
+--------+--------+---------+
```

OCTET_LENGTH( )

OCTET_LENGTH(*string*)

This function returns the number of bytes contained in the given string. Note that there are eight bits to a byte and there is one byte to a letter. An *octet* is a term used to describe the components of a IP address. This function is an alias of LENGTH( ).

OLD_PASSWORD( )

OLD_PASSWORD(*string*)

This function encrypts a given string based on the password encryption method used prior to Version 4.1 of MySQL. The result is not decryptable.

```
UPDATE teachers
    SET pwd = OLD_PASSWORD('test')
    WHERE teacher_id = '730522';
```

ORD( )

ORD(*string*)

This function returns an ordinal value, the position of a character in the ASCII character set, of the first character from the left in a string given.

```
SELECT ORD('A'), ORD('a');
```

```
+----------+----------+
| ORD('A') | ORD('a') |
+----------+----------+
|       65 |       97 |
+----------+----------+
```

PASSWORD( )

PASSWORD(*string*)

This function encrypts a password given as an argument. The result is not decryptable. This function is used for encrypting data in the *password* column of the *user* table in the *mysql* database.

```
UPDATE teachers
SET pwd = PASSWORD('test')
WHERE teacher_id = '730522';
```

POSITION( )

POSITION(*substring* IN *string*)

This function returns the numeric starting point from the left of the first occurrence of the string given in the first argument of the function found in the string given in the second. MySQL does not search beyond this point. This function is similar to LOCATE( ).

```
SELECT name_last AS 'Name',
        POSITION('n' IN name_last) AS 'First n'
FROM teachers
WHERE teacher_id = '730522';
```

```
+--------+---------+
| Name   | First n |
+--------+---------+
| Vernon |       4 |
+--------+---------+
```

In this SQL statement, the last name of the teacher selected contains the letter "n" twice, but only the position of the first occurrence is returned.

QUOTE( )

QUOTE(*string*)

This function returns a value as an input-safe string for a given string enclosed in single quotes. Single quotes, backslashes, ASCII NULLs, and Ctrl-Zs contained in the string are escaped with a backslash. This is a useful security measure when accepting values from a public web interface.

```
SELECT QUOTE(course_name) AS Courses
FROM courses
WHERE course_name LIKE "%'%" LIMIT 1;
+-------------------+
| Courses           |
+-------------------+
| Works of O\'Henry |
+-------------------+
```

In the WHERE clause of this SQL statement, the LIKE operator is used to find courses with a single quote in their names. The % is a wildcard. Because of the QUOTE( ) function, the single quote in the field returned is escaped with a backslash.

REPEAT( )

REPEAT(*string, count*)

This function returns the string given in the first argument of the function, as many times as specified in the second argument. It returns an empty string if *count* is less than or equal to 0. It returns NULL if either argument is NULL.

```
SELECT REPEAT('Urgent! ', 3)
AS 'Warning Message';
```

REPLACE( )

REPLACE(*string, old_element, new_element*)

This function replaces occurrences of an element given in the second argument, that exists in the string given in first argument, with a new element given in the third.

```
SELECT student_id,
CONCAT(REPLACE(title, 'Mrs.', 'Ms.'),
   ' ', name_first, ' ', name_last) AS Name
FROM students;
```

This SQL statement will retrieve each student's title and replace any occurrences of "Mrs." with "Ms.," but will leave all other titles unchanged.

REVERSE( )

REVERSE(*string*)

This function returns characters of *string* given in reverse order.

```
SELECT REVERSE('MUD');

+----------------+
| REVERSE('MUD') |
+----------------+
| DUM            |
+----------------+
```

RIGHT( )

RIGHT(*string, length*)

This function returns characters from *string* given in the first argument for the length specified in the second argument, starting from the right end of the string.

```
SELECT RIGHT(soc_sec, 4)
FROM students
WHERE student_id = '43325146122';
```

This SQL statement retrieves the last four digits of the student's Social Security number as an identity verification.

RPAD( )

RPAD(*string, length, padding*)

This function adds padding specified in the third argument of the function to left end of the string given in the first argument, until the maximum length (second argument) of *string* and *padding* combined is reached.

```
SELECT RPAD(course_name, 25, '.') AS Courses
FROM courses LIMIT 3;

+---------------------------+
| Courses                   |
+---------------------------+
| Creative Writing......... |
| Professional Writing..... |
| American Literature...... |
+---------------------------+
```

This SQL statement presents a list of three course names that are retrieved. The results are padded with dots to the right of each.

RTRIM( )

RTRIM(*string*)

This function returns the string given with any trailing spaces removed.

```
UPDATE students
SET name_last = RTRIM(name_last);
```

In this example, the last names of several students have been entered inadvertently with a space at the end of the names. This SQL statement will remove any trailing spaces from each name retrieved and then write the trimmed text over the existing data.

SHA( )

SHA(*string*)

This function returns the Secure Hash Algorithm (SHA) 160-bit checksum for the given string. The results are a string composed of 40 hexadecimal digits. NULL is returned if the given string is NULL. This function is synonymous with SHA1( ).

```
SELECT SHA('test');
```

```
+------------------------------------------+
| SHA('test')                              |
+------------------------------------------+
| a94a8fe5ccb19ba61c4c0873d391e987982fbbd3 |
+------------------------------------------+
```

SHA1( )

SHA(*string*)

This function returns the SHA 160-bit checksum for the given string. The results are a string composed of 40 hexadecimal digits. NULL is returned if the given string is NULL. This function is synonymous with SHA( ).

SOUNDEX( )

SOUNDEX(*string*)

This function returns an alphanumeric equivalent of a string based on an algorithm.

```
SELECT IF(SOUNDEX('him') = SOUNDEX('hymm'),
'Sounds Alike', 'Does not sound alike')
AS 'Sound Comparison';
```

```
+------------------+
| Sound Comparison |
+------------------+
| Sounds Alike     |
+------------------+
```

SOUNDEX( ) was designed to allow comparisons between fuzzy input, but it's rarely used.

SPACE( )

SPACE(*count*)

This function returns a string of spaces. The number of spaces returned is set by the argument.

```
SELECT CONCAT(name_first, SPACE(1), name_last)
AS Name
FROM students LIMIT 1;
```

```
+------------------+
| Name             |
+------------------+
| Richard Stringer |
+------------------+
```

Although this requires more typing than just placing a space within quotes, it's more visible to a human reader. Also, you could substitute the count with a variable in a program, and adjust it for the length of the name or some other factor.

STRCMP( )

STRCMP(*string, string*)

This function compares two strings to determine whether the first string is before or after the second string in ASCII sequence. If the first string precedes the second, -1 is returned. If it follows the second, 1 is returned. If they are equal, 0 is returned. This function is often used for alphanumeric comparisons, but is case-sensitive.

```
SELECT STRCMP('test','text')
AS Comparison;
+------------+
| Comparison |
+------------+
|         -1 |
+------------+
```

SUBSTRING( )

SUBSTRING(*string, position[, length]*)

SUBSTRING(*string* FROM *position* FOR *length*)

This function returns the characters of a given string, starting from the left position given. The first character is numbered 1. You can restrict the length of the string retrieved by specifying a limit. This function is similar to MID( ).

```
SELECT CONCAT(SUBSTRING(soc_sec, 1, 3), '-',
       SUBSTRING(soc_sec FROM 4 FOR 2), '-',
       SUBSTRING(soc_sec FROM 6))
          AS 'Social Security Nbr.'
FROM students LIMIT 1;

+----------------------+
| Social Security Nbr. |
+----------------------+
| 433-12-3456          |
+----------------------+
```

This example shows the three types of syntax of SUBSTRING( ) for reformatting a Social Security number stored without dashes.

SUBSTRING_INDEX( )

SUBSTRING_INDEX(*string, delimiter, count*)

This function returns a substring of the string given in the first argument that contains delimited data. The delimiter needs to be given in the second argument of the function. The number of elements starting from the left end of the string to extract is given in the third argument. A negative number instructs MySQL to count from the right end.

```
SELECT SUBSTRING_INDEX(pre_req, '|', -1)
       AS 'Last Prerequisite',
    pre_req AS 'All Prerequisites'
FROM courses WHERE course_id = '1245';
```

```
+--------------------+----------------------------+
| Last Prerequisite  | All Prerequisites          |
+--------------------+----------------------------+
| ENGL-202           | ENGL-101|ENGL-201|ENGL-202 |
+--------------------+----------------------------+
```

In this example, the last prerequisite course for the course selected is displayed, because -1 was entered for the count.

TRIM( )

TRIM([[BOTH | LEADING | TRAILING] [*padding*] FROM] *string*)

This function returns the string given with any trailing or leading padding removed, depending on which are specified. The default padding is a space if none is specified.

```
SELECT TRIM(LEADING '.' FROM col1),
       TRIM(TRAILING FROM col2),
       TRIM(BOTH '-' FROM col3),
       TRIM(col4)
FROM table1;
```

In this generic example, leading dots will be removed from the output of *col1*, spaces will be eliminated from *col2*, leading and trailing hyphens will be removed from *col3*, and leading and trailing spaces will be removed from *col4*.

UCASE( )

UCASE(*string*)

This function converts the given string of text or a string from a column to all upper-case letters. It is synonymous with UPPER( ) function.

```
SELECT course_id AS 'Course ID',
       UCASE(course_name) AS Course
FROM courses LIMIT 3;
```

```
+-----------+---------------------+
| Course ID | Course              |
+-----------+---------------------+
|      1245 | CREATIVE WRITING    |
|      1255 | PROFESSIONAL WRITING |
|      1244 | AMERICAN LITERATURE |
+-----------+---------------------+
```

UNCOMPRESS( )

UNCOMPRESS(*string*)

This function returns uncompressed string. It reverses the results of the COMPRESS( ) function. It requires MySQL to have been compiled with a compression library (i.e., zlib), and it returns NULL if the string is not compressed or if MySQL wasn't compiled with zlib.

```
SELECT UNCOMPRESS(essay)
FROM applications_archive
WHERE applicant_id = '1748';
```

UNCOMPRESSED_LENGTH( )

UNCOMPRESSED_LENGTH(*string*)

This function returns the number of characters contained in the given string after decompression. You can compress strings using the COMPRESS( ) function. This function is available as of Version 4.1 of MySQL.

```
SELECT UNCOMPRESSED_LENGTH(essay)
FROM applications
WHERE applicant_id = '1748';
```

UNHEX( )

UNHEX(*string*)

This function converts hexadecimal numbers to their character equivalent. It reverses the results of the HEX( ) function. This function is available as of Version 4.1.2 of MySQL.

```
SELECT ORD(UNHEX(MID('#FFFFFF', 2,2))) AS 'Red Value',
ORD(UNHEX(MID('#FFFFFF', 4,2))) AS 'Green Value',
ORD(UNHEX(RIGHT('#FFFFFF', 2))) AS 'Blue Value';
```

```
+-----------+-------------+------------+
| Red Value | Green Value | Blue Value |
+-----------+-------------+------------+
|       255 |         255 |        255 |
+-----------+-------------+------------+
```

This SQL statement returns the RGB values for the color white. The ORD( ) function is used to convert the results of UNHEX( ) to plain text.

UPPER( )

UPPER(*string*)

This function converts the given string of text or a string from a column to all uppercase letters. It is synonymous with the UCASE( ) function.

6

Date and Time Functions

The ability to record dates and times in a MySQL database is a very common requirement. This chapter presents the date and time functions for MySQL.

Date and time data comprises only numeric strings, so it can be stored in a regular character column. However, by using temporal datatype columns, you can use several built-in functions offered by MySQL. Currently, five temporal datatypes are available: date, time, datetime, timestamp, and year. The date column type is only for recording the date and uses the format *yyyy-mm-dd*. The time column type is for recording time in the format *hhh:mm:ss*. To record a combination of date and time, you can use the datetime column type: *yyyy-mm-dd hh:mm:ss*. The timestamp column is similar to datetime, but is a little limited in its range of allowable time: it starts at the Unix epoch time (i.e., 1970-01-01) and ends at the end of 2037. Finally, the year datatype is used only for recording the year in a column.

Incidentally, any function that calls for a date or a time datatype will also accept a combined datetime datatype. For more information on date and time datatypes, see Appendix A.

Validation of date strings is limited: MySQL makes sure that months range only from 0 to 12, and days range from 0 to 31. Therefore, a date such as February 30 would be accepted. Version 5.0.2 of MySQL will offer more refined validation that would reject such a date.

At the end of this introduction is a listing of date and time functions, grouped by type of function. The bulk of this chapter consists of an alphabetical listing of date and time functions, with explanations of each. Many functions come with examples, along with a resulting display. For help in locating functions, see the index at the back of this book.

For the examples in this chapter, I used the scenario of a professional services firm (e.g., a law firm or an investment advisory firm) that tracks appointments and seminars in MySQL.

Date and Time Functions Grouped by Type

This section lists the functions according to their purpose: to retrieve a time, extract an element of one, or perform calculations on it.

Determining the Date and Time

CURDATE( ), CURRENT_DATE, CURTIME( ), CURRENT_TIME, CURRENT_TIMESTAMP, NOW( ), LOCALTIME( ), LOCALTIMESTAMP( ), SYSDATE( ), UNIX_TIMESTAMP( ), UTC_DATE( ), UTC_TIME( ), UTC_TIMESTAMP( )

Extracting and Formatting the Date and Time

DATE( ), DATE_FORMAT( ), DAY( ), DAYNAME( ), DAYOFMONTH( ), DAYOFWEEK( ), DAYOFYEAR( ), EXTRACT( ), GET_FORMAT( ), HOUR( ), LAST_DAY( ), MAKEDATE( ), MAKETIME( ), MINUTE( ), MONTH( ), MONTHNAME( ), QUARTER( ), SECOND( ), STR_TO_DATE( ), TIME_FORMAT( ), TIMESTAMP( ), WEEK( ), WEEKDAY( ), WEEKOFYEAR( ), YEAR( ), YEARWEEK( )

Calculating and Modifying the Date and Time

ADDDATE( ), ADDTIME( ), CONVERT_TZ( ), DATE_ADD( ), DATE_SUB( ), DATEDIFF( ), FROM_DAYS( ), FROM_UNIXTIME( ), PERIOD_ADD( ), PERIOD_DIFF( ), SEC_TO_TIME( ), SUBDATE( ), SUBTIME( ), TIME_TO_SEC( ), TO_DAYS( ), TIMEDIFF( ), TIMESTAMPADD( ), TIMESTAMPDIFF( )

Date and Time Functions in Alphabetical Order

The rest of the chapter lists each function in alphabetical order.

ADDDATE( )

ADDDATE(date,INTERVAL value type)

This function adds the given interval of time to the date or time provided. This is an alias for DATE_ADD( ); see its definition for details and interval types.

```
UPDATE seminars
    SET seminar_date = ADDDATE(seminar_date, INTERVAL 7 DAY)
    WHERE seminar_date = '2004-12-15'';
```

This example postpones the seminar that was scheduled for December 15, 2004 to December 22—seven days later. As of Version 4.1 of MySQL, for adding days the second argument of the function may simply be the number of days (i.e., just 7 instead of INTERVAL 7 DAY).

ADDTIME( )

ADDTIME(*datetime, datetime*)

This function returns the date and the time for given string or column, incremented by the time given as the second argument (*d hh:mm:ss*). If a negative number is given, the time is subtracted, and the function is the equivalent of SUBTIME( ). This function is available as of Version 4.1.1 of MySQL.

```
SELECT NOW( ) AS Now,
       ADDTIME(NOW( ), '1:00:00.00') AS 'Hour Later';
```

```
+---------------------+---------------------+
| Now                 | Hour Later          |
+---------------------+---------------------+
| 2005-01-11 23:20:30 | 2005-01-12 00:20:30 |
+---------------------+---------------------+
```

Notice that the hour was increased by one, and because the time is near midnight, the function causes the date to be altered by one day, as well. To increase the date, add the number of days before the time (separated by a space) like so:

```
SELECT NOW( ) AS Now,
       ADDTIME(NOW( ), '30 0:0:0') AS 'Thirty Days Later';
```

```
+---------------------+---------------------+
| NOW( )              | Thirty Days Later   |
+---------------------+---------------------+
| 2005-01-11 23:20:30 | 2005-02-10 23:20:30 |
+---------------------+---------------------+
```

CONVERT_TZ( )

CONVERT_TZ(*datetime, day*)

This function converts a given date and time from one given time zone to another. It requires time-zone tables to be installed in the *mysql* database. If they're not already installed on your system, go to MySQL AB's site (*http://dev.mysql.com/downloads/time-zones.html*) to download the tables. Copy them into the *mysql* subdirectory of the *data* directory of MySQL. Change the ownership to the system *mysql* user with a system command like *chmod* and restart the server. This function is available as of Version 4. 1.3 of MySQL.

```
SELECT NOW( ) AS 'New Orleans',
       CONVERT_TZ(NOW( ), 'US/Central', 'Europe/Berlin')
           AS Berlin;
```

```
+---------------------+---------------------+
| New Orleans         | Berlin              |
+---------------------+---------------------+
| 2005-01-12 01:37:11 | 2005-01-12 08:37:11 |
+---------------------+---------------------+
```

This example retrieves the current time of the server located in New Orleans and converts it to the time in Berlin.

CURDATE( )

CURDATE( )

This function returns the current system date in *yyyy-mm-dd* format. It will return the date in a *yyyymmdd* format if it's used as part of a numeric calculation (see example). You can use the function in SELECT statements as shown here, in INSERT and UPDATE statements to set a value, or in a WHERE clause. CURDATE( ) is synonymous with CURRENT_ DATE; see its definition for more details.

```
SELECT CURDATE( ) AS Today,
       CURDATE( ) + 1 AS Tomorrow;
```

```
+------------+----------+
| Today      | Tomorrow |
+------------+----------+
| 2005-01-15 | 20050116 |
+------------+----------+
```

Because the second use of the function involves a numeric calculation, tomorrow's date is displayed without dashes.

CURRENT_DATE( )

CURRENT_DATE( )

This function returns the current date. The usual parentheses are not required. This function is synonymous with CURDATE( ). You can use both in SELECT statements to dynamically set values or in WHERE clauses.

```
UPDATE appointment
SET appt_date = CURRENT_DATE( )
WHERE rec_id = '1250';
```

This statement changes the appointment date for a client that came in today unexpectedly.

CURRENT_TIME( )

CURRENT_TIME( )

This function returns the current time in *hh:mm:ss* format. It will return the time in an *hhmmss* format if it's used as part of a numeric calculation. The usual parentheses are not required. It's synonymous with CURTIME( ).

```
INSERT INTO appointments
    (client_id, appt_date, start_time)
    VALUES('1403', CURRENT_DATE( ), CURRENT_TIME);
```

In this example, we're logging an unscheduled appointment that has just begun so that we can bill the client later.

CURRENT_TIMESTAMP( )

CURRENT_TIMESTAMP( )

This function returns current date and time in *yyyy-mm-dd hh:mm:ss* format. It will return the time in a *yyyymmddhhmmss* format if it's used as part of a numeric calculation (see example). Parentheses aren't required.

```
SELECT CURRENT_TIMESTAMP( ) AS Now,
       CURRENT_TIMESTAMP( ) + 10000 AS 'Hour Later';
```

```
+---------------------+----------------+
| Now                 | Hour Later     |
+---------------------+----------------+
| 2005-01-12 16:41:47 | 20050112174147 |
+---------------------+----------------+
```

By adding 10,000 to the current time, the hour is increased by 1 and the minutes and seconds by zero each, and the time is displayed in the second field without dashes.

CURTIME( )

CURTIME( )

This function returns the current system time in *hh:mm:ss* format. It will return the time in an *hhmmss* format if it's used as part of a numeric calculation (see example). This is an alias for CURRENT_TIME( ).

```
SELECT CURTIME( ) AS Now,
       CURTIME( ) + 10000 AS 'Hour Later';
```

```
+----------+------------+
| Now      | Hour Later |
+----------+------------+
| 16:35:43 |     163643 |
+----------+------------+
```

By adding 10,000 to the current time, this statement increases the hour by 1 and the minutes and seconds by zero each, and displays the time in the second field without dashes.

DATE( )

DATE(*date*)

This function returns the date from a given string. This function is available as of Version 4.1.1 of MySQL.

```
SELECT appointment, DATE(appointment)
    FROM appointments
    WHERE client_id = '8639' LIMIT 1;
```

```
+---------------------+-------------------+
| appointment         | DATE(appointment) |
+---------------------+-------------------+
| 2005-01-11 14:11:43 | 2005-01-11        |
+---------------------+-------------------+
```

In this SQL statement, the value of the *appointment* column, which is a `DATETIME` type column, is shown first. The second field is the date extracted by the function from the same column.

DATE_ADD( )

DATE_ADD(*date*, INTERVAL *value type*)

This function extracts time or date information and, thereby, adds time to the value extracted. It's synonymous with the `ADDDATE( )` function.

```
UPDATE appointments
    SET appt_date = DATE_ADD(appt_date, INTERVAL 1 DAY)
    WHERE rec_id='1202';
```

In this example, the appointment date is changed to its current value plus, one additional day (i.e., we're postponing the appointment by one day). If we changed the 1 to a -1, MySQL would subtract a day instead. The format of value depends on the type and is shown in Table 6-1.

Table 6-1. DATE_ADD intervals and formats of values

Type of increment	Description
DAY	dd
DAY_HOUR	dd hh
DAY_MINUTE	dd hh:mm
DAY_SECOND	dd hh:mm:ss
HOUR	hh
HOUR_MINUTE	hh:mm
HOUR_SECOND	hh:mm:ss
MINUTE	mm
MINUTE_SECOND	mm:ss
MONTH	mm
SECOND	ss
YEAR	yyyy
YEAR_MONTH	yy-mm

DATE_FORMAT( )

DATE_FORMAT(*date*, '*format_code*')

This function returns date and time information in a format desired, based on formatting codes listed in the second argument of function.

```
SELECT DATE_FORMAT(appointment, '%W - %M %e, %Y at %r')
       AS 'Appointment'
    FROM appointments
    WHERE client_id = '8392'
       AND appointment > CURDATE( );
```

```
+----------------------------------------+
| Appointment                            |
+----------------------------------------+
| Tuesday - June 15, 2004 at 01:00:00 PM |
+----------------------------------------+
```

Using the formatting codes, we're specifying that we want the name of the day of the week followed by a dash and then the date of the appointment in a typical U.S. format, with the month name and a comma after the day. We're ending with the word "at" followed by the full non-military time. Table 6-2 contains a list of all the formatting codes you can use with DATE_FORMAT( ). You can also use these codes with TIME_FORMAT( ) and EXTRACT( ).

Table 6-2. DATE_FORMAT( ) format codes and resulting formats

Code	Example
%%	A literal '%'
%a	Abbreviated weekday name (Sun...Sat)
%b	Abbreviated month name (Jan...Dec)
%c	Month, numeric (1...12)
%d	Day of the month, numeric (00...31)
%D	Day of the month with English suffix (1st, 2nd, 3rd, etc.)
%e	Day of the month, numeric (0...31)
%h	Hour (01...12)
%H	Hour (00...23)
%i	Minutes, numeric (00...59)
%I	Hour (01...12)
%j	Day of the year (001...366)
%k	Hour (0...23)
%l	Hour (1...12)
%m	Month, numeric (01...12)
%M	Month name (January...December)
%p	AM or PM
%r	Time, 12-hour (hh:mm:ss [AP]M)
%s	Seconds (00...59)
%S	Seconds (00...59)
%T	Time, 24-hour (hh:mm:ss)
%u	Week (0...52), where Monday is the first day of the week
%U	Week (0...52), where Sunday is the first day of the week
%v	Week (1...53), where Monday is the first day of the week; used with '%x'
%V	Week (1...53), where Sunday is the first day of the week; used with '%X'
%w	Day of the week (0=Sunday...6=Saturday)
%W	Weekday name (Sunday...Saturday)
%x	Year for the week, where Monday is the first day of the week, numeric, 4 digits; used with '%v'
%X	Year for the week, where Sunday is the first day of the week, numeric, 4 digits; used with '%V'
%y	Year, numeric, 2 digits
%Y	Year, numeric, 4 digits

Date/Time
Functions

DATE_SUB( )

DATE_SUB(*date*, INTERVAL *value type*)

Use this function to subtract from the results of a date or time datatype column. See DATE_ADD( ) for a table of incremental types.

```
SELECT DATE_SUB(NOW( ), INTERVAL 1 DAY)
        AS Yesterday;
```

```
+---------------------+
| Yesterday           |
+---------------------+
| 2004-05-08 07:05:08 |
+---------------------+
```

This statement was entered on the morning of May 9, a little after 7 a.m. Notice that the time remains unchanged, but the date was reduced by one day. By placing a negative sign in front of the value the reverse effect would occur, giving a result of May 10 in this example. Whatever intervals that can be used with DATE_ADD( ) can be used with DATE_SUB( ).

DATEDIFF( )

DATEDIFF(*date*, *date*)

This function returns the number of days in the difference between the two dates given. Although a parameter may be given in date and time format, only the date is used for determining the difference. This function is available as of Version 4.1. 1 of MySQL.

```
SELECT CURDATE( ) AS Today,
        DATEDIFF('2005-12-25', NOW( ))
        AS 'Days to Christmas';
```

```
+------------+-------------------+
| Today      | Days to Christmas |
+------------+-------------------+
| 2005-01-11 |               348 |
+------------+-------------------+
```

DAY( )

DAY(*date*)

This function returns the day of the month for a given date provided. This function is available as of Version 4.1.1 of MySQL. It's synonymous with the DAYOFMONTH( ) function.

```
SELECT DAY('2005-12-15') AS 'Day';
```

```
+-------+
| Day   |
+-------+
|    15 |
+-------+
```

This function is more meaningful when you apply it to a date column where the date is unknown before entering the SQL statement.

DAYNAME( )

DAYNAME(*date*)

This function returns the name of the day for the date provided.

```
SELECT DAYNAME(appt_date) AS Appointment
FROM appointments
WHERE rec_id = '1439';
```

```
+-------------+
| Appointment |
+-------------+
| Saturday    |
+-------------+
```

DAYOFMONTH( )

DAYOFMONTH(*date*)

This function returns the day of the month for the date given. It returns NULL if the day for the date is greater than 31. It will accept a date like 2005-02-31 as valid and will return 31. Future releases of MySQL will resolve this problem.

```
SELECT DAYOFMONTH('2005-03-01')
       AS 'Day of Month';
```

```
+--------------+
| Day of Month |
+--------------+
|            1 |
+--------------+
```

This is more meaningful when you apply it to a date column where the date is unknown before entering the SQL statement.

DAYOFWEEK( )

DAYOFWEEK(*date*)

This function returns numerical day of the week for a given date. Sunday returns a value of 1, and Saturday returns a value of 7.

```
SELECT DAYOFWEEK('2005-03-01')
       AS 'Day of Week',
       DAYNAME('2005-03-01')
       AS 'Name of Day';
```

```
+-------------+-------------+
| Day of Week | Name of Day |
+-------------+-------------+
|           3 | Tuesday     |
+-------------+-------------+
```

In this example, the date is on the third day of the week, which is a Tuesday.

DAYOFYEAR( )

DAYOFYEAR(*date*)

This function returns the day of the year. January 1 would give a value of 1, and December 31 would normally be 365, except on leap years, when it would be 366.

```
SELECT (DAYOFYEAR('2004-03-01') -
        DAYOFYEAR('2004-02-28'))
            AS 'Difference for Leap Year';
```

```
+--------------------------+
| Difference for Leap Year |
+--------------------------+
|                        2 |
+--------------------------+
```

Here we are using the function to calculate the number of days from the first date, March 1, 2004, to the second date, February 28 of the same year. 2004 was a leap year, so the result is 2 days.

EXTRACT( )

EXTRACT(*type* FROM *date*)

This function extracts date or time information from a date in the format type requested. The acceptable types are the same as for DATE_ADD( ).

```
SELECT EXTRACT(HOUR_MINUTE FROM NOW( ))
        AS 'Time Now';
```

```
+-----------+
| Time Now |
+-----------+
|      1121 |
+-----------+
```

When this SQL statement was run, it was 11:21 a.m.

FROM_DAYS( )

FROM_DAYS(*value*)

This function returns the date based on the number of days given, which are from the beginning of the currently used standard calendar. Problems occur for dates before 1582 when the Gregorian calendar became the standard. The opposite of this is TO_DAYS( ).

```
SELECT FROM_DAYS((365.25*2005))
        AS 'Start of 2005?';
```

```
+----------------+
| Start of 2005? |
+----------------+
| 2005-01-15     |
+----------------+
```

Assuming that there are 365.25 days in a year on average (allowing for the leap year), you would think that multiplying that factor by 2005 would give a result of January 1, 2005, but it doesn't because of the calendar changes centuries ago. This function is useful for comparing dates, not for determining static information on one date.

FROM_UNIXTIME( )

FROM_UNIXTIME(*unix_timestamp*[, *format*])

This function returns the date based on Unix time, which is the number of seconds since January 1, 1970, Greenwich Mean Time (GMT), with 12:00:01 being the first second of Unix time (the epoch). Optionally the results may be formatted using the formatting codes from DATE_FORMAT( ). It will return the date and time in a *yyyy-mm-dd hh:mm:ss* format, but will return the data in a *yyyymmdd* format if it's used as part of a numeric calculation.

```
SELECT FROM_UNIXTIME(0)
        AS 'My Epoch Start';
```

```
+----------------------+
| My Epoch Start       |
+----------------------+
|  1969-12-31 18:00:00 |
+----------------------+
```

Here we're selecting the date based on zero seconds since the start of Unix time. The results are off by six hours because I'm not located in the GMT zone. This function is typically used on columns in which their values were derived from UNIXTIME_STAMP( ).

GET_FORMAT( )

GET_FORMAT(*data_type*, *format_type*)

This function returns the format for a format type given as the second argument for a datatype given as the first. The format codes returned are the same codes used by the DATE_FORMAT( ) function. Four datatypes may be given: DATE, TIME, DATETIME, and TIMESTAMP. Five format types may be given as the second argument: EUR, INTERNAL, ISO, JIS, and USA. This function is available as of Version 4.1.1 of MySQL. The TIMESTAMP datatype isn't acceptable until Version 4.1.4. Here's an example using the function that returns the USA format:

```
SELECT GET_FORMAT(DATE, 'USA');
```

```
+------------------------+
| GET_FORMAT(DATE, 'USA') |
+------------------------+
| %m.%d.%Y               |
+------------------------+
```

You can hand off to the DATE_FORMAT( ) function for formatting the value of a date column like so:

```
SELECT DATE_FORMAT(appointment, GET_FORMAT(DATE, 'USA'))
            AS Appointment LIMIT 1;
```

```
+-------------+
| Appointment |
+-------------+
| 01.11.2005  |
+-------------+
```

Table 6-3 lists the results for the different combinations. The datetype of TIMESTAMP is
not listed, because the results are the same as DATETIME.

Table 6-3. DATE_FORMAT arguments and their results

Combination	Results
DATE, 'EUR'	%d.%m.%Y
DATE, 'INTERNAL'	%Y%m%d
DATE, 'ISO'	%Y-%m-%d
DATE, 'JIS'	%Y-%m-%d
DATE, 'USA'	%m.%d.%Y
TIME, 'EUR'	%H.%i.%S
TIME, 'INTERNAL'	%H%i%s
TIME, 'ISO'	%H:%i:%s
TIME, 'JIS'	%H:%i:%s
TIME, 'USA'	%h:%i:%s %p
DATETIME, 'EUR'	%Y-%m-%d-%H.%i.%s
DATETIME, 'INTERNAL'	%Y%m%d%H%i%s
DATETIME, 'ISO'	%Y-%m-%d %H:%i:%s
DATETIME, 'JIS'	%Y-%m-%d %H:%i:%s
DATETIME, 'USA'	%Y-%m-%d-%H.%i.%s

HOUR( )

HOUR(*time*)

This function returns the hour for the time given. For column types containing the
time of day (e.g., DATETIME), the range of results will be from 0 to 23. For TIME datatype
columns that contain data not restricted to day limits, this function may return values
greater than 23.

```
SELECT HOUR(appointment)
FROM appointments
WHERE client_id = '3992'
   AND appointment > CURDATE( );
```

```
+-------------------+
| HOUR(appointment) |
+-------------------+
|                13 |
+-------------------+
```

This statement is selecting the upcoming appointment for a particular client. The hour
is returned in military time (i.e., 13 is 1 p.m.).

LAST_DAY( )

LAST_DAY(*date*)

This function returns the date of the last day of the month for a given date. This function is available as of Version 4.1.1 of MySQL.

```
SELECT LAST_DAY('2005-12-15')
   AS 'End of Month';
```

```
+--------------+
| End of Month |
+--------------+
| 2005-12-31   |
+--------------+
```

This function is more meaningful when you apply it to a date column where the date is unknown before entering the SQL statement.

LOCALTIME( )

LOCALTIME( )

This function returns the current system date in *yyyy-mm-dd hh:mm:ss* format. You can use it in SELECT statements as shown here, in INSERT and UPDATE statements to set a value, or in a WHERE clause. This statement is available as of Version 4.0.6 of MySQL. Incidentally, the parentheses are not required. This function is synonymous with LOCALTIMESTAMP( ) and NOW( ).

```
SELECT LOCALTIME( );
```

```
+---------------------+
| LOCALTIME( )        |
+---------------------+
| 2005-01-10 14:27:41 |
+---------------------+
```

LOCALTIMESTAMP( )

LOCALTIMESTAMP( )

This function returns the current system date in *yyyy-mm-dd hh:mm:ss* format. You can use it in SELECT statements as shown, in INSERT and UPDATE statements to set a value, or in a WHERE clause. This statement is available as of Version 4.0.6 of MySQL. Incidentally, the parentheses are not required. This function is synonymous with LOCALTIME( ) and NOW( ).

```
SELECT LOCALTIMESTAMP( );
```

```
+---------------------+
| LOCALTIMESTAMP( )   |
+---------------------+
| 2005-01-10 14:49:56 |
+---------------------+
```

MAKEDATE( )

MAKEDATE(*year*, *day*)

This function converts a given day of the year of a given year to a date in *yyyy-mm-dd* format. The day given can be from 1 to 365 (366 for leap years). It returns NULL if a value less is than 1 or greater than the maximum number of days allowed. This function is available as of Version 4.1.1 of MySQL.

```
SELECT MAKEDATE(2005, 1) AS 'First Day',
       MAKEDATE(2005, 365) AS 'Last Day';
```

```
+------------+------------+
| First Day  | Last Day   |
+------------+------------+
| 2005-01-01 | 2005-12-31 |
+------------+------------+
```

MAKETIME( )

MAKETIME(*hour*, *minute*, *second*)

This function converts a given hour, minute, and second to *hh:mm:ss* format. It returns NULL if the value for *minute* is greater than 60 or if *second* is greater than 59. It will accept an hour greater than 24. This function is available as of Version 4.1.1 of MySQL.

```
SELECT MAKETIME(14, 32, 5)
    AS Time;
```

```
+----------+
| Time     |
+----------+
| 14:32:05 |
+----------+
```

MICROSECOND( )

MICROSECOND(*time*)

This function extracts the microseconds value of a given time. This function is available as of Version 4.1.1 of MySQL.

```
SELECT MICROSECOND('2005-01-11 19:28:45.80')
        AS 'MicroSecond';
```

```
+-------------+
| MicroSecond |
+-------------+
|      800000 |
+-------------+
```

MINUTE( )

MINUTE(*time*)

This function returns the minute value (0–59) of a given time.

```
SELECT CONCAT(HOUR(appointment), ':',
        MINUTE(appointment)) AS 'Appointment'
    FROM appointments
    WHERE client_id = '3992'
        AND appointment > CURDATE( );
```

```
+-------------+
| Appointment |
+-------------+
|       13:30 |
+-------------+
```

This statement is using the string function CONCAT( ) to paste together the hour and the minute, with a colon as a separator.

MONTH( )

MONTH(*date*)

This function returns the numeric value of the month (1–12) for the date provided.

```
SELECT MONTH(appointment)
            AS Appointment
    FROM appointments
    WHERE client_id = '8302'
        AND appointment > CURRDATE( );
```

```
+-------------+
| Appointment |
+-------------+
|           6 |
+-------------+
```

This SQL statement is retrieving the month of any appointments after the current date for a particular client. There's only one appointment, and it's in June.

MONTHNAME( )

MONTHNAME(*date*)

This function returns the name of the month for the date provided.

```
SELECT MONTHNAME(appointment)
        AS 'Appointment'
    FROM appointments
    WHERE client_id = '8302'
        AND appointment > NOW( );
```

```
+-------------+
| Appointment |
+-------------+
| June        |
+-------------+
```

In this example, the client has only one appointment after the current date, and it's in June. As you can with any date and time function, you can use this one in conjunction with other formatting functions like CONCAT( ) for human formatting of data.

NOW( )

NOW( )

This function returns the current date and time. It will return the date and time in a *yyyy-mm-dd hh:mm:ss* format, but will return the data in a *yyyymmdd* format if it's used as part of a numeric calculation. It's synonymous with LOCALTIME( ).

```
SELECT NOW( ) AS Now,
    NOW( ) + 10000 AS 'Hour Later';
```

```
+---------------------+----------------+
| Now                 | Hour Later     |
+---------------------+----------------+
| 2005-01-12 17:10:28 | 20050112181028 |
+---------------------+----------------+
```

By adding 10,000 to the current time, the hour is increased by 1 and the minutes and seconds by zero each, and the time is displayed in the second field, without dashes.

PERIOD_ADD( )

PERIOD_ADD(*yearmonth, value*)

This function adds a specified number of months to the year and month given. The date must be in string format and can contain only the year and month in either *yyyymm* or *yymm* format. The value for the second argument of the function specifies the number of months to add to the period given.

```
SELECT PERIOD_ADD(200412, 1)
    AS 'Next Accounting Period';
```

```
+-----------------------+
| Next Accounting Period |
+-----------------------+
|                200501 |
+-----------------------+
```

Functions such as this one are particularly useful when you're building a script or program, and you need to design an SQL statement that will account for accounting periods that roll into new years.

PERIOD_DIFF( )

PERIOD_DIFF(*yearmonth*,*yearmonth*)

This function returns the number of months between periods. The dates must be in string format and contain only the year and month, in either *yyyymm* or *yymm* format.

```
SELECT PERIOD_DIFF(200403, 200401)
       AS 'Accounting Periods Apart';
```

```
+--------------------------+
| Accounting Periods Apart |
+--------------------------+
|                        2 |
+--------------------------+
```

The first period is for March 2004 and the second is for January 2004. This function doesn't work on standard date columns unless you put them into the format shown here. An example of doing this conversion is:

```
SELECT PERIOD_DIFF(EXTRACT(YEAR_MONTH FROM CURDATE( )),
       EXTRACT(YEAR_MONTH FROM appointment))
       AS 'Accounting Periods Apart'
   FROM appointments
   WHERE client_id = '5620'
   ORDER BY appointment DESC;
```

```
+--------------------------+
| Accounting Periods Apart |
+--------------------------+
|                       -2 |
+--------------------------+
```

This SQL statement determines that it's been two months since this client's last appointment. This works, but it's cumbersome.

QUARTER( )

QUARTER(*date*)

This function returns the number of quarters (1–4) for the date provided. The first three months of each year have a value of 1.

```
SELECT COUNT(appointment)
       AS 'Appts. Last Quarter'
   FROM appointments
   WHERE QUARTER(appointment) = (QUARTER(NOW( )) - 1)
       AND client_id = '7393';
```

```
+---------------------+
| Appts. Last Quarter |
+---------------------+
|                  16 |
+---------------------+
```

In this example, we're having MySQL calculate the total number of appointments for a particular client that occurred before this quarter. The flaw in this SQL statement is that it doesn't work when it's run during the first quarter of a year. In the first quarter, the calculation on the fourth line would produce a quarter value of 0. This statement also doesn't consider appointments in previous quarters of previous years. To solve these problems, we could set up user-defined variables for the values of the previous quarter and for its year:

```
SET @LASTQTR:=IF((QUARTER(CURDATE( ))-1) = 0,
    4, QUARTER(CURDATE( ))-1);

SET @YR:=IF(@LASTQTR = 4,
    YEAR(NOW( ))-1, YEAR(NOW( )));

SELECT COUNT(appointment)
    AS 'Appts. Last Quarter'
FROM appointments
WHERE QUARTER(appointment) = @LASTQTR
    AND YEAR(appointment) = @YR
    AND client_id = '7393';
```

In the first SQL statement here, we're using an IF statement to test whether reducing the quarter by one would yield us a 0 value. If so, we'll set the user variable for the last quarter to 4. In the second statement we're establishing the year for the last quarter, based on the value determined for @LASTQTR. The last SQL statement selects rows and counts them where the QUARTER( ) function yields a value equal to the @LASTQTR variable and where the YEAR( ) function yields a value equal to the @YR variable based on the appointment date, and where the client is the one for which we are running the statement.

SEC_TO_TIME( )

SEC_TO_TIME(*seconds*)

This function returns the period for a given number of seconds, in the format *hh:mm:ss*. It will return the time in *hhmmss* format if it's used as part of a numeric calculation.

```
SELECT SEC_TO_TIME(3600)
        AS 'Actual Time';

+-------------+
| Actual Time |
+-------------+
| 01:00:00    |
+-------------+
```

In this example, we have a value of 3,600 seconds into the day, which the function has translated to 1 a.m. Incidentally, if the number of seconds exceeds 86,400, or one day's worth, the value for hours will result in an amount greater than 23 and will not be reset back to 0.

SECOND( )

SECOND(*time*)

This function returns seconds value (0–59) for a given time.

```
SELECT NOW( ), SECOND(NOW( ));
```

```
+---------------------+----------------+
| NOW( )              | SECOND(NOW( )) |
+---------------------+----------------+
| 2004-05-09 14:56:11 |             11 |
+---------------------+----------------+
```

The first column generated shows the time that this statement was entered, using NOW( ) function. The second column displays only the seconds value for the results of NOW( ).

STR_TO_DATE( )

STR_TO_DATE(*datetime*, '*format_code*')

This function returns the date and time of a given string for a given format. The function takes a string containing a date or time, or both. So that the function may convert the string given, the formatting code for the string needs to be provided. The formatting codes are the same codes used by the DATE_FORMAT( ) function. This function is available as of Version 4.1.1 of MySQL.

```
SELECT STR_TO_DATE('January 15, 2005 1:30 PM',
                   '%M %d, %Y %h:%i %p')
            AS Anniversary;
```

```
+---------------------+
| Anniversary         |
+---------------------+
| 2005-01-15 13:30:00 |
+---------------------+
```

SUBDATE( )

SUBDATE(*date*, INTERVAL *value type*)

Use this function to subtract a time interval from the results of a date or time datatype column. If a negative value is given, the interval is added and is equivalent to the ADDDATE( ) function. This is an alias for the DATE_SUB( ) function. See DATE_ADD( ) for a table of incremental types.

```
SELECT SUBDATE(NOW( ), INTERVAL 1 DAY)
            AS 'Yesterday',
       SUBDATE(NOW( ), INTERVAL -1 DAY)
            AS 'Tomorrow';
```

```
+---------------------+---------------------+
| Yesterday           | Tomorrow            |
+---------------------+---------------------+
| 2004-05-09 16:11:56 | 2004-05-11 16:11:56 |
+---------------------+---------------------+
```

As of Version 4.1 of MySQL, for subtracting days the second argument of the function may simply be the number of days (i.e., just 1 instead of INTERVAL 1 DAY).

SUBTIME( )

SUBTIME(*datetime, datetime*)

This function returns the date and time for the given string or column, decreased by the time given as the second argument (*d hh:mm:ss*). If a negative number is given, the time is added and the function is the equivalent of ADDTIME( ). This function is available as of Version 4.1.1 of MySQL.

```
SELECT NOW( ) AS Now,
       SUBTIME(NOW( ), '1:00:00.00') AS 'Hour Ago';
```

```
+---------------------+---------------------+
| Now                 | Hour Ago            |
+---------------------+---------------------+
| 2005-01-12 00:54:59 | 2005-01-11 23:54:59 |
+---------------------+---------------------+
```

Notice that the hour was decreased by one, and because the time is just after midnight, the function causes the date to be altered by one day, as well. To decrease the date, add the number of days before the time (separated by a space) like so:

```
SELECT NOW( ) AS Now,
       SUBTIME(NOW( ), '30 0:0.0') AS 'Thirty Days Ago';
```

```
+---------------------+---------------------+
| Now                 | Thirty Days Ago     |
+---------------------+---------------------+
| 2005-01-12 00:57:04 | 2004-12-13 00:57:04 |
+---------------------+---------------------+
```

SYSDATE( )

SYSDATE( )

This function returns the system date. It will return the date and time in a *yyyy-mm-dd hh:mm:ss* format, but will return the data in a *yyyymmdd* format if it's used as part of a numeric calculation. This function is an alias for the NOW( ) function.

```
SELECT SYSDATE( );
```

```
+---------------------+
| SYSDATE( )          |
+---------------------+
| 2004-05-09 18:44:51 |
+---------------------+
```

TIME( )

TIME(*time*)

This function returns the time from a given string or column containing date and time data. This function is available as of Version 4.1.1 of MySQL.

```
SELECT TIME(NOW( )) , NOW( );
```

```
+-------------+---------------------+
| TIME(NOW( )) | NOW( )             |
+-------------+---------------------+
| 21:14:20    | 2005-01-11 21:14:20 |
+-------------+---------------------+
```

TIMEDIFF( )

TIMEDIFF(*time, time*)

This function returns the time difference between the two times given. Although the arguments may be given in time or date-and-time format, both arguments must be of the same datatype. This function is available as of Version 4.1.1 of MySQL.

```
SELECT appointment AS Appointment, NOW( ) AS Now,
       TIMEDIFF(appointment, NOW( )) AS 'Time Remaining'
    FROM appointments
    WHERE rec_id='3783';
```

```
+--------------------+--------------------+----------------+
| Appointment        | Now                | Time Remaining |
+--------------------+--------------------+----------------+
| 2005-01-11 10:30:00| 2005-01-11 22:28:09| 12:01:51       |
+--------------------+--------------------+----------------+
```

TIMESTAMP( )

TIMESTAMP(*date, time*)

This function returns date and time (in *yyyy-mm-dd hh:mm:ss* format) from a given string or column containing date and time data, respectively. If only the date or only the time is given, the function will return zeros for the missing parameters. This function is available as of Version 4.1.1 of MySQL.

```
SELECT TIMESTAMP(appt_date, appt_time)
    FROM appointments LIMIT 1;
```

```
+-------------------------------+
| TIMESTAMP(appt_date, appt_time) |
+-------------------------------+
| 2005-01-15 10:30:00           |
+-------------------------------+
```

TIMESTAMPDIFF( )

TIMESTAMPDIFF(*interval, datetime, datetime*)

This function returns the time difference between the two times given but only for the interval being compared. The intervals accepted are the same as those for the TIMESTAMPADD( ) function. This function is available as of Version 5 of MySQL.

```
SELECT NOW( ) AS Today,
       TIMESTAMPDIFF(DAY, NOW( ), LAST_DAY(NOW( )))
           AS 'Days Remaining in Month';
```

```
+---------------------+-------------------------+
| Today               | Days Remaining in Month |
+---------------------+-------------------------+
| 2005-01-12 02:19:26 | 19                      |
+---------------------+-------------------------+
```

This SQL statement retrieves the current date and time and uses the LAST_DAY( ) function to determine the date of the last day of the month. Then TIMESTAMPDIFF( ) function determines the difference between the day of the date now and the day for the date at the end of the month.

TIMESTAMPADD( )

TIMESTAMPADD(*interval, value, datetime*)

This function adds the given interval of time to the given date or time. The intervals accepted are FRAC_SECOND, SECOND, MINUTE, HOUR, DAY, WEEK, MONTH, QUARTER, and YEAR. For compatibility with other systems, you can add the SQL_TSI_ prefix to these interval names (e.g., SQL_TSI_YEAR). This function is available as of Version 5 of MySQL. This function is similar to DATE_ADD( ). In this example, an appointment is set to an hour later.

```
UPDATE appointments
    SET appointment = TIMESTAMPADD(HOUR, 1, appointment)
    WHERE rec_id = '8930';
```

TIME_FORMAT( )

TIME_FORMAT(*time, format*)

This function returns the time value of a time element provided and formats it according to formatting codes given as the second argument in parentheses. See the DATE_FORMAT( ) function for formatting codes but only those related to time values. This function will return NULL for other formatting codes.

```
SELECT TIME_FORMAT(appointment, '%r')
       AS 'Appt. Time' FROM appointments
WHERE client_id = '8373'
   AND appointment > SYSDATE( );
```

```
+-------------+
| Appt. Time  |
+-------------+
| 01:00:00 PM |
+-------------+
```

TIME_TO_SEC( )

TIME_TO_SEC(*time*)

This function returns the number of seconds that the given time represents. This function is the inverse of SEC_TO_TIME( ).

```
SELECT TIME_TO_SEC('01:00')
        AS 'Seconds up to 1 a.m.';

+----------------------+
| Seconds up to 1 a.m. |
+----------------------+
|                 3600 |
+----------------------+
```

Here we're calculating the number of seconds up until the time of 1 a.m. (i.e., 60 seconds times 60 minutes) or one hour into the day.

TO_DAYS( )

TO_DAYS(*date*)

This function returns the date based on the number of days given, which are from the beginning of the currently used standard calendar. Problems occur for dates before 1582 when the Gregorian calendar became the standard. The opposite of this function is FROM_DAYS( ).

```
SELECT (TO_DAYS('2005-01-15') -
        TO_DAYS('2005-01-01'))
          AS 'Difference';

+------------+
| Difference |
+------------+
|         14 |
+------------+
```

In this example, the TO_DAYS( ) function is employed to calculate the difference in the number of days between the two dates.

UNIX_TIMESTAMP( )

UNIX_TIMESTAMP([*datetime*])

This function returns the number of seconds since the start of the Unix epoch (January 1, 1970, Greenwich Mean Time). Without a given time, this function will return the Unix time for the current date and time. Optionally, a date and time value (directly or by way of a column value) may be given for conversion to Unix time with this function.

```
SELECT UNIX_TIMESTAMP( )
        AS 'Now',
      UNIX_TIMESTAMP('2004-05-09 20:45:00')
        AS 'Same Time';
```

```
+-----------------+-----------------+
|           Now   |     Same Time   |
+-----------------+-----------------+
|      1084153500 |      1084153500 |
+-----------------+-----------------+
```

The first column uses the function to determine the Unix time for the moment that the statement was entered. The second column uses the same function to determine the Unix time for the same date and time provided in a usual, readable format.

UTC_DATE( )

UTC_DATE( )

This function returns the current Universal Time Clock (UTC) date in *yyyy-mm-dd* format. This function will return the UTC date in a *yyyymmdd* format if it's used as part of a numeric calculation (see example). You can use this in SELECT statements as shown here, in INSERT and UPDATE statements to set a value, or in a WHERE clause. This function is available as of Version 4.1.1 of MySQL. The pair of parentheses is optional.

```
SELECT UTC_DATE( ) + 1, UTC_DATE( );
```

```
+-----------------+------------+
| UTC_DATE( ) + 1 | UTC_DATE( ) |
+-----------------+------------+
|        20050112 | 2005-01-11 |
+-----------------+------------+
```

UTC_TIME( )

UTC_TIME( )

This function returns the current UTC time in *hh:mm:ss* format. It will return the UTC time in an *hhmmss* format if it's used as part of a numeric calculation (see example). You can use this in SELECT statements as shown here, in INSERT and UPDATE statements to set a value, or in a WHERE clause. This statement is available as of Version 4.1.1 of MySQL. The pair of parentheses is not required.

```
SELECT UTC_TIME( ) + 1, UTC_TIME( );
```

```
+-----------------+------------+
| UTC_TIME( ) + 1 | UTC_TIME( ) |
+-----------------+------------+
|          195858 | 19:58:57   |
+-----------------+------------+
```

UTC_TIMESTAMP( )

UTC_TIMESTAMP( )

This function returns the current UTC date and time in *yyyy-mm-dd hh:mm:ss* format. It will return the UTC date and time in a *yyyymmddhhmmss* format if it's used as part of a numeric calculation (see example). You can use this in SELECT statements as shown here, in INSERT and UPDATE statements to set a value, or in a WHERE clause. This statement is available as of Version 4.1.1 of MySQL. The pair of parentheses is not required. Use UTC_TIME( ) for only the UTC time and UTC_DATE( ) for only the UTC date.

```
SELECT UTC_TIMESTAMP( ) + 1, UTC_TIMESTAMP( );
```

```
+--------------------+--------------------+
| UTC_TIMESTAMP( ) + 1 | UTC_TIMESTAMP( )   |
+--------------------+--------------------+
|       20050111200238 | 2005-01-11 20:02:37 |
+--------------------+--------------------+
```

WEEK( )

WEEK(*date*[, *value*])

This function returns the number of the week starting from the beginning of the year for a date provided. By default, Sunday is considered to be the first day of a week for this calculation. To set the first day to Monday, enter a value of 1 as a second argument to this function. This function returns 0–52 by default. However, when the start is set to Monday, the range is 1–53.

```
SELECT WEEK('2004-01-15') AS 'Sunday Start',
       WEEK('2004-01-15',1) AS 'Monday Start';
```

```
+--------------+--------------+
| Sunday Start | Monday Start |
+--------------+--------------+
|            2 |            3 |
+--------------+--------------+
```

Notice in the first column, that the first day of the week is the default of Sunday, so the date January 15, 2004 returns a value of 2. When the first day of the week is set to Monday, though, the value of 3, or the third week, is returned for the same date.

WEEKDAY( )

WEEKDAY(*date*)

This function returns the number for the day of the week. Monday is considered the first day of the week for this function and it returns a value of 0; Sunday returns 6.

```
SELECT WEEKDAY('2005-01-01')
       AS 'Saturday, Jan. 1';
```

```
+------------------+
| Saturday, Jan. 1 |
+------------------+
|                5 |
+------------------+
```

WEEKOFYEAR( )

WEEKOFYEAR(*date*)

This function returns the calendar week of the year for the given date. This function was added in Version 4.1.1 of MySQL.

```
SELECT CURDATE( ) AS Date,
       WEEKOFYEAR(CURDATE( )) AS Week;
```

```
+------------+------+
| Date       | Week |
+------------+------+
| 2005-01-11 |    2 |
+------------+------+
```

YEAR( )

YEAR(*date*)

This function returns the year of the given date provided. It returns values from 1,000–9,999.

```
SELECT YEAR('2005-01-01')
       AS 'Year';
```

```
+------+
| Year |
+------+
| 2005 |
+------+
```

YEARWEEK( )

YEARWEEK(*date*[, *value*])

This function returns the year coupled with the number of the week into the year: *yyyyww*. By default, the first day of the week is Sunday and the basis of the calculation. Optionally, you can set this to Monday as the first day of the week by entering a value of 1 for the second argument.

```
SELECT YEARWEEK('2005-01-07')
       AS 'YearWeek';
```

```
+----------+
| YearWeek |
+----------+
|   200501 |
+----------+
```

This function may be useful in conjunction with the PERIOD_ADD( ) and PERIOD_DIFF( ) functions.

7

Mathematical and Aggregate Functions

MySQL has many built-in mathematical and aggregate functions that you can use in SQL statements for performing calculations on values in databases. Functions in this chapter include those used for statistical information, such as counting rows and determining the average of a given column's value.

You should be aware of a few factors regarding some of these functions: all mathematical functions return NULL when there is an error. If an aggregate function is used without a GROUP BY clause, it operates on all rows. The following aggregate functions require a GROUP BY clause: AVG( ), BIT_AND( ), BIT_OR( ), BIT_XOR( ), COUNT( ), GROUP_CONCAT( ), MIN( ), MAX( ), STD( ), STDDEV( ), SUM( ), VARIANCE( ).

Functions in Alphabetical Order

The rest of the chapter describes each function with examples.

ABS( )

ABS(*number*)

This function returns the absolute value of a given number.

```
SELECT ABS(-10);
```

```
+----------+
| ABS(-10) |
+----------+
|       10 |
+----------+
```

ACOS( )

ACOS(*number*)

This function returns the arc cosine of a given number. For numbers given that are greater than 1 or less than -1, NULL is returned.

```
SELECT ACOS(.5), ACOS(1.5);
```

```
+-----------+-----------+
| ACOS(.5)  | ACOS(1.5) |
+-----------+-----------+
| 1.047198  |      NULL |
+-----------+-----------+
```

ASIN( )

ASIN(*number*)

This function returns the arc sine of a given number. For numbers given that are greater than 1 or less than -1, NULL is returned.

```
SELECT ASIN(1);
```

```
+-----------+
| ASIN(1)   |
+-----------+
| 1.570796  |
+-----------+
```

ATAN( )

ATAN(*number*[, ...])

This function returns the arc tangent of a given number. To determine the arc tangent of two numbers (Y and X), add the optional second argument to the function or use ATAN2( ). The value of Y for a Cartesian plane is given as the first argument and X as the second.

```
SELECT ATAN(2);
```

```
+-----------+
| ATAN(2)   |
+-----------+
| 1.107149  |
+-----------+
```

ATAN2( )

ATAN2(*number, number*)

This function returns the arc tangent in radians of X and Y for a point on a Cartesian plane. The value for Y is given as the first argument and X as the second. The reverse function is TAN( ).

```
SELECT ATAN2(10, 5);

+--------------+
| ATAN2(10, 5) |
+--------------+
|     1.107149 |
+--------------+
```

AVG( )

AVG(*column*)

This function returns the average or mean of a set of numbers given as the argument.
Use it in conjunction with GROUP BY clause.

```
SELECT col1, AVG(col2)
FROM table1
GROUP BY col1;
```

BIT_AND( )

BIT_AND(*column*)

This function returns the bitwise AND of all elements in *column*. Use this in conjunction
with the GROUP BY clause. The function has a 64-bit precision. If there are no matching
rows, before Version 4.0.17 of MySQL, a -1 is returned. Newer versions return
18446744073709551615, which is the maximum value for an unsigned BIGINT
column.

BIT_OR( )

BIR_OR(*column*)

This function returns the bitwise OR of all elements in *column*. It calculates with a 64-bit
precision. It returns 0 if no matching rows are found. Use it in conjunction with GROUP
BY clause.

BIT_XOR( )

BIR_XOR(*column*)

This function returns the bitwise XOR of all elements in *column*. It calculates with a 64-
bit precision. It returns 0 if no matching rows are found. Use it in conjunction with the
GROUP BY clause. This function is available as of Version 4.1.1 of MySQL.

CEIL( )

CEIL(*number*)

This function rounds a given floating-point number up to the next higher integer. It's
an alias to CEILING( ).

```
SELECT CEIL(1), CEIL(1.1);
```

```
+---------+-----------+
| CEIL(1) | CEIL(1.1) |
+---------+-----------+
|       1 |         2 |
+---------+-----------+
```

CEILING( )

CEILING(number)

This function rounds a given floating-point number up to the next higher integer. It's an alias to CEIL( ).

COS( )

COS(number)

This function returns cosine of number, where number is expressed in radians.

```
SELECT COS(2 * PI( ));
```

```
+---------------+
| COS(2 * PI( )) |
+---------------+
|             1 |
+---------------+
```

COT( )

COT(number)

This function returns the cotangent of a number.

```
SELECT COT(1);
```

```
+------------+
| COT(1)     |
+------------+
| 0.64209262 |
+------------+
```

COUNT( )

COUNT([DISTINCT] column)

This function returns the number of rows retrieved in the SELECT statement for the column given. Rows in which the column given is NULL are not counted. If the wildcard * is used as the argument, the function counts all rows, including ones with NULL values. Use this in conjunction with the GROUP BY clause. The second syntax returns the number of unique non-NULL values found. This function is set to optimal performance for MyISAM tables if a WHERE clause is not included in a statement.

```
SELECT col1, COUNT(col2),
       COUNT(DISTINCT col2)
  FROM table1
  GROUP BY col1;
```

CRC32( )

CRC32(*string*)

This function returns a 32-bit unsigned value for the given string's cyclic redundancy check value. This function is available as of Version 4.1 of MySQL.

```
SELECT CRC32('test');
```

```
+---------------+
| CRC32('test') |
+---------------+
|    3632233996 |
+---------------+
```

DEGREES( )

DEGREES(*number*)

This function converts radians to degrees.

```
SELECT DEGREES(PI( ));
```

```
+------------------+
| DEGREES(PI( ))   |
+------------------+
|       180.000000 |
+------------------+
```

EXP( )

EXP(*number*)

This function returns the value of the natural logarithm base number *e* to the power of the given number.

```
SELECT EXP(1);
```

```
+----------+
| EXP(1)   |
+----------+
| 2.718282 |
+----------+
```

FLOOR( )

FLOOR(*number*)

This function rounds a given floating-point number down to the next lower integer. It's a counterpart to CEILING( ).

FORMAT( )

FORMAT(*number, decimal*)

This function returns the floating-point *number* given with a comma inserted between every three digits and a period before the number of decimal places specified in the second argument.

```
SELECT FORMAT(1000.375, 2)
       AS Amount;
```

```
+----------+
| Amount   |
+----------+
| 1,000.38 |
+----------+
```

Notice that the function rounded the number given to two decimal places.

GREATEST( )

GREATEST(*value, value, ...*)

Use this function to compare two or more values and return the greatest value. In an INTEGER datatype context, all values are treated as integers for comparison. In a REAL datatype context, all values are treated as REAL values for comparison. If any parameter contains a case-sensitive string (i.e., with a BINARY flag), all values are compared as case-sensitive strings.

```
SELECT GREATEST(col1, col2, col3);
```

GROUP_CONCAT( )

GROUP_CONCAT([DISTINCT] *expression*[, ...]

   [ORDER BY {*unsigned_integer*|*column*|*expression*}

   [ASC|DESC] [,*column* ...]]

   [SEPARATOR *character*])

This function returns non-NULL values of a group concatenated together, separated by commas. It returns NULL if the group doesn't contain non-NULL values. Duplicates are omitted with the DISTINCT flag. The ORDER BY clause for the function instructs MySQL to sort values before concatenating. Ordering may be based on an integer value, column, or expression. The sort order can be set to ascending with the ASC flag (default), or to descending with the DESC flag. To change the default separator of a comma, use the SEPARATOR flag followed by the preferred separator. This function is available as of Version 4.1 of MySQL.

```
SELECT item_nbr AS Item,
       GROUP_CONCAT(quantity) AS Quantities
  FROM orders
  GROUP BY item_nbr LIMIT 1;
```

```
+------+------------+
| Item | Quantities |
+------+------------+
| 100  | 7,12,4,8   |
+------+------------+
```

The results here are limited only to one item by the LIMIT clause. Notice that the quantities aren't sorted—it's the item numbers that are sorted by the GROUP BY clause. To sort the quantities within each field and to use a different separator, enter something like the following instead:

```
SELECT item_nbr AS Item,
       GROUP_CONCAT(quantity
                    ORDER BY quantity ASC
                    SEPARATOR '|')
          AS Quantities
FROM table3
  GROUP BY item_nbr;
```

```
+------+------------+
| Item | Quantities |
+------+------------+
| 100  | 4|7|8|12   |
+------+------------+
```

LEAST( )

LEAST(*value, value, ...*)

Use this function to compare two or more values and return the smallest value. In an INTEGER datatype context, all values are treated as integers for comparison. In a REAL data type context, all values are treated as REAL values for comparison. If any parameter contains a case-sensitive string (i.e., with a BINARY flag), all values are compared as case-sensitive strings.

```
SELECT LEAST(col1, col2, col3);
```

LN( )

LN(*number*)

This function returns the natural logarithm of a given number.

```
SELECT LN(5);
```

```
+----------+
| LN(5)    |
+----------+
| 1.609438 |
+----------+
```

LOG( )

LOG(number[, base])

This function returns the natural logarithm of a given number. If a second argument is given, a natural logarithm is returned for the first argument for the arbitrary base given in the second argument. This is the same as using LOG(number)/LOG(base).

```
SELECT LOG(5,4);

+------------+
|  LOG(5,4)  |
+------------+
| 1.16096405 |
+------------+
```

LOG2( )

LOG2(number)

This function returns the base-two logarithm of a given number.

LOG10( )

LOG10(number)

This function returns the base 10 logarithm of a given number.

MAX( )

MAX(column)

This function returns the lowest number in the values for *column*. Use this in conjunction with the GROUP BY clause.

```
SELECT col1, MAX(col2)
FROM table1
GROUP BY col1;
```

MIN( )

MIN(column)

This function returns the lowest number in the values for *column*. Used in conjunction with the GROUP BY clause.

```
SELECT col1, MIN(col2)
    FROM table1
    GROUP BY col1;
```

MOD( )

MOD(*number*, *number*)

number MOD *number*

This function returns the remainder of a number given in the first argument divided evenly by the number given in the second argument, the modulo. It works the same as using the % operator between two given numbers. The second syntax shown is available as of Version 4.1 of MySQL. Starting with Version 4.1.7, fractional values may be given.

```
SELECT MOD(10, 3);
```

```
+------------+
| MOD(10, 3) |
+------------+
|          1 |
+------------+
```

Here's an example of the alternate syntax:

```
SELECT 10 MOD 3;
```

```
+----------+
| 10 MOD 3 |
+----------+
|        1 |
+----------+
```

PI( )

PI( )

This function returns by default the first five decimal places of the number *pi*. You can adjust it to include more decimal places by adding a mask to the end of the function. There is no argument within the parentheses of the function.

```
SELECT PI( ), PI( )+0.0000000000;
```

```
+----------+--------------------+
| PI( )    | PI( )+0.0000000000 |
+----------+--------------------+
| 3.141593 |       3.1415926536 |
+----------+--------------------+
```

POW( )

POW(*number*, *exponent*)

This function returns the result of raising the number given in the first argument to the exponent given in the second argument. It's an alias for POWER( ).

```
SELECT POW(2, 4);
```

```
+----------+
| POW(2, 4) |
+----------+
| 16.000000 |
+----------+
```

POWER( )

POWER(*number, exponent*)

This function returns the result of raising the number given in the first argument to the power of the number given in the second argument. It's an alias for POW( ).

RADIANS( )

RADIANS( )

This function converts degrees to radians.

```
SELECT RADIANS(180);
```

```
+------------------+
| RADIANS(180)     |
+------------------+
| 3.1415926535898 |
+------------------+
```

RAND( )

RAND([*seed*])

This function returns a random floating-point number from 0 to 1. A seed number may given with the function, but the results will be the same each time.

```
SELECT RAND( ), RAND( );
```

```
+------------------+------------------+
| RAND( )          | RAND( )          |
+------------------+------------------+
| 0.29085519843814 | 0.45449978900561 |
+------------------+------------------+
```

Note that rerunning this statement with the same seeds will produce the same results.

ROUND( )

ROUND(*number*[, *precision*])

This function rounds a number given in the first argument to the nearest integer. The number may be rounded to the number of decimal places given in the second argument.

```
SELECT ROUND(2.875), ROUND(2.875, 2);
```

```
+-------------+-----------------+
| ROUND(2.875) | ROUND(2.875, 2) |
+-------------+-----------------+
|           3 |            2.88 |
+-------------+-----------------+
```

SIGN( )

SIGN(*number*)

This function returns -1 if the given number is a negative and 1 if it is positive.

```
SELECT SIGN(-5);
```

```
+----------+
| SIGN(-5) |
+----------+
|       -1 |
+----------+
```

SIN( )

SIN(*number*)

This function returns the sine of the number given, where *number* is expressed in radians.

```
SELECT SIN(.5 * PI( ));
```

```
+----------------+
| SIN(.5 * PI()) |
+----------------+
|              1 |
+----------------+
```

SQRT( )

SQRT(*number*)

This function returns the square root of a given, positive number.

```
SELECT SQRT(25);
```

```
+----------+
| SQRT(25) |
+----------+
| 5.000000 |
+----------+
```

STD( )

STD(*column*)

This function returns the standard deviation of the column given. Use it in conjunction with the GROUP BY clause. It's an alias for STDDEV( ).

```
SELECT col1, STD(col2)
    FROM table1
    GROUP BY col1;
```

STDDEV( )

STDDEV( )

This function returns the standard deviation of the column given. Use it in conjunction with the GROUP BY clause. It's an alias for STD( ).

SUM( )

SUM(*column*)

This function returns the sum of the value of the column given. Use it in conjunction with the GROUP BY clause.

```
SELECT col1, SUM(col2)
    FROM table1
    GROUP BY col1;
```

TAN( )

TAN(*number*)

This function returns the tangent of an angle, of a given number in radians. It's the reverse of ATAN2( ).

```
SELECT ATAN2(1), TAN(0.785398);
```

```
+----------+---------------+
| ATAN2(1) | TAN(0.785398) |
+----------+---------------+
| 0.785398 |      1.000000 |
+----------+---------------+
```

TRUNCATE( )

TRUNCATE(*number, number*)

This function returns a number given in the first argument with the digits beyond the number of decimal places specified in the second argument, truncated. It does not round the number—use the ROUND( ) function instead. If a 0 is given for the second argument, the decimal point and the fractional value are dropped. If a negative number is given as the second argument, the decimal point and the fractional value is dropped, and the number of positions given is zeroed out for the integer.

```
SELECT TRUNCATE(321.1234, 2) AS '+2',
       TRUNCATE(321.1234, 0) AS '0',
       TRUNCATE(321.1234, -2) AS '-2';
```

```
+--------+-----+-----+
| +2     | 0   | -2  |
+--------+-----+-----+
| 321.12 | 321 | 300 |
+--------+-----+-----+
```

Notice that for the first field, the last two decimal places are dropped. For the second field, the decimal point and all of the fractional value are dropped. For the third, the decimal point and the fractional value are dropped, and because the second parameter is -2, the first two numbers (starting from the right) of the integer are changed to zeros.

VARIANCE( )

VARIANCE(*column*)

The function returns the standard variance of *column*, based on the rows selected as a whole population. Use it in conjunction with the GROUP BY clause. This function is available as of Version 4.1 of MySQL.

```
SELECT col1, VARIANCE(col2)
    FROM table1
    GROUP BY col1;
```

8

Flow Control Functions

MySQL has a few built-in flow control functions that you can use in SQL statements for more precise and directed results. This chapter lists these functions, provides the syntax of each, and gives examples of their use. For the examples in this chapter, a fictitious database for a stock broker is used.

Functions in Alphabetical Order

The following are the MySQL flow control functions.

CASE( )

```
CASE value

  WHEN [value] THEN result

  ...

  [ELSE result]

END

CASE

  WHEN [condition] THEN result

  ...

 [ELSE result]

END
```

This function allows a particular result from a list of results to be chosen based on various conditions. It is similar to the IF( ) function except that multiple conditions and results may be strung together. In the first syntax shown, *value* is compared to each WHEN value. The second syntax tests each condition independently, and they are not based on a single value. Both syntaxes return NULL if there is no match and no ELSE clause.

Here is an example of the first syntax:

```
SELECT CONCAT(name_first, SPACE(1), name_last) AS Client,
       telephone_home AS Telephone,
       CASE type
         WHEN 'RET' THEN 'Retirement Account'
         WHEN 'REG' THEN 'Regular Account'
         WHEN 'CUS' THEN 'Minor Account'
       END AS 'Account Type'
FROM clients;
```

This SQL statement retrieves a list of clients and their telephone numbers, along with a description of their account type. However, the account type is a three-letter abbreviation, so CASE( ) is used to substitute each type with a more descriptive name.

The previous example uses the syntax in which a common parameter is evaluated to determine the possible result. The following SQL statement utilizes the other syntax for the function:

```
SELECT CONCAT(name_last, SPACE(1), name_first) AS Prospect,
CASE
  WHEN YEAR(NOW( )) - YEAR(birth_date) < 18 THEN 'Minor'
  WHEN YEAR(NOW( )) - YEAR(birth_date) > 17 < 26 THEN 'Too Young'
  WHEN YEAR(NOW( )) - YEAR(birth_date) > 60 THEN 'Elderly'
  ELSE home_telephone;
END
  AS Telephone
FROM prospects;
```

In this example, the SQL statement analyzes a table containing a list of people that the broker might call to buy an investment. The table contains the birth dates and the telephone numbers of each prospect. The SQL statement provides the telephone numbers only for prospects aged 26 to 60—anyone younger or older would not be suitable for this particular investment. However, a message for each prospect that is disqualified is given based on the clauses of the CASE( ) statement.

IF( )

IF(*condition*, *result*, *result*)

This function returns the second argument *result* if *condition* (the first argument) is met, and the third argument is not. Note that the value of *condition* is converted to an integer. It will return a numeric or a string value depending on its use. As of Version 4. 0.3 of MySQL, if the second or the third argument is NULL, the other non-NULL argument will be returned.

```
SELECT clients.client_id AS ID,
CONCAT(name_first, SPACE(1), name_last) AS Client,
telephone_home AS Telephone, SUM(qty) AS Shares,
IF(
    (SELECT SUM(qty * price)
     FROM investments, stock_prices
     WHERE stock_symbol = symbol
     AND client_id = ID )
```

```
      > 100000, 'Large', 'Small') AS 'Size'
FROM clients, investments
WHERE stock_symbol = 'GT'
AND clients.client_id = investments.client_id
GROUP BY clients.client_id LIMIT 2;
```

```
+------+---------------+-----------+--------+-------+
| ID   | Client        | Telephone | Shares | Size  |
+------+---------------+-----------+--------+-------+
| 8532 | Jerry Neumeyer | 834-8668 |    200 | Large |
| 4638 | Rusty Osborne  | 833-8393 |    200 | Small |
+------+---------------+-----------+--------+-------+
```

This SQL statement is designed to retrieve the names and telephone numbers of clients who own Goodyear stock (the stock symbol is *GT*), because the broker wants to call them to recommend that they sell it. The example utilizes a subquery (available as of Version 4.1) to tally the value of all the client's stocks first (not just Goodyear stock), as a condition of the IF( ) function. It does this by joining the *investments* table (which contains a row for each stock purchase and sale) and the *stock_prices* table (which contains current prices for all stocks). If the sum of the value of all stocks owned by the client (the results of the subquery) is more than $100,000, a label of *Large* is assigned to the *Size* column. Otherwise, the client is labeled *Small*. The broker wants to call her large clients first. Notice in the results shown that both clients own the same number of shares of Goodyear, but one has a large portfolio.

IFNULL( )

IFNULL(*condition, result*)

This function returns the results of the condition given in the first argument of the function if not NULL. If the condition results are NULL, the results of the expression or string given in the second argument are returned. It will return a numeric or a string value depending on the context.

```
SELECT CONCAT(name_first, SPACE(1), name_last) AS Client,
telephone_home AS Telephone,
IFNULL(goals, 'No Goals Given') AS Goals
FROM clients LIMIT 2;
```

```
+----------------+-----------+----------------+
| Client         | Telephone | Goals          |
+----------------+-----------+----------------+
| Janice Sogard  | 835-1821  | No Goals Given |
| Kenneth Bilich | 488-3325  | Long Term      |
+----------------+-----------+----------------+
```

This SQL statement provides a list of clients and their telephone numbers, along with their investment goals. If the client never told the broker of an investment goal (i.e., the *goals* column is NULL), the text "No Goals Given" is displayed.

NULLIF( )

NULLIF(*condition1, condition2*)

This function returns NULL if the two arguments given are equal. Otherwise, it returns the value or results of the first argument.

```
SELECT clients.client_id AS ID,
CONCAT(name_first, SPACE(1), name_last) AS Client,
telephone_home AS Telephone,
NULLIF(
    (SELECT SUM(qty * price)
     FROM investments, stock_prices
     WHERE stock_symbol = symbol
     AND client_id = ID ), 0)
AS Value
FROM clients, investments
WHERE clients.client_id = investments.client_id
GROUP BY clients.client_id;
```

In this example, NULL is returned for the *Value* column if the value of the client's stocks is 0 (i.e., the client had stocks but sold them all). If there is a value to the stocks, however, the sum of their values is displayed.

This function is the same as:

```
CASE WHEN condition1 = condition2
THEN NULL
ELSE condition1;
```

9

Miscellaneous Functions

In addition to the built-in functions covered in the previous chapters, MySQL has a few others that don't fit in any convenient category. This chapter lists those miscellaneous functions, provides the syntax of each, and gives examples of their use.

Functions in Alphabetical Order

Functions not covered in earlier chapters are described in the following sections.

ANALYSE( )

ANALYSE([*column*[, *memory*]])

This function returns an analysis of a results table from a SELECT statement. The \G at the end of the following statement provides a vertical output. Use this function only as part of a PROCEDURE clause. The default values are 256 per column and 8,192 for memory.

```
SELECT col1
FROM table1
PROCEDURE ANALYSE( ) \G

*************************** 1. row ***************************
           Field_name: table1.col1
            Min_value: 1
            Max_value: 82
           Min_length: 1
           Max_length: 2
     Empties_or_zeros: 0
                Nulls: 0
Avg_value_or_avg_length: 42.8841
                  Std: 24.7600
      Optimal_fieldtype: TINYINT(2) UNSIGNED NOT NULL
```

You can specify the maximum number of elements to analyze for each column in the optional first argument, and the maximum amount of memory that may be used in the optional second argument.

BENCHMARK( )

BENCHMARK(*number, expression*)

Use this function to evaluate the performance of a MySQL server. The expression given as the second argument of the function is repeated for the number of times given in the first argument. The results are always 0. It's the processing time reported that is meaningful. This function is meant to be used from within the *mysql* client.

```
SELECT BENCHMARK(1000000,PI( ));
+-------------------------+
| BENCHMARK(1000000,PI( )) |
+-------------------------+
|                       0 |
+-------------------------+
1 row in set (0.04 sec)

SELECT BENCHMARK(1000000,PI( ));
+-------------------------+
| BENCHMARK(1000000,PI( )) |
+-------------------------+
|                       0 |
+-------------------------+
1 row in set (0.02 sec)
```

In these two examples, the first SQL statement took .04 seconds and the second one took .02 seconds to determine the value of *pi* 1 million times. The difference is due to a variety of factors unrelated to the SQL statement. The function is useful when run several times to determine an average time before making changes to a server and then afterward to see the effect of the changes. For a much better performance indicator, try the Perl scripts provided in the *sql-bench* directory of the MySQL source files. For more information on these benchmark scripts, see *High Performance MySQL* (O'Reilly) by Jeremy D. Zawodny and Derek J. Balling.

BIT_COUNT( )

BIT_COUNT(*number*)

This function returns the number of bits set in a given number, an integer that is treated as a binary number.

```
SELECT BIT_COUNT(10), BIT_COUNT(11);

+---------------+---------------+
| BIT_COUNT(10) | BIT_COUNT(11) |
+---------------+---------------+
|             2 |             3 |
+---------------+---------------+
```

Miscellaneous Functions

CAST( )

CAST(*expression* AS *type*)

Use this function to convert a value from one datatype to another. This function is available as of Version 4.0.2 of MySQL. For the first syntax shown, the datatype given as the second argument can be BINARY, CHAR, DATE, DATETIME, SIGNED [INTEGER], TIME, or UNSIGNED [INTEGER]. BINARY converts a string to a binary string. CHAR conversion is available as of Version 4.0.6 of MySQL. This function is synonymous with CONVERT( ), although the syntax is different.

CHARSET( )

CHARSET(*string*)

This function returns the character set used by a given string. This function is available as of Version 4.1.0 of MySQL.

```
SELECT CHARSET('test');
```

```
+-----------------+
| CHARSET('test') |
+-----------------+
|          latin1 |
+-----------------+
```

COALESCE( )

COALESCE(*column*[, ...])

This function returns the leftmost non-NULL string or column in a comma-separated list. If all elements are NULL, the function returns NULL.

```
SELECT COALESCE(col1, col2, col3)
    FROM table1;
```

COERCIBILITY( )

COERCIBILITY(*string*)

This function returns the collation coercibility value of a given string. A value of 0 is returned for explicit collation, 1 for no collation, 2 for implicit collation, and 3 for coercible. This function is available as of Version 4.1.1 of MySQL.

```
SELECT COERCIBILITY('test');
```

```
+----------------------+
| COERCIBILITY('test') |
+----------------------+
|                    3 |
+----------------------+
```

COLLATION( )

COLLATION(*string*)

This function returns the collation for the character set of a given string. This function is available as of Version 4.1.0 of MySQL.

```
SELECT COLLATION('test');
```

```
+-------------------+
| COLLATION('test') |
+-------------------+
| latin1_swedish_ci |
+-------------------+
```

CONNECTION_ID( )

CONNECTION_ID( )

This function returns the MySQL connection identification number for the MySQL session. There are no arguments. Connection identifiers are unique.

```
SELECT CONNECTION_ID( );
```

```
+-----------------+
| CONNECTION_ID( ) |
+-----------------+
|           11266 |
+-----------------+
```

CONVERT( )

CONVERT(*expression, type*)

CONVERT(*expression* USING *transcoding*)

Use this function to convert a value from one datatype to another. This function is available as of Version 4.0.2 of MySQL. For the first syntax shown, the datatype given as the second argument can be BINARY, CHAR, DATE, DATETIME, SIGNED [INTEGER], TIME, or UNSIGNED [INTEGER]. BINARY converts a string to a binary string. CHAR conversion is available as of Version 4.0.6 of MySQL. The second syntax shown allows for transcoding (character set) names to be given instead of datatypes. This function is synonymous with CAST( ), although the syntax is different.

CURRENT_USER( )

CURRENT_USER( )

This function returns the username and the hostname that were given by the user for the current MySQL connection. There are no arguments for the function. This function may not always return the same results as USER( ).

```
SELECT CURRENT_USER( ), USER( );
```

```
+----------------+------------------+
| CURRENT_USER() | USER()           |
+----------------+------------------+
| ''@localhost   | russel@localhost |
+----------------+------------------+
```

In this example, the user logged in to the *mysql* client with the username *russel* (missing one l in the name), but because there isn't an account for that user, the client logged in with the anonymous (i.e., '') account.

DATABASE( )

DATABASE( )

This function returns the name of the database currently in use for the session. There are no arguments. If no database has been set to default yet, it returns NULL; prior to Version 4.1.1 of MySQL, it returns an empty string.

```
SELECT DATABASE();
```

```
+------------+
| DATABASE() |
+------------+
| bookstore  |
+------------+
```

FOUND_ROWS( )

FOUND_ROWS( )

Use this function in conjunction with the SQL_CALC_FOUND_ROWS option of a SELECT statement to determine the number of rows an SQL statement using a LIMIT clause would have generated without the limitation. There are no arguments for the function. It's available as of Version 4 of MySQL.

```
SELECT SQL_CALC_FOUND_ROWS *
    FROM table1 LIMIT 5;
...
SELECT FOUND_ROWS();
```

GET_LOCK( )

GET_LOCK(*string, seconds*)

This function attempts to get a lock on the name given in the first argument. The number of seconds to attempt the lock is given in the second argument. If successful, 1 is returned. If the function is unsuccessful due to the attempt timing out, 0 is returned. If the lock fails due to an error of any kind, NULL is returned. The function RELEASE_ LOCK( ), may be used to release a lock. It's also released when the same client issues another GET_LOCK( ) or when the client's connection is terminated.

```
SELECT GET_LOCK('my_lock', 10);
```

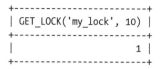

```
+--------------------------+
| GET_LOCK('my_lock', 10) |
+--------------------------+
|                        1 |
+--------------------------+
```

INTERVAL( )

INTERVAL(*search, column, ...*)

This function returns the index of the value of the string or column given in the first argument for where it would be located in the list of strings or columns given in subsequent arguments, which must be listed from lowest to highest. If the search element would be located before the first element, 0 is returned. All arguments are treated as integers.

```
SELECT INTERVAL('4', '1','3','5','7','9');
```

```
+----------------------------------+
| INTERVAL('4', '1','3','5','7','9') |
+----------------------------------+
|                                2 |
+----------------------------------+
```

In this example, the value of 4 would fall after the second position, after the 3 in the list.

IS_FREE_LOCK( )

IS_FREE_LOCK(*string*)

Use this function to determine if the name of the lock given in parentheses is free and available as a lock name. It returns 1 if the lock name is free; 0 if it's not free. It returns NULL if there is an error. This function is available as of Version 4.0.2 of MySQL. Locks are created by GET_LOCK( ).

```
SELECT IS_FREE_LOCK('my_lock');
```

```
+------------------------+
| IS_FREE_LOCK('my_lock') |
+------------------------+
|                      0 |
+------------------------+
```

IS_USED_LOCK( )

IS_USED_LOCK(*string*)

Use this function to determine if the name given is already in use as a lock name. If the lock name is in use, it returns the connection identifier of the client holding the lock. It returns NULL if it is not in use. Locks are created by GET_LOCK( ).

```
SELECT IS_USED_LOCK('my_lock');
+-------------------------+
| IS_USED_LOCK('my_lock') |
+-------------------------+
|                       1 |
+-------------------------+
```

ISNULL( )

ISNULL(*column*)

Use this function to determine if the value of the argument given in parentheses is NULL. Returns 1 if it is NULL; 0 if it is not NULL.

```
SELECT ISNULL(col2)
FROM table1;
```

LAST_INSERT_ID( )

LAST_INSERT_ID([*id*])

This function returns the identification number of the last row inserted using the MySQL connection. The identification number for rows inserted by other clients will not be returned to the other connections. Identification numbers that were set manually when rows are inserted, without the aid of AUTO_INCREMENT, won't register and therefore won't be returned by LAST_INSERT_ID( ). If multiple rows are inserted by one SQL statement, LAST_INSERT_ID( ) returns the identification number for the first row inserted.

```
SELECT LAST_INSERT_ID( );

+------------------+
| LAST_INSERT_ID( ) |
+------------------+
|             1039 |
+------------------+
```

MASTER_POS_WAIT( )

MASTER_POS_WAIT(*filename, position*[, *timeout*])

Use this function to synchronize MySQL master and slave server logging. The function causes the master to wait until the slave server has read and applied all updates to the position (given in the second argument) in the master log (named in the first argument). You can specify a third argument to set the number of seconds the master will wait. The function returns the number of log entries that were made by the slave while the master was waiting. A value of NULL is returned if there is an error.

RELEASE_LOCK( )

RELEASE_LOCK(*string*)

This function releases a lock created by GET_LOCK( ). The name of the lock is given in parentheses. If successful, 1 is returned; if unsuccessful, 0 is returned. If the lock specified does not exist, NULL is returned.

```
SELECT RELEASE_LOCK('my_lock');
```

```
+------------------------+
| RELEASE_LOCK('my_lock') |
+------------------------+
|                      1 |
+------------------------+
```

As an alternative to using SELECT, you can use DO; no results are returned.

```
DO RELEASE_LOCK('my_lock');
```

SESSION_USER( )

SESSION_USER( )

This function returns the username and the hostname for the current MySQL connection. There are no arguments for the function. It's synonymous with SYSTEM_USER( ) and USER( ).

SYSTEM_USER( )

SYSTEM_USER( )

This function returns the username and the hostname for the current MySQL connection. There are no arguments for the function. It's synonymous with SESSION_USER( ) and USER( ).

USER( )

USER( )

This function returns the username and the hostname for the current MySQL connection. There are no arguments for the function. It's synonymous with SESSION_USER( ) and SYSTEM_USER( ).

```
SELECT USER( );
```

```
+------------------+
| USER( )          |
+------------------+
| russell@localhost |
+------------------+
```

UUID ( )

UUID( )

This function returns a Universal Unique Identifier (UUID), a 128-bit number composed of five hexadecimal numbers. This number is intended to be unique per invocation and is based on values that are both temporal and spatial. There are no arguments for the function. It's available as of Version 4.1.2 of MySQL.

```
SELECT UUID( );
```

```
+----------------------------------------+
| UUID( )                                |
+----------------------------------------+
| '8bde367a-caeb-0933-1031-7730g3321c32' |
+----------------------------------------+
```

VERSION( )

VERSION( )

This function returns the MySQL server version. There are no arguments for the function.

```
SELECT VERSION( );
```

```
+-------------------------+
| VERSION( )              |
+-------------------------+
| 5.0.2-alpha-standard-log |
+-------------------------+
```

10

MySQL Server and Client

The primary program of the MySQL server is the *mysqld* daemon, which listens for requests from clients and processes them. The general-purpose client provided with MySQL is the *mysql* program. This chapter presents the many options available for both the MySQL server and the *mysql* client. A few scripts provided with MySQL that are used to start the server (e.g., mysqld_multi and mysqld_safe) are also explained. The daemons and scripts are listed in alphabetical order.

mysql

mysql *options* [*database*]

You can use the *mysql* client to interface with MySQL in terminal or console mode. To enter terminal mode, you would enter something like the following from the command line:

```
mysql -u russell -p
```

After entering this, if the MySQL server is running the user will be prompted for a password. Once in terminal mode, SQL statements may be entered to view or to change data.

As an alternative to terminal mode, when performing straightforward tasks in MySQL one can still use the *mysql* client from the command line. For instance, to execute a batch file that contains several SQL statements that will insert data into a database, you could do something like this:

```
mysql -u russell -ppassword db1 < stuff.sql
```

In this example, the password is given so that the user isn't prompted. It's entered immediately after the -p option, without a space in between. Next the database name *db1* is given. The redirect (the less-than sign) tells the shell to input the text file *stuff. sql* to the command. When the client has finished processing the text file, the user is returned to the command prompt.

Several options may be given when calling the *mysql* client. They are listed alphabetically here:

--auto-rehash
> Generates a hash of table and column names to complete the names for users when typing in terminal mode by pressing the Tab key after having entered the first few letters of the name.

--batch, -B
> This default option displays data selected with fields separated by tabs and rows by carriage returns. It won't prompt the user, won't display error messages to stdout, and won't save to the history file.

--debug=*filename*, -# *filename*
> Instructs the client to record debugging information to the logfile specified.

--debug-info, -T
> Causes the client to display debugging information when finished.

--exec='*statement*', -e '*statement*'
> Executes an SQL statement contained in single or double quotes. The equals sign may be replaced optionally with a space in the long form.

--force, -f
> With this option, the client is to continue executing or processing, even if there are SQL errors.

--help, -?
> Displays basic help information.

--hostname=*host*, -h *host*
> Specifies the hostname (e.g., *localhost*) or Internet Protocol (IP) address of the MySQL server.

--no-auto-rehash, -A
> Automatic rehashing is normally used to let the user complete table and column names when typing in terminal mode by pressing the Tab key after having entered the first few letters of the name. The --no-auto-rehash option will disable this feature and, thereby, decrease the startup time for the client. This option is deprecated as of Version 4 of MySQL.

--password=[*password*], -p[*password*]
> Provides the password to give to the MySQL server. No spaces are allowed between the -p and the password. If a password is not given, the user will be prompted for one.

--port=*port*, -P *port*
> Specifies the port to use for connecting to the server. The default is 3306.

--quick, -q
> This option has the client retrieve and display data one row at a time rather than buffering the entire results set before displaying data. With this option, the history file isn't used, and it may slow the server if the output is suspended.

--raw, -r
> For data that may contain characters that would normally be converted in batch mode to an escape-sequence equivalent (e.g., newline to \n), you can use this option to have the client print out the characters without converting them.

--set-variable *var=value*, -o *var=value*
>   Sets a server variable. Enter mysql --help for the current values for a particular server's variables.

--silent, -s
>   Reduces the number of messages displayed. Including this several times will further reduce messages.

--socket=*socket*, -S *socket*
>   Provides the path and name of the server's socket file.

--table, -t
>   Causes data from a query that is executed to be displayed in ASCII format, which is the format normally used in terminal mode.

--unbuffered, -n
>   This option has the client flush the memory buffer after each query is performed.

--user=*user*, -u *user*
>   Instructs the client to access MySQL with a user different from the current system user.

--verbose, -v
>   Displays more information. Use -vv or -vvv to increase verbosity.

--version, -V
>   Displays the version of the utility.

--wait, -w
>   If the client cannot connect to the server, this option tells the client to wait and retry repeatedly until it can connect.

mysqld

mysqld [*options*]

When mysqld is started, you can use various options. Although these options may be given on the command line, it's common practice to enter them into a configuration file. On Unix-based systems, the main configuration file typically is */etc/my.cnf*. For Windows systems, the main file is usually either *c:\systems\my.ini* or *c:\my.conf*. Options are entered on separate lines and follow a *variable=value* format. They are grouped under headings contained within square brackets. The *mysqld* daemon reads options from the configuration file under the headings of [mysqld] and [server] as it's started. The following is an alphabetical list of options that apply to the *mysqld* daemon and an explanation of each. The options are shown as you would enter them from the command line. If an option is used in a configuration file, you should use the long form (not the dash with a single letter) and omit the double-dash prefix. For example, you could enter --basedir=/data/mysql from the command line. In a configuration file, though, you would enter basedir=/data/mysql on its own line.

--ansi
>   Instructs the server to use standard ANSI SQL syntax, rather than MySQL syntax.

--basedir=*path*, -b *path*
>   Specifies the base directory for MySQL installation.

--big-tables
>   Instructs the server to save temporary results sets to a file to solve errors where results are large and tables are said to be full.

--bind-address=*address*
> Specifies the IP address upon which the server is to bind. Use it to restrict network access on a host with multiple IP addresses.

--character-set-server=*set*
> Start a server with a particular character set. It's available as of Version 4.1.3 of MySQL.

--character-sets-dir=*path*
> Specifies the directory containing character sets.

--chroot=*path*
> Runs the daemon with chroot( ) from the filesystem so as to start it in a closed environment for additional security. This is a recommended security measure as of Version 4 of MySQL. This option has vulnerabilities under Version 3.23.

--collation-server=*collation*
> Starts a server with a particular collation. It's available as of Version 4.1.3 of MySQL.

--console
> Displays the error messages to stdout and stderr.

--core-file
> Instructs the server to create a core file if the daemon dies. Some systems also require the --skip-stack-trace option to be set, as well. Some systems also require the --core-file-size option when using mysqld_safe. On Solaris systems, if the --user option is used also, the server will not create the core file.

--datadir=*path*, -h *path*
> Specifies the directory that contains datafiles (i.e, database directories and table files).

--debug[=*options*], -# [*options*]
> Obtains a trace file of the daemon's activities. The debug options are typically 'd:t:o,filename'. MySQL has to be compiled for debugging using the --with-debug option when configuring.

--default-character-set=*set*
> Specifies the default character set. This option is deprecated as of Version 4.1.3 of MySQL. Use the --character-set-server option instead.

--default-collation=*collation*
> Specifies the collation to use as default. This option is deprecated as of Version 4.1.3 of MySQL. Use the --collation-server option instead.

--default-storage-engine=*type*
> Specifies the default table type. It's synonymous with the --default-table-type option.

--default-table-type=*type*
> Changes the default table type. MyISAM is the default unless you change it with this option.

--default-time-zone=*zone*
> Specifies the default time zone for the server. The filesystem time zone is used by default.

--delay-key-write[=*option*]
> Instructs the server on how to handle key buffers between writes for MyISAM tables. The choices are OFF, ON, and ALL. The ON choice delays writes for tables

created with DELAYED KEYS. The ALL choice delays writes for all MyISAM tables regardless. MyISAM tables should not be accessed by another server or clients like myisamcheck when the ALL choice is used. It may cause corruption of indexes.

`--delay-key-write-for-all-tables`

Instructs the server not to flush key buffers between writes for MyISAM tables. As of Version 4.0.3 of MySQL, use `--delay-key-write=ALL` instead.

`--des-key-file=`*filename*

Instructs the server to obtain the default keys from the file named when the MySQL functions DES_ENCRYPT( ) or DES_DECRYPT( ) are used.

`--enable-named-pipe`

This enables support for named pipe connections with the mysqld-nt and mysqld-max-nt servers, which support them.

`--exit-info[=`*flags*`], -T [`*flags*`]`

Displays debugging information when the daemon exits.

`--external-locking`

Previously called `--enable-locking`, this option allows system locking. Be careful when using this option on a platform with problems with lockd (e.g., Linux): the *mysqld* daemon may lock and you might have to reboot the server to unlock it.

`--flush`

Use this to have the server flush all changes to disk after each SQL statement and not to wait for the filesystem to determine the frequency of writes.

`--help, -?`

Displays basic help information and more information when it's combined with the `--verbose` option.

`--init-file=`*filename*

Instructs the server to read the SQL commands contained in the file named at startup. Each SQL statement in the file must be on one line only and cannot include comments.

`--innodb-safe-binlog`

Ensures consistency between the content of InnoDB tables and the binary log.

`--language=`*language*`, -L `*language*

Provides the name of the language preferred for user messages and, optionally, the path to the language file.

`--log[=`*filename*`], -l [`*filename*`]`

Instructs the server to log connection information and queries to the path and file named, or to the default (*host.log*) if none is given.

`--log-bin[=`*filename*`]`

Enables binary logging of changes to databases to the path and name of the file given. If a filename isn't provided, the default name of *host-bin.index* will be used, where *host* is the hostname of the server and *index* is a numeric count.

`--log-bin-index[=`*filename*`]`

Names the path and filename for the index file for the binary log filenames. The default name for the log if none is specified with this option is *host-bin.index*, where *host* is the server's hostname and *index* is a numeric count.

--log-error[=*filename*]

Activates logging of error messages and server start-up messages to the path and filename given. The default name for the log if none is specified with this option is *host.err*, where *host* is the server's hostname.

--log-isam[=*filename*]

Activates logging of changes to ISAM and MyISAM tables to the path and filename given. This option is used only when debugging.

--log-long-format

Instructs the server to be more verbose in logs. This is the default setting as of Version 4.1 of MySQL. Use the --log-short-format option to disable this option.

--log-queries-not-using-indexes

When you use this with the --log-slow-queries option, all queries that do not use indexes are logged to the slow query log. This option is available as of Version 4.1 of MySQL.

--log-short-format

Instructs the server to be less verbose in logs. This option is available as of Version 4.1 of MySQL.

--log-slow-queries[=*filename*]

Instructs the server to log queries that take longer than the maximum number of seconds specified in the value of the long_query_time variable. If *filename* is specified, entries are recorded in the logfile named.

--log-update[=*filename*]

Activates logging of updates to the path and filename given. This feature is deprecated in favor of binary logging.

--log-warnings, -W

Activates logging of warning messages. Prior to Version 4 of MySQL, this option was invoked with the --warnings option. After Version 4.1.2, this option is enabled by default and can be disabled with the --skip-log-warnings option.

--low-priority-updates

Sets all SQL statements that modify data to a lower priority by default than SELECT statements.

--memlock

Use this on filesystems that support mlockall( ) system calls (e.g., Solaris) to lock the daemon in memory and thereby avoid the use of disk swapping and improving performance. It requires the daemon to be started by *root*, which may be a security problem.

--myisam-recover[=*options*]

Sets the MyISAM storage engine's recovery mode so that all MyISAM tables will be automatically checked and repaired if needed when the server starts. The choices of settings are BACKUP (makes backups of recovered tables that were changed), DEFAULT (disables this option), FORCE (runs recovery regardless of the risk of losing data), and QUICK (doesn't check rows for tables without any deletions). Multiple choices may be given in a comma-separated list.

--ndbcluster

Enables support for the NDB Cluster storage engine.

--nbd-connectstring=*string*

Specifies the connect string when using the NDB Cluster storage engine.

--new, -n

At the time of this writing, this option tests queries before upgrading from Version 4 to 4.1 of MySQL.

--old-protocol, -o

Has the server use Version 3.2 protocol of MySQL for compatibility with older clients.

--one-thread

Instructs the server to allow only one thread when debugging a Linux system.

--open-files-limit=*number*

Specifies the maximum number of file descriptors for the daemon.

--pid-file=*path*

Specifies the path to the process identifier file when using mysqld_safe.

--port=*port*, -P *port*

Specifies the port on which the server will listen for client connections.

--safe-mode

Disables some optimization at startup.

--safe-show-database

Hides database names that a user does not have permission to access.

--safe-user-create

Prevents a user from creating new users without INSERT privileges for the *user* table in the *mysql* database.

--secure

Enables reverse host lookup of IP addresses.

--secure-auth

Prevents authentication of users with passwords created prior to Version 4.1 of MySQL.

--set-variable *variable=value*

Sets a server variable. Enter mysqld --verbose --help for the current values for a particular server's variables.

--shared-memory

Allows shared memory connections by Windows clients locally. This option is available as of Version 4.1 of MySQL.

--shared-memory-base-name=*name*

Sets the name to use for shared memory connections in Windows. This option is available as of Version 4.1 of MySQL.

--skip-bdb

Disables the BDB storage engine.

--skip-concurrent-insert

Prevents simultaneous SELECT and INSERT statements for MyISAM tables.

--skip-delay-key-write

Disregards tables marked as DELAY_KEY_WRITE. As of Version 4.0.3 of MySQL, use --delay-key-write=OFF instead.

--skip-external-locking

Previously called --skip-locking, this option prevents system locking.

`--skip-grant-tables`

Instructs the server not to use the grants table and thus give all users full access. This is a security risk. If this option is used, restarting the server without this option or running the FLUSH PRIVILEGES statement from the terminal mode will re-enable privileges. You can use this option if you have lost the *root* password. It lets you log in without the password and then reset it.

`--skip-host-cache`

Disables the use of the internal host cache and requires DNS lookup for each new connection.

`--skip-innodb`

Disables the InnoDB storage engine.

`--skip-isam`

This option disables the ISAM storage engine. As of Version 4.1 of MySQL, this option is on by default.

`--skip-locking`

Disables server system locking.

`--skip-name-resolve`

This option requires a client's IP address to be named in the privileges tables for tighter security and faster connections.

`--skip-ndbcluster`

This option disables the NDB Cluster storage engine.

`--skip-networking`

Prevents network connections of clients and allows local connections only.

`--skip-new`

Instructs the server not to use new, questionable routines.

`--skip-safemalloc`

Prevents the server from checking for memory overruns when performing memory allocation and memory-freeing activities.

`--skip-show-database`

Prevents the SHOW DATABASES statement from being executed by users without that specific privilege.

`--skip-stack-trace`

Prevents the writing of stack traces.

`--skip-symlink`

Disables support for symbolic links. As of Version 4.0.3 of MySQL, use `--symbolic-links` to enable symbolic links and `--skip-symbolic-links` to disable them.

`--skip-thread-priority`

Prevents prioritizing of threads.

`--socket=filename`

Provides the path and name of the socket file to be generated (*/tmp/mysql.sock* on Unix systems by default). On Windows systems, this option is used to provide the pipe name (*MySQL* by default) for local connections.

`--sql-mode=value`

Sets the SQL mode. Multiple values may be given in a comma-separated list.

`--temp-pool`

Instructs the server to utilize a small set of names for temporary file naming rather than unique names for each file.

--tmpdir=*path*, -t *path*
: Names the directory for the server to write temporary files. Multiple paths may be given in a colon-separated list.

--transaction-isolation=*option*
: Sets the default transaction isolation level. The various levels available are READ-UNCOMMITTED, READ-COMMITTED, REPEATABLE-READ, and SERIALIZABLE.

--user=*user*, -u *user*
: Starts the daemon with the filesystem username or user identifier number given. This is particularly useful when starting the daemon while logged in as *root*.

--version, -v
: Displays the version of the server.

mysqld_multi

mysqld_multi [*options*] {start|stop|report} [*server_id*]

Use this to run multiple MySQL servers on different socket files and ports. To set up multiple servers, a different section of server options must be entered into a configuration file (e.g., */etc/my.cnf*). The naming scheme for each section must be [mysqld*n*] where *n* is a different number for each server. Options must be entered separately for each server in its own section, even when servers use the same options. At a minimum, each server should use a different socket file and a different TCP/IP port. To see an example of how a configuration file might be set up for multiple servers, enter the following from the command line:

    mysqld_multi --example

Once multiple servers have been configured, to start a server, you can enter something like the following from the command line:

    mysqld_multi start 3

This line would start server number 3 listed in the configuration file as [mysqld3]. By entering report for the first argument, you can obtain the status on the server. For starting and stopping the server, this script uses the *mysqladmin* utility. Here is an alphabetical list of options specific to mysqld_multi that you can enter from the command line, along with a brief explanation of each:

--config-file=*filename*
: Specifies the path and name of the server's configuration file if it is different from the default.

--example
: Displays a sample configuration file.

--help
: Displays basic help information.

--log=*filename*
: Sets the path and name of the logfile. The default is */tmp/mysqld_multi.log*.

--mysqladmin=*path*
: Sets the path to the *mysqladmin* utility.

--mysqld=*path*
: Specifies the path to *mysqld*.

`--no-log`
> Instructs the utility not to save messages to a log, but to send them to `stdout` instead.

`--password=password`
> Provides the password for using *mysqladmin*.

`--tcp-ip`
> Enables TCP/IP communication with the server instead of using a Unix-domain socket.

`--user=user`
> Provides the username for using *mysqladmin*. The same user must be used for all servers.

`--version`
> Displays the version of the utility.

---

mysqld_safe

`mysqld_safe [options]`

Use this to start the MySQL server and to restart automatically it if it dies unexpectedly. By default, the script will first attempt to start *mysqld-max*. If *mysqld-max* is not installed on the server, it will then start *mysqld* instead. Although options may be entered from the command line, to ensure that any options that are to be passed to the daemon are used when it's reloaded after a crash, they should be included in a configuration file (e.g., *my.cnf*). There are just a few options (listed here) relative to the `mysqld_safe` script. They should be included in the configuration file under the heading `[mysqld_safe]` but without the leading double dashes. In previous distributions of MySQL, this script was named `safe_mysqld`.

`--basedir=path`
> Specifies the path to the MySQL installations.

`--core-file-size=size`
> Specifies the maximum size of the core file to create if the daemon dies.

`--datadir=path`
> Specifies the directory which contains datafiles (i.e, table files).

`--defaults-extra-file=path`
> Specifies an additional configuration file to use after the default file is read.

`--defaults-file=path`
> Specifies the path to the default configuration file for the server.

`--err-log=path`
> Specifies the path to the error log for error messages outside of the daemon, such as errors when starting.

`--ledir=path`
> Specifies the path where the daemons may be found.

`--log-error=filename`
> Enables logging of error messages and server startup messages to the path and filename given.

`--mysqld=daemon`
> Specifies which daemon to start (i.e., *mysqld-max* or *mysqld*).

`--mysqld-version=`*suffix*

Specifies which daemon to use by providing the suffix of the daemon's name (i.e., mysqld-*suffix*). A value of max ensures *mysqld-max* is started. A blank value ensures *mysqld* is started.

`--nice=`*number*

Employs the *nice* utility to set scheduling priority to the value given.

`--no-defaults`

Instructs the script not to refer to configuration files for options.

`--open-files-limit=`*number*

Limits the number of files the daemon may open. Only *root* may use this option.

`--pid-file=`*filename*

Specifies the path and the name of the file containing the process identifier.

`--port=`*port*

Specifies the port number to use for connecting to the server.

`--socket=`*filename*

Provides the path and name of the server's socket file.

`--timezone=`*zone*

Sets the environment variable for the time zone of the server.

`--user=`*user*

Specifies the username for connecting to the server.

11

Command-Line Utilities

This chapter describes the utilities that you can use to administer the MySQL server and data. Some interact with the server and others manipulate the datafiles directly for MySQL. Others can be used to make backups of data (e.g., *mysqldump* and *mysqlhotcopy*). These utilities are listed here in alphabetical order, with descriptions.

Some of these utilities are provided with MySQL and are typically installed in a standard directory for executables so that they are automatically on the user's command path. Other utilities have to be downloaded and installed from MySQL AB's site or from a third-party site.

comp_err

comp_err *source destination*

Use this to compile text files that contain mappings of error codes into a format necessary for MySQL. This is particularly useful for creating error code messages in spoken languages for which error message files do not already exist. You can also use it to modify error messages to a particular liking. To do this, just edit the appropriate *errmsg.txt* file in its default directory. For English messages on Unix systems, the source text file and the compiled system file are found typically in */usr/share/mysql/english*. The following demonstrates how to compile a text file containing error messages in Pig Latin:

```
comp_err /usr/share/mysql/piglatin/errmsg.txt \
        /usr/share/mysql/piglatin/errmsg.sys
```

To make the new set of error messages the default set, add the following line to the MySQL configuration file (e.g., */etc/my.cnf*) under the [mysqld] section:

```
language=/usr/share/mysql/piglatin
```

Notice that only the path is given and not the filename.

isamchk

isamchk *options table*[.MYI]

Use this to check ISAM tables, to repair them if there are problems, and to optimize them if possible. ISAM tables, however, are deprecated. Therefore, this utility functions very much like myisamchk with the same options, so see the explanation of myisamchk for use of isamchk.

make_binary_distribution

make_binary_distribution

Use this to make a binary distribution of MySQL from the source code. This can be useful, for instance, to a developer who has modified the source code for her needs and wants to make a customized binary version for use by her associates. Executing the script from the directory containing the modified source code generates a GNU zipped tar file for distribution.

msql2mysql

msql2mysql *program.c*

Use this to convert mSQL C API function calls in programs written in C to the MySQL equivalent functions. The only argument to the utility is the name of the source to convert. The utility does not create a copy of the source file. Instead, it converts the given source file itself. Therefore, you should make a backup of the source before connecting. This utility isn't always effective in converting all mSQL functions. So, manual inspection of the code and testing may be required after a conversion. Note that the replace utility is used by msql2mysql.

my_print_defaults

my_print_defaults *options filename*

Use this to parse a configuration file so as to convert key/value pairs into command-line equivalent options. For instance, a line from the *my.cnf* file that reads basedir=/data/mysql will be converted to the --basedir=/data/mysql. To export the MySQL daemon (i.e., *mysqld*) section of *my.cnf* file, enter the following from the command line (the output follows):

```
my_print_defaults --config-file=/etc/my.cnf mysqld

--basedir=/data/mysql
--datadir=/data/mysql
--socket=/tmp/mysql.sock
--tmpdir=/tmp
--log-bin=/data/mysql/logs/log-bin
```

Notice that only the *mysqld* section is parsed and the header [mysqld] and the blank lines are not included in the output. Also, each key/value pair is printed on separate lines. To parse more than one section, you can list additional section names at the end of the command line, separated by spaces.

myisamchk

myisamchk *options table*[.MYI][...]

Use this to check and repair MyISAM tables, as well as to optimize them. This utility works with the table files directly and does not require interaction with the MySQL server. Therefore, it may be necessary to specify the path along with the table or table names in the second argument. Also, tables that are being checked should be locked or the MySQL server daemon should be stopped. This utility works with the index files for the tables, so the suffix *.MYI* may be given for table names to prevent it from attempting to analyze other files. Providing no suffix (e.g., *table1*, not *table1.**) will have the same effect as giving a specific one (*table1.MYI*). To check all of the tables in a database, use the wildcard (i.e., **.MYI*). Here is a basic example of how you can use myisamchk to check one table:

```
myisamchk /data/mysql/workrequests/requests
Checking MyISAM file: /data/mysql/workrequests/requests
Data records:    531   Deleted blocks:      0
myisamchk: warning: 3 clients is using or hasn't closed the table properly
- check file-size
- check key delete-chain
- check record delete-chain
- check index reference
- check data record references index: 1
- check record links
MyISAM-table '/data/mysql/workrequests/requests' is usable but should be
fixed
```

No options are specified here, so the default of --check is used. Notice that myisamchk detected a problem with the table. To fix this problem, you can run the utility again, but with the --recover option like so:

```
myisamchk --recover /data/mysql/workrequests/requests
- recovering (with sort) MyISAM-table
 '/data/mysql/workrequests/requests'
Data records: 531
- Fixing index 1
```

The following sections list of the options available with myisamchk.

Check options

--check, -c

Instructs the utility to check tables for errors.

--check-only-changed, -C

Instructs the utility to check only tables that have changed since the last check.

--extend-check, -e

Instructs the utility to check tables thoroughly. Use this option only in extreme cases.

--fast, -F

Use this option to have the utility check only tables that haven't been closed properly.

--force, -f

    Instructs the utility to repair tables that report errors during check mode. It restarts the utility with the --recover option if any errors occur.

--information, -i

    Displays statistical information about tables being checked.

--medium-check, -m

    Instructs the utility to check tables more thoroughly than --check, but not as thoroughly as --extend-check.

--read-only, -T

    Tells the utility not to mark tables with status information so that tables may be used while checking. Tables are not marked as checked when using this option.

--update-state, -U

    Has the utility update tables to indicate when they were checked and mark them as crashed if any errors are found.

Repair options

--backup, -B

    Instructs the utility to make a copy of datafiles (*table.MYD*), naming them *table-datetime.BAK*.

--character-sets-dir=*path*

    Sets the directory where character sets are located.

--correct-checksum

    Corrects a table's checksum information.

--data-file-length=*number*, -D *number*

    Sets the maximum length of a datafile for when rebuilding a full datafile.

--extend-check, -e

    Instructs the utility to attempt to recover all rows, including intentionally deleted ones.

--force, -f

    Instructs the utility to ignore error messages and to overwrite temporary files.

--keys-used=*bitfield*, -k *bitfield*

    Instructs the utility to have MyISAM updates use only specific keys for faster data inserts.

--max-record-length=*number*

    Tells the utility to skip rows larger than the length specified if there is not enough memory.

--parallel-recover, -p

    This option is the same as the --recover option, but instructs the utility to create all keys in parallel with different threads.

--quick, -q

    Repairs indexes only and not datafiles of tables that are not corrupted.

-qq

    Repairs indexes only and updates datafiles only when duplicates are found.

--safe-recover, -o

    Repairs rows that the --sort-recover option cannot handle (e.g., duplicate values for unique keys).

`--set-character-set=set`
> Specifies the character set to use.

`--sort-recover, -n`
> Instructs the utility to use the sort buffer regardless of whether the temporary file would be too large based on default limits.

`--unpack, -u`
> Unpacks tables that were packed with the `myisampack` utility.

Other options

`--analyze, -a`
> Instructs the utility to optimize the use of keys in tables. This option can help with some joins. Use the `--description` and the `--verbose` options to show the calculated distribution.

`--block-search=offset, -b offset`
> Searches for a row based on a given offset.

`--description, -d`
> Displays information about the table.

`--set-auto-increment[=value], -A [value]`
> Sets the value of an auto-increment column for the next row created. If no value is given, the next value above the highest value found for column is used.

`--sort-index, -S`
> Sorts indexes.

`--sort-records=index, -R index`
> Sorts rows based on the index given.

Global options

`--debug=options, -# options`
> Sets debug option to log (e.g., 'd:t:o, filename').

`--character-sets-dir=path`
> Specifies the directory containing character sets.

`--help, -?`
> Displays basic help information.

`--silent, -s`
> Displays only print error messages. With `-ss` even less information will be displayed.

`--sort-index, -S`
> Sorts indexes.

`--sort-records=value, -R value`
> Instructs the utility to sort records based on the index given.

`--tmpdir=path, -t path`
> Sets the path for temporary files. Additional paths may be given in a colon-separated list.

`--verbose, -v`
> Displays more information. Additional vs (e.g., `-vv`) will provide more information.

`--version, -V`
> Displays the version of the utility.

`--wait, -w`
> Instructs the utility to wait before proceeding if the table is locked.

myisamlog

`myisamlog options [filename [table ...]]`

Use this to scan and extract information from the *myisam.log* file, which logs debugging messages for the MyISAM table handler. The path and name of the logfile may be given. Also, the command can list specific tables to limit scanning to these tables. To activate the log, add the following line to the MySQL server configuration file (e.g., *my.cnf*) under the [server] section or the [mysqld] section:

> `log-isam=/data/mysql/logs/myisam.log`

This utility has several options for retrieving data from the log. Here is a list of them along with a brief explanation of each:

`-?, -I`
> Displays basic help information.

`-c number`
> Limits the output to *number* commands.

`-D`
> Use this with a server that was compiled with debugging in effect.

`-F path`
> Provides the file path to use. The path should end with a trailing slash.

`-f files`
> Sets the maximum number of open files allowed.

`-o offset`
> Specifies where in the log to begin the scan.

`-P`
> Displays information about processes.

`-p number`
> Instructs the utility to remove the given number of components from the path.

`-R`
> Displays the current record position.

`-r`
> Displays recovery activities.

`-u`
> Displays update activities.

`-V`
> Displays the version of the utility.

`-v`
> Displays more information. Additional vs (e.g., -vv) will increase the amount of information.

`-w`
> Displays file write activities.

myisampack

`myisampack options table[.MYI]`

Use this to create compressed, read-only tables to reduce table sizes and to increase retrieval speed. When reading compressed tables, MySQL decompresses the data in memory. To decompress tables packed with myisampack, use myisamchk with the --unpack option. Note that tables that are compressed and later decompressed should be reindexed using myisamchk. The pack_isam utility works very much like myisampack with the same options, but on ISAM tables, which are deprecated. Here is an alphabetical list of options for myisampack, along with a brief explanation of each:

`--backup, -b`
Has the utility create a backup of the given table (*table.OLD*).

`--debug=options, -# options`
Sets debug options to log (e.g., 'd:t:o, filename').

`--force, -f`
Forces a compressed table to be created, even if the results are larger than the original, and to overwrite a temporary table (*table.TMD*) if it exists.

`--help, -?`
Displays basic help information.

`--join=table, -j table`
Instructs the utility to join tables given into one compressed table. The table structures must be identical.

`--packlength=bytes, -p bytes`
Sets the size of the pointers for records to the number of bytes given (1, 2, or 3).

`--silent, -s`
Suppresses all information except error messages.

`--temp_dir=path, -T path`
Instructs the utility to use the path given for the directory where it is to write temporary tables.

`--test, -t`
Has the utility test the compression process without actually compressing the table.

`--verbose, -v`
Displays information about the compression process.

`--version, -V`
Displays the version of the utility.

`--wait, -w`
Instructs the utility to wait before compressing if the table is locked by another client or utility.

mysqlaccess

`mysqlaccess [host] user database [options]`

Use this to check privileges of a user for a specific host and database. This utility is executed from the command line, so it can be useful, for instance, as a preliminary tool to check for user permissions before proceeding with a customized program that uses one of the APIs.

With regard to the syntax, the hostname is the first argument and is optional. If not given, *localhost* is assumed. The username given in the second argument is the name of the user for which the utility is checking privileges. The third argument is the database for which it is checking against. The fourth argument involves several possible options, one of which could be the username by which the utility will access the server to gather information on the user named in the second argument. Here is an example of how you might use this utility:

```
mysqlaccess localhost marie db1 -U russell -P
```

In this example, the utility is given the hostname, then the user for which I'm inquiring about, then the database name for which I want user privilege information. The -U option is used to specify the username with which to access the server to gather information. This user has full access to the *mysql* database. The -P instructs the utility to prompt me for a password. The results of the preceding inquiry is shown here:

```
Access-rights
for USER 'marie', from HOST 'localhost', to DB 'ANY_NEW_DB'
        +-----------------+---+ +-----------------+---+
        | Select_priv     | Y | | Shutdown_priv   | N |
        | Insert_priv     | N | | Process_priv    | N |
        | Update_priv     | N | | File_priv       | N |
        | Delete_priv     | N | | Grant_priv      | N |
        | Create_priv     | N | | References_priv | N |
        | Drop_priv       | N | | Index_priv      | N |
        | Reload_priv     | N | | Alter_priv      | N |
        +-----------------+---+ +-----------------+---+
NOTE:   A password is required for user `reader' :-(

The following rules are used:
db    : 'No matching rule'
host  : 'Not processed: host-field is not empty in db-table.'
user:'localhost','marie','6ffa06534985249d','Y','N','N','N','N','N','N','N',
'N','N','N','N','N','N'
```

First, a table is presented displaying the privileges for the combination of the database named, the host given, and the user. This user has only SELECT privileges.

Additionally, the results are given in raw form for each component. This user's privileges are the same for all databases and hosts (i.e., there are no entries in the *db* or the *host* tables in the *mysql* database), so there aren't any results for those particular components. For the user component, the command displays details without labels, but they are presented in the order that they are found in the *user* table in the *mysql* database. The third field is the password in the encrypted format that it stored. The Ys and Ns are the settings for each user privilege.

Several options are available with this utility. Here is an alphabetical list:

--brief, -b
> Provides a brief display of results from an inquiry.

--commit
> Copies grant rules from temporary tables to the grant tables.

--copy
> Reloads temporary tables with original data from the grant tables so that privileges take effect.

--db=*database*, -d *database*
    Explicitly specifies the database against which to query the user privileges.

--debug=*level*
    Sets the debugging level. The choices are from 0 to 3.

--help, -?
    Displays basic help information.

--host=*host*, -h *host*
    Specifies the host on which to obtain privilege information. The *localhost* is the default.

--howto
    Displays basic examples of usage with sample results.

--old-server
    Stipulates that the server to which the utility is connecting is running an older version of MySQL (prior to 3.21) requiring a different method with regard to WHERE clauses in SQL statements.

--password=*password*, -p *password*
    Provides the password of the user logging into the server, not the user on which to check for privileges.

--plan
    Displays plans for further development of the utility by its developers.

--preview
    Displays the differences in temporary grant tables before they are committed.

--relnotes
    Displays notes on each release of the utility.

--rhost=*host*, -H *host*
    If the utility is not being run on the same server as the MySQL server that's being queried, use this option to specify the address of the MySQL server to query.

--rollback
    Undoes the last change to user privileges.

--spassword=*password*, -P *password*
    Provides the password when using a superuser.

--superuser=*user*, -U *user*
    Provides a superuser's username.

--table, -t
    Instructs the utility to display data in an ASCII table format.

--user=*user*, -u *user*
    Provides the username for logging in to the server, not the user on which to check for privileges.

--version, -v
    Displays the version of the utility.

mysqladmin

mysqladmin [*options*] *command* [*command-options*]

Use this to perform MySQL server administration tasks from the command line. You can use it to check the server's status and settings, flush tables, change passwords, shut down the server, and perform a few other administrative functions. This utility interacts with the MySQL server. Here is an alphabetical list of options that you can give as the first argument to the utility:

--character-sets-dir=*path*
> Specifies the directory that contains character sets.

--compress, -C
> Instructs the utility to compress data passed between it and the server if supported.

--connect_timeout=*number*
> Sets the number of seconds a connection may be idle before it will time out.

--count=*number*, -c *number*
> Specifies the number of iterations of commands to perform in conjunction with the --sleep option.

--debug=*settings,filename*, -# *settings, filename*
> Instructs the utility to write debugging information to the log specified along with various settings (e.g., 'd:t:o,logname').

--force, -f
> Forces execution of the DROP DATABASE statement and others despite error messages.

--help, -?
> Displays basic help information.

--host=*host* , -h *host*
> Specifies the name or IP address of the server for connection.

--password[=*password*], -p[*password*]
> Provides the password to give to the server. No spaces are allowed between the -p and the password. If a password is not given, the user will be prompted for one.

--port=*port*, -P *port*
> Specifies the port on which to connect to the server. The default is 3306.

--relative, -r
> Instructs the utility to display the differences between values with each iteration of commands issued with the --sleep option.

--shutdown_timeout=*number*
> Sets the number of seconds the client should wait before shutting down.

--silent, -s
> Tells the utility to exit without error messages if a connection to the server cannot be established.

--sleep=*seconds*, -i *seconds*
> Specifies the number of seconds to wait between the repeated execution of commands. The number of iterations is set by the --count option.

--socket=*filename*, -S *filename*
> Provides the path and name of the server's socket file.

`--user=user, -u user`
> Specifies a MySQL user other than the current filesystem user.

`--verbose, -v`
> Displays more information.

`--version, -V`
> Displays the version of the utility.

`--vertical, -E`
> Displays output in a vertical format with a separate line for each column of data.

`--wait[=number], -w [number]`
> Instructs the utility to wait until it can connect to the server. It will retry once unless the number of times it is to retry is given with this option.

Commands

The main focus of `mysqladmin` are the commands that perform administrative tasks. Commands are given as the second argument. You can issue one or more commands on the same line. Here is an alphabetical list of commands (with options for some) and an explanation of each:

`create database`
> Creates the new database specified.

`drop database`
> Deletes the database specified.

`extended-status`
> Displays the MySQL server's extended status information.

`flush-hosts`
> Flushes all cached hosts.

`flush-logs`
> Instructs the utility to flush all logs.

`flush-privileges`
> Reloads the grant tables.

`flush-status`
> Flushes status variables.

`flush-tables`
> Has the utility flush all tables.

`flush-threads`
> Flushes the thread cache.

`kill id`
> Kills the server thread specified by an identifier. Additional threads may be given in a comma-separated list.

`password password`
> Changes the password of the user currently connected to the server through the utility to the password given.

`ping`
> Determines if the server is running.

`processlist`
> Displays a list of active server threads. With the `--verbose` option, more information is provided on each thread.

refresh
> Flushes all tables and reloads logfiles.

reload
> Reloads the grant tables.

shutdown
> Shuts down the MySQL server.

start-slave
> Starts a replication slave server.

status
> Displays the server's status.

stop-slave
> Stops a replication slave server.

variables
> Displays the variables and the values of the server.

version
> Displays the version of the utility.

mysqlbinlog

`mysqlbinlog [options] filename`

Use this to format the display of the binary log for a MySQL server. Customized applications also can use it for monitoring server activities. The path to the logfile to format is given as the second argument for the utility. Additional logfiles may be given either with filesystem wildcards or by listing them individually, separated by spaces. Here is an alphabetical list of the options that you can give as the first argument, along with a brief explanation of each:

--database=database, -d database
> Displays information regarding only the database given.

--disable-log-bin, -D
> Disables binary logging.

--force-read, -f
> Forces the reading of unknown log information.

--help, -?
> Displays basic help information.

--host=host, -h host
> Specifies the hostname or IP address of a remote server containing the logfile to format.

--local-load=path, -l path
> Specifies local directory in which temporary files are to be prepared for LOAD DATA INFILE statements.

--offset=number, -o number
> Specifies the number of entries to skip in the logfile.

--open_files_limit
> Sets the maximum number of open files allowed. The default is 64.

--password=*password*, -p *password*
Provides the password to the remote server that is being accessed.

--port=*port*, -P *port*
Specifies the port to use for connecting to a remote server.

--position=*number*, -j *number*
Sets the number of bytes to skip in the log file. This option is deprecated. Use --start-position instead.

--protocol=*protocol*
Specifies the protocol to use when connecting to the server. The choices are TCP, SOCKET, PIPE, and MEMORY.

--short-form, -s
Changes the output to a shorter format.

--start-date=*datetime*
Instructs the utility to begin reading the log from the first event recorded with a date and time equal to or greater than the one given. The time can be in DATETIME or TIMESTAMP format. Use the time zone of the server.

--start-position=*number*
Sets the position to start reading the logfile.

--stop-date=*datetime*
Instructs the utility to stop reading the log at the first event recorded with a date and time equal to or greater than the one given. The time can be in DATETIME or TIMESTAMP format. Use the time zone of the server.

--stop-position=*number*
Sets the position to stop reading the log file.

--table=*table*, -t *table*
Obtains information on the table named.

--user=*user*, -u *user*
Specifies the username to use when connecting to a remote server.

--version, -V
Displays the version of the utility.

---

mysqlbug

mysqlbug

This is a script for reporting bugs to MySQL AB developers. Executed at the command line of the server, this script gathers information on the version of MySQL and related libraries installed, the operating system, as well as how MySQL was compiled.

To run the utility, simply type the command without any options or arguments. After a few moments a text editor (e.g., Emacs) will be started with a form for reporting the bug. Several of the details will be filled in with information gathered by the script. You can modify this information, and you are expected to answer questions about the bug discovered. This includes a description of how to reproduce the problem or what circumstances occurred that may have caused or contributed to the problem. If you discovered a workaround solution, report this, as well. The report created (saved in the */tmp* directory on Unix systems) should be emailed to *dev-bugs@mysql.com*. Go to *http://bugs.mysql.com* to report bugs online.

mysqlcheck

mysqlcheck [*options*] *database* [*table*]

Use this to check and to repair MyISAM tables, as well as to optimize them. This utility is similar in use and purpose to myisamchk. Instead of working with the table files directly like myisamchk, though, this utility interacts with the MySQL server instead. It uses the ANALYZE TABLE, the CHECK TABLE, and REPAIR TABLE statements.

The name of the database containing the tables to check is given as the second argument to the utility. The table to check is given as the third argument. Additional tables may be given in a space-separated list. Here is a list of options that you can give and a brief explanation of each:

--all-databases, -A
> Instructs the utility to check all databases.

--all-in-1, -1
> Instructs the utility to execute all queries for all tables in each database in one statement rather than in separate queries for each table.

--analyze, -a
> Has the utility analyze tables.

--auto-repair
> Instructs the utility to automatically repair any corrupted tables found.

--character-sets-dir=*path*
> Specifies the directory containing character sets.

--check, -c
> Instructs the utility to check tables for errors.

--check-only-changed, -C
> Has the utility check only tables that have changed since the last check, as well as tables that were not closed properly.

--compress
> Instructs the utility to compress data passed between it and the server if supported.

--databases *databases*, -B *databases*
> Specifies more than one database for checking. To specify tables with this option, use the --tables option.

--debug[=*options*], -# [*options*]
> Instructs the utility to write debugging information to the log specified, along with various settings (e.g., 'd:t:o,logname').

--default-character-set=*set*
> Specifies the default character set.

--extended, -e
> Ensures consistency of data when checking tables. When repairing tables with this option, the utility will attempt to recover all rows, including intentionally deleted ones.

--fast, -F
> Instructs the utility to check only tables that were improperly closed.

--force, -f
> Forces processing of tables regardless of SQL errors encountered.

`--help, -?`
> Displays basic help information.

`--host=host, -h host`
> Specifies the name or IP address of the server for connection.

`--medium-check, -m`
> This option is more thorough than the `--check` option and is less thorough than the `--extended` option.

`--optimize, -o`
> Instructs the utility to optimize tables.

`--password[=password], -p[password]`
> Provides the password to pass to the server. A space is not permitted after `-p` if the password is given.

`--port=port, -P port`
> Specifies the port to use for connecting to the server. The default is 3306.

`--protocol=protocol`
> Specifies the protocol to use when connecting to the server. The choices are `TCP`, `SOCKET`, `PIPE`, and `MEMORY`.

`--quick, -q`
> Checks tables faster by not scanning rows for incorrect links. When used to repair tables, it has the utility repair only the index tree. This option is the fastest method.

`--repair, -r`
> Instructs the utility to repair tables. Note that it can't repair unique keys containing duplicates.

`--silent, -s`
> Suppresses all messages except for error messages.

`--socket=filename, -S filename`
> Provides the path and name of the server's socket file.

`--tables`
> Specifies table names when using the `--databases` option.

`--user=user, -u user`
> Specifies the username for connecting to the server.

`--verbose, -v`
> Displays more information.

`--version, -V`
> Displays the version of the utility.

mysqldump

`mysqldump [options] database [table]`

Use this to export data and table structures from MySQL. Typically, you use this utility to make backups of databases or to move databases from one server to another. You can run it on an active server. For consistency of data between tables, the tables should be locked (see the `--lock-tables` option) or the daemon should be shutdown. To make a backup of a database, enter something like the following from the command line:

```
mysqldump -u russell -p -l db1 > /tmp/db1.sql
```

In this example, the username is given with the -u option. The -p option tells the utility to prompt the user for a password. The -l option is the same as the --lock-tables option. It has the server lock the tables, making the backup, and then unlock them when it's finished. Next the database to back up (*db1*) is specified. Finally, using the redirect (the greater-than sign), the output is saved to the path and filename given.

The dump file created will be in the text file format. It will contain a CREATE TABLE statement for each table in the database, along with a separate INSERT statement for each row of data. To restore the data from a dump file created by mysqldump, you can use the *mysql* client. To restore the file created by the preceding statement, you can enter the following from the command line:

```
mysql -u russell -p < /tmp/db1.sql
```

This example redirects the stdin through the use of the less-than sign. This instructs the *mysql* client to take input from the file given.

The contents of the dump file can be determined by the options chosen. Here is a list of options, along with an explanation of each:

--add-drop-table
> Instructs the utility to add a DROP TABLE statement to the export file before each set of INSERT statements for each table.

--add-locks
> Instructs the utility to add a LOCK statement before each set of INSERT statements and an UNLOCK after each set.

--all, -a
> Instructs the utility to include all MySQL-specific statements in the export file. This option is deprecated as of Version 4.1.2 of MySQL. It is replaced with the --create-options option.

--all-databases, -A
> Instructs the utility to export all databases.

--allow-keywords
> Makes keywords allowable for column names by including the table name and a dot before such column names in the export file.

--character-sets-dir=*path*
> Specifies the directory containing character sets.

--comments[=0|1]
> If this option is set to a value of 1 (default), any comments from a table's schema will be included in the export file. If it is set to 0, they won't be included.

--compatible=*type*
> Use this to have the utility make the export file's contents compatible with other database systems. The choices currently are: mysql323, msyql40, postgresql, oracle, mssql, db2, sapdb, no_key_options, no_table_options, and no_field_options. More than one type may be given in a comma-separated list.

--complete-insert, -c
> Instructs the utility to generate complete INSERT statements in the export file.

--compress, -C
> Instructs the utility to compress data passed between it and the server if supported.

--create-options

Instructs the utility to include all MySQL-specific statements (e.g., CREATE TABLE) in the export file. It's synonymous with the --all option.

--databases, -B

Names more than one database to export. Table names may not be given with this option unless using the --tables option.

--debug[=options], -# [options]

Instructs the utility to write debugging information to the log specified along with various settings (e.g., 'd:t:o,logname').

--default-character-set=set

Specifies the default character set.

--delayed

Instructs the utility to add the DELAYED flag to INSERT statements in the export file.

--delete-master-logs

Instructs the utility to lock all tables on all servers and then to delete the binary logs of a master replication server after completing the export.

--disable-keys, -K

For MyISAM tables, this option instructs the utility to add an ALTER TABLE... DISABLE KEYS statement to the export file before each set of INSERT statements, and an ALTER TABLE...ENABLE KEYS statement after each set to optimize later restoration.

--extended-insert, -e

Instructs the utility to bundle INSERT statements together for each table in the export file to make the export faster.

--fields-enclosed-by=characters

Use this with the --tab option to identify the characters to use to indicate the start and end of fields in the data text file.

--fields-escaped-by=character

Use this with the --tab option to identify the character to use to escape special characters in the data text file. Backslash is the default.

--fields-optionally-enclosed-by=characters

Use this with the --tab option to identify the characters that may indicate the start and end of fields in the data text file.

--fields-terminated-by=character

Use this with the --tab option to identify the characters that indicate the end of fields in the data text file.

--first-slave, -x

Locks all tables on all servers.

--flush-logs, -F

Instructs the utility to flush all logs.

--force, -f

Instructs the utility to continue processing data despite errors.

--help, -?

Displays basic help information.

--host=host, -h host

Specifies the name or IP address of the server for connection.

`--lines-terminated-by=`*`character`*

Use this with the `--tab` option to identify the characters that indicate the end of records in the data text file.

`--lock-tables, -l`

Instructs the utility to lock all tables before exporting data.

`--no-create-db, -n`

Instructs the utility not to add `CREATE DATABASE` statements to the export file when the `--all-databases` option or the `--databases` option is used.

`--no-create-info, -t`

Instructs the utility not to add `CREATE TABLE` statements to the export file.

`--no-data, -d`

Instructs the utility to export only database and table schema and not data.

`--opt`

Instructs the utility to use several options with just this one option: `--add-drop-table`, `--add-locks`, `--all` (or `--create-options` instead as of MySQL Version 4.1.2), `--extended-insert`, `--lock-tables`, and `--quick`. As of Version 4.1, the `--opt` option is enabled by default.

`--password[=`*`password`*`], -p[`*`password`*`]`

Provides the password to pass to the server. A space is not permitted after `-p` if the password is given. If the password is not given, the user will be prompted for one.

`--port=`*`port`*`, -P `*`port`*

Specifies the port number to use for connecting to the server.

`--quick, -q`

Instructs the utility not to buffer data into a complete results set before exporting. Instead, data is exported one row at a time directly to the export file.

`--quote-names, -Q`

Instructs the utility to place the names of databases, tables, and columns within backticks ('). This is the default option.

`--result-file=`*`filename`*`, -r `*`filename`*

Provides the path and the name of the file to which data should be exported.

`--single-transaction`

Instructs the utility to run a `BEGIN` statement before exporting.

`--skip-comments`

Instructs the utility not to export any comments from a table's schema to the export file.

`--skip-opt`

Disables the `--opt` option.

`--skip-quote-names`

Disables the `--quote-names` option.

`--socket=`*`filename`*`, -S `*`filename`*

Provides the path and name of the server's socket file.

`--tab=`*`path`*`, -T `*`path`*

Instructs the utility to create two separate export files: one for the table schema (e.g., *table.sql*) and another for the data (e.g., *table.txt*). The data text file will contain data in a tab-separated format.

--tables

Names specific tables with the --databases option. All names after the --tables option are treated as table names.

--user=*user*, -u *user*

Specifies the username for connecting to the server.

--verbose, -v

Displays more information.

--version, -V

Displays the version of the utility.

--where='*condition*', -w '*condition*'

Sets a WHERE condition for selecting rows for export.

--xml, -X

Exports databases in XML format.

mysqldumpslow

mysqldumpslow [*options*] [*filename*]

Use this to display a summary of the slow query log. The path and name of the logfile may be given in the second argument. Otherwise, the utility will look to the server's configuration file (i.e., *my.cnf*) for this information. The following options can narrow the summary or change what is displayed.

-a

Instructs the utility not to combine queries with similar SQL statements.

-d

Enables debugging mode.

-g *expression*

Extracts information on queries that meet the given expression.

-h *host*

Specifies the host's name for which the utility is to scan. By default, logfiles are named with the server's hostname as the filename's prefix.

-i *host*

Specifies the hostname of the server.

-l

With this option, the lock time is added to the execution time for the utility's summary.

-n *number*

Sets the minimum number of occurrences for reporting.

-r

Reverses the order of sorts for reporting.

-s *type*

Specifies the type of queries on which to report. The choices are al for average lock time, ar for average rows, at for average execution time, l for lock time, r for rows, and t for execution time.

-t

Sets the number of queries on which to display.

-v

Displays more information.

mysqlhotcopy

mysqlhotcopy *database* [*path*]

Use this to make backup copies of databases while the server is active. It only works on MyISAM and ISAM tables, though. It makes a simple copy of each database directory and each table file. This results in a separate directory for each database and usually three files for each table: one for the schema, another for the data, and a third for the index. It places a read lock on all of the tables in the database while copying them. Here is an example of how you can copy a database with mysqlhotcopy:

mysqlhotcopy -u russell -p password db1 /tmp/backup

Note that unlike other MySQL utilities, there is a space between the -p and the password. Next the database (*db1*) is specified. Finally, the path to write the backup directories is given. To restore databases or tables that were copied by mysqlhotcopy, just copy the table files to be restored to their original data directories. Here are the following options:

--addtodest

Instructs the utility not to abort the session or to rename the backup directory, but to add new files to the directory.

--allowold

Instructs the utility to rename an existing backup directory to *_old so that the copying may be completed. If the new copy is successful, the old directory is deleted. If it's unsuccessful, the old directory is restored.

--checkpoint=*database.table*

Instructs the utility to save logging information to the named database and table.

--debug

Used to enable debugging information.

--dryrun, -n

This option has the utility test the backup process without actually making a copy.

--flushlog

Instructs the utility to flush logs after all tables are locked.

--help, -?

Displays basic help information.

--keepold

Instructs the utility when using the --allowold option not to delete the old directory if the copying is successful.

--method=*method*

Sets the method used by the utility for copying files. The choices are cp or scp.

--noindices

Instructs the utility to copy only the headers of index files. Indexes may be rebuilt when restoring copies.

`--password=password, -p password`
> Provides the password to pass to the server. A space is permitted after the -p option, before the password.

`--port=port, -P port`
> Specifies the port number to use for connecting to the server.

`--quiet, -q`
> Suppresses all messages except for error messages.

`--regexp=expression`
> Provides a regular expression for determining which databases to copy based on the name.

`--resetmaster`
> Instructs the utility to execute a RESET MASTER statement after tables are locked.

`--resetslave`
> Instructs the utility to execute a RESET SLAVE statement after tables are locked.

`--socket=filename, -S filename`
> Provides the path and name of the server's socket file.

`--sufix=string`
> Specifies the suffix for the copies of databases. The default is _copy.

`--tmpdir=path`
> Specifies the temporary directory to use. The default is /tmp.

`--user=user, -u user`
> Specifies the username for connecting to the server.

mysqlimport

`mysqlimport [options] database filename`

Use this to import data and table structures from a text file given as the third argument, into a database named in the second argument of the utility. This utility interacts with the server and uses the LOAD DATA INFILE statement. The root name of the text file being imported must be the same as the table name. Additional text files may be given in a space-separated list. Options may be given on the command line as the first argument to the utility or they may be provided in the server's configuration file (e.g., my. cnf) under the heading [client] or [mysqlimport]. When included in the configuration file, options appear without the leading double dashes. Here is an alphabetical list of options you can give for the first argument along with an explanation of each:

`--character-sets-dir=name`
> Specifies the directory containing character sets.

`--columns=columns, -c columns`
> Identifies the order of fields in the text file as they relate to the columns in the table. Columns are given in a comma-separated list.

`--compress, -C`
> Instructs the utility to compress data passed between it and the server if supported.

`--debug[=options], -# options`
> Instructs the utility to write debugging information to the log specified along with various settings (e.g., 'd:t:o,logname').

`--default-character-set=set`
> Specifies the default character set.

`--defaults-extra-file=filename`
> Instructs the utility to accept additional options from the text file named.

`--defaults-file=filename`
> Instructs the utility to accept options only from the text file named.

`--delete, -d`
> Instructs the utility to delete all of the data from each target table before importing data from the text file.

`--fields-enclosed-by=characters`
> Identifies the characters that indicate the start and end of fields in the text file being imported.

`--fields-escaped-by=character`
> Identifies the character that will escape special characters in the text file being imported. Backslash is the default.

`--fields-optionally-enclosed-by=characters`
> Identifies the characters that indicate the start and end of fields in the text file being imported.

`--fields-terminated-by=character`
> Identifies the character that indicates the end of fields in the text file being imported.

`--force, -f`
> Instructs the utility to continue importing data despite errors encountered.

`--help, -?`
> Displays basic help information.

`--host=host, -h host`
> Specifies the name or IP address of the server for connection.

`--ignore, -i`
> Instructs the utility to ignore error messages regarding rows containing duplicate keys and thereby not to replace such rows with imported data.

`--ignore-lines=number`
> Instructs the utility to ignore the first number of lines specified. It's useful in skipping headings in the text file being imported.

`--lines-terminated-by=character`
> Identifies the character that indicates the end of records in the text file being imported.

`--local, -L`
> Tells the utility that the text file to import is located locally on the client and not on the server, which is the default assumption.

`--lock-tables, -l`
> Instructs the utility to lock all tables before importing data.

`--low-priority`
> Has the utility use the LOW PRIORITY flag when importing data.

`--no-defaults`
> Tells the utility not to accept options from a configuration file.

`--password[=password], -p[password]`
> Provides the password to pass to the server. A space is not permitted after the -p option if the password is given. If the password is not given, the user will be prompted for one.

`--port=port, -P port`
> Specifies the port number to use for connecting to the server.

`--print-defaults`
> Displays related options found in the server's configuration files.

`--protocol=protocol`
> Used to specify the protocol to use when connecting to the server. The choices are TCP, SOCKET, PIPE, and MEMORY.

`--replace, -r`
> Instructs the utility to replace rows that contain duplicate keys with the imported data.

`--silent, -s`
> Suppress all messages except for error messages.

`--socket=filename, -S filename`
> Provides the path and name of the server's socket file.

`--user=user, -u user`
> Specifies the username for connecting to the server.

`--verbose, -v`
> Displays more information.

`--version, -V`
> Displays the version of the utility.

mysqlshow

`mysqlshow [options] [database [table [column]]]`

Use this to obtain a list of databases, tables, or descriptions of tables. This utility interacts with the server and uses the SHOW DATABASES, SHOW TABLES, and SHOW TABLE statements. If no database name is given for the second argument, all database names will be listed. If a database name is given along with a table name, the table named will be described. To limit information to specific columns, list the columns desired in the fourth argument:

    mysqlshow --user=russell -ppassword db1 table1

The results of this command will be the same as entering the following SQL statement from the *mysql* client:

    SHOW TABLE db1.table1;

Here is an alphabetical list of options that you can give as part of the first argument to the utility along with a brief explanation of each:

`--character-sets-dir=path`
> Specifies the directory containing character sets.

`--compress, -C`
> Instructs the utility to compress data passed between it and the server if supported.

--debug[=*options*], -# *options*
: Instructs the utility to write debugging information to the log specified along with various settings (e.g., 'd:t:o,logname').

--default-character-set=*set*
: Specifies the default character set.

--help, -?
: Displays basic help information.

--host=*host*, -h *host*
: Specifies the name or IP address of the server for connection.

--keys, -k
: Instructs the utility to display table indexes.

--password[=*password*], -p[*password*]
: Provides the password to pass to the server. A space is not permitted after the -p option if the password is given. If the password is not given, the user will be prompted for one.

--port=*port*, -P *port*
: Specifies the port number to use for connecting to the server.

--protocol=*protocol*
: Specifies the protocol to use when connecting to the server. The choices are TCP, SOCKET, PIPE, and MEMORY.

--socket=*filename*, -S *filename*
: Provides the path and name of the server's socket file.

--status, -i
: Displays additional information regarding tables.

--user=*user*, -u *user*
: Specifies the username for connecting to the server.

--verbose, -v
: Displays more information.

--version, -V
: Displays the version of the utility.

perror

perror [*options*] *code*

Use this to obtain descriptions of system error codes that MySQL received. Multiple error codes may be given in a space-separated list as the second argument. The only options are for help (--help), the version (--version), and verbosity (--verbose).

12

Perl API

The easiest method of connecting to MySQL with the programming language Perl is to use the Perl DBI module, which is part of the core Perl installation. You can download both Perl and the DBI module from CPAN (*http://www.cpan.org*). This chapter was written with the assumption that the reader has Perl installed along with DBI.pm and that the reader has a basic knowledge of Perl. Its focus, therefore, is on how to connect to MySQL, how to run SQL statements, and how to effectively retrieve data from MySQL using Perl and DBI. For the examples here, the scenario of a bookstore's inventory is used.

Using Perl DBI with MySQL

This section presents basic tasks that you can perform with Perl DBI.

Connecting to MySQL

To interface with MySQL, first you must call the DBI module and then connect to MySQL. To make a connection to the *bookstore* database using the Perl DBI, only the following lines are needed in a Perl script:

```perl
#!/usr/bin/perl -w
use strict;
use DBI;

my $dbh = DBI->connect ("DBI:mysql:bookstore:localhost",
                        "username","password")
        or die "Could not connect to database: "
        . DBI->errstr;
```

The first two lines start Perl and set a useful condition for reducing scripting errors (use strict). The third line calls the DBI module. The next statement (spread over more than one line here) sets up a database handle that specifies the database engine (*mysql*), the name of the database (*bookstore*), the hostname (*localhost*), the username, and the password. Incidentally, the name of the database handle doesn't have to be called *$dbh*—anything will do. Next, the or operator provides alternate instructions to be performed if the connection fails. That is, the script will terminate (die) and then display the message in quotes along with whatever error message is generated by the driver using the errstr method from the DBI—the dot (.) merges them together.

Executing an SQL Statement

Making a connection to MySQL does little good unless an SQL statement is executed. Any SQL statement that can be entered from the *mysql* client may be executed through the API. Continuing the previous example, let's look at how an SQL statement that retrieves a list of books and their authors might look:

```
my $sql_stmnt = "SELECT title, author
                 FROM books";
my $sth = $dbh->prepare($sql_stmnt);
$sth->execute();
```

The first line (terminated by the semicolon) sets up a variable ($sql_stmnt) to store the SQL statement. The next line puts together the database handle created earlier and the SQL statement to form the SQL statement handle ($sth). Finally, the third line executes the statement handle in the notational method of the DBI module.

Capturing Data

Having connected to MySQL and invoked an SQL statement, what remains is to capture the data results and to display them. MySQL returns the requested data to Perl in columns and rows, as it would with the *mysql* client, but without table formatting. In Perl, rows are returned one at a time by MySQL and are processed usually by a loop in Perl. Each row is returned as an array, one element per column in the row. For each array, each element can be parsed into variables for printing and manipulation before receiving or processing the next row. You can do this with a while statement like so:

```
while (my($title, $author) = $sth->fetchrow_array())
{ print "$title ($author) \n"; }
```

At the core of this piece of code is the fetchrow_array() method belonging to the DBI module. As its name suggests, it fetches each row or array of columns, one array at a time. The while statement executes its block of code repeatedly so long as there are arrays to process. The value of each element of each array is stored in the two variables $title and $author. Then the variables are printed to the screen with a newline character after each pair.

Disconnecting from MySQL

Once there is no longer a need to maintain a connection to the MySQL database, it should be terminated. If the connection stays idle for too long, MySQL will eventually break the connection on its own. To minimize the drain on system resources, however, it's good practice to have scripts end their sessions like so:

```
$sth->finish( );
$dbh->disconnect( );
exit( );
```

This first line closes the SQL statement handle. As long as the connection to MySQL is not broken, as it will be in the second line here, more SQL statement handles could be issued, prepared, and executed without having to reconnect to MySQL. The last line of code here ends the Perl script.

Temporarily Storing Results

Perhaps a cleaner method of retrieving data from MySQL than the one just explained involves capturing all of the data in memory for later use, thus allowing the connection to MySQL to end before processing and displaying the data. Putting MySQL on hold while processing each row as shown earlier can slow down a script. It's sometimes better to create a complex data structure (an array of arrays) and then leave the data structure in memory, just passing around a reference number to its location in memory. To do this, instead of using fetchrow_array( ), you'd use the fetchall_arrayref( ) method. As the method's name indicates, it fetches all of the data at once, puts it into an array, and returns the array's starting location in memory. Here is a Perl script that uses fetchall_arrayref( ):

```
#!/usr/bin/perl -w
use strict;
use DBI;

# Connect to MySQL and execute SQL statement
my $dbh = DBI->connect("DBI:mysql:bookstore:localhost",
                       "username","password")
            || die "Could not connect to database: "
            . DBI->errstr;

my $sql_stmnt = "SELECT title, author
                    FROM books";
my $sth = $dbh->prepare($sql_stmnt);
$sth->execute( );

# Retrieve reference number to results
my $books = $sth->fetchall_arrayref( );
$sth->finish( );
$dbh->disconnect( );

# Loop through array of arrays containing data

foreach my $book (@$books){

    # Parse each row and display
    my ($title, $author) = @$book;
    print "$title by $author\n";
}
exit;
```

Instead of embedding the fetch method within a flow control statement, the results of the SQL statement using fetchall_arrayref( ) are stored in memory. A reference number to the location of those results is stored in the $books variable and the connection to MySQL is then closed. A foreach statement is employed to extract each reference to each array (i.e., each row) of the complex array. Each record's array is parsed into separate variables. The the values of the variables are displayed. Incidentally, to learn more about references, see Randal Schwartz's book *Learning Perl Objects, References & Modules* (O'Reilly).

This kind of batch processing of an SQL statement has the added advantage of allowing multiple SQL statements to be performed without them tripping over each other, while still performing complex queries. For instance, suppose that we want to get a list of books written by Henry James, ordered by title, then by publisher, and then by year. This is easy enough in MySQL. Suppose that we also want the inventory count of each title, bookstore by bookstore, with some address information to be displayed between the listing for each store. This becomes a little complicated. One way to do this is to use a SELECT statement that retrieves a list of store locations and their relevant information (i.e., their address and telephone number) and to save a reference to the data in memory. Then we could issue another SQL statement to retrieve the book inventory data and then close the MySQL connection. With a flow control statement, we could then print a store header followed by the store's relevant inventory information for each book before moving on to the next store. It would basically look like this:

```
...  # Start script and connect to MySQL

# Retrieve list of stores
my $sql_stmnt = "SELECT store_id, store_name,
                address, city, state, telephone
                FROM stores";
my $sth = $dbh->prepare($sql_stmnt);
$sth->execute( );
my $stores = $sth->fetchall_arrayref( );
$sth->finish( );

# Retrieve list of books
my $sql_stmnt = "SELECT title, publisher,
                pub_year, store_id, quantity
                FROM books, inventory
                WHERE author = 'Henry James'
                AND books.book_id = inventory.book_id
                ORDER BY title, publisher, pub_year";
my $sth = $dbh->prepare($sql_stmnt);
$sth->execute( );
my $books = $sth->fetchall_arrayref( );
$sth->finish( );
$dbh->disconnect( );

foreach my $store (@$stores){

    my ($store_id, $store_name, $address,
        $city, $state, $telephone) =
```

```
        @$store;
    print "$store_name\n
            $address\n$city, $state\n
            $telephone\n\n";

    foreach my $book (@$books){

        my ($title, $publisher,
            $pub_year, $store, $qty) = @$book;
        if($store ne $store_id) { next; }
            print "$title ($publisher $pub_year) $qty\n";
        }
    }
    exit;
```

To save space, I left out the opening lines for the script, because they are the same as in the previous script. In the first SQL statement here, we're selecting the store information. With the fetchall_arrayref( ) method, we're storing the reference for the data in $stores. If we were to print out this variable, we would see only a long number and not the actual data. Although an SQL statement may retrieve many rows of data, all of the data will be stored in memory. Therefore, we can issue finish( ) and, as long as we don't disconnect from MySQL, we can issue another SQL statement. The next SQL statement selects the book inventory information. Once this has been collected, the connection to MySQL is terminated and we can begin displaying the data with the use of flow control statements.

The first foreach statement loops through the data of each store and prints out the address information. Within each loop is another foreach loop for processing all of the titles for the particular store. Notice the if statement for the book inventory loop. The first record or array for the first store is read and the basic store information is displayed. Then the first array for the inventory is retrieved from its complex array and the elements parsed into variables. If store (which is the store_id) doesn't match the one that its on, Perl moves on to the next record. The result is that a store header is displayed and all of the inventory information requested is displayed for the store before going on to the next store's data.

You can accomplish this task in many ways—some simpler and some tighter—but this gives you a general idea of how to perform such a task, without keeping the connection to MySQL open while processing data. For more details on using the Perl DBI with MySQL, see Alligator Descartes and Tim Bunce's book, *Programming the Perl DBI* (O'Reilly).

Perl DBI Method and Function Reference

The following is a list of DBI methods and functions in alphabetical order. The syntax and an explanation of each as well as examples of the use of most is provided. However, to save space, the examples are only excerpts and are missing some components, such as the calling of the DBI module and the creation of a database handle. See the previous tutorial for an example of a complete Perl DBI script. In addition to passing parameters, you can affect the behavior of several methods by setting global values called *attributes*. See the end of this chapter for a list of attributes.

available_drivers( )

```
DBI->available_drivers([nowarn])
```

This returns a list of available DBD drivers. Any warning messages may be suppressed by providing the text *nowarn* as an argument.

```
...
my @drivers = DBI->available_drivers( )
              || die "No drivers found.";
foreach my $driver(@drivers) {
    print "$driver\n";
}
exit;
```

begin_work( )

```
$database_handle->begin_work( )
```

This temporarily turns AutoCommit off until commit( ) or rollback( ) is run. There are no arguments to this database handle method.

bind_col( )

```
$statement_handle->bind_col(index, \$variable[, \%attributes])
```

This associates or binds a column from a statement handle to a given variable. The values are updated when the related row is retrieved using a fetch method, without extra copying of data.

```
...
my $sql_stmnt = "SELECT title, author FROM books";
my $sth = $dbh->prepare($sql_stmnt);
$sth->execute( );

$sth->bind_col(1, \$title);
$sth->bind_col(2, \$author);

while($sth->fetch( )) {
    print "$title by $author \n";
}
```

A separate statement has to be issued for each bind. To bind multiple columns in one statement, use bind_columns( ).

bind_columns( )

```
$statement_handle->bind_columns([\%attributes,] @references)
```

This associates or binds columns from a statement handle to a given list (*@references*) of variables. The values are updated when the related row is retrieved using a fetch method without extra copying of data. The number of variables given must match the number of columns selected and the columns are assigned to variables in the order the columns are returned. Attributes common to all DBI handles may be stated as the first argument.

```
...
my $sql_stmnt = "SELECT title, author FROM books";
my $sth = $dbh->prepare($sql_stmnt);
$sth->execute();

$sth->bind_columns(\$title, \$author);

while($sth->fetch()) {
    print "$title by $author \n";
}
```

bind_param()

$statement_param(*index, values*[, *type*])

This associates or binds a value in an SQL statement to a placeholder. Placeholders are indicated by ? in SQL statements and are numbered in the order they appear in the statement, starting with 1. The first argument indicates which placeholder to replace with a given value, the second argument. The datatype may be specified as a third argument.

```
...
my $sql_stmnt = "SELECT title, publisher
                    FROM books WHERE author = ?";
my $sth = $dbh->prepare($sql_stmnt);
$sth->bind_param(1, $author);
$sth->execute();

while($sth->fetch()) {
    print "$title ($publisher) \n";
}
```

In this example, a placeholder (a question mark) is given in the SQL statement and is replaced with the actual value of $author using bind_param(). This must be done before the execute() is issued.

bind_param_array()

$statement_handle->bind_param_array(*index, values*[,

$$\%attributes|type])$$

This associates or binds an array of values in an SQL statement within a prepare() using placeholders. The first argument indicates which placeholder to replace with the array of given values, the second argument. The values are updated when the related row is retrieved using a fetch method. Attributes may be added or the datatype given as a third argument.

bind_param_inout( )

$statement_handle->bind_param_inout(*index, values*[, *length,*

\%*attributes*|*type*])

This associates or binds a value in an SQL statement using a placeholder. The first argument indicates which placeholder to replace with a given value, the second argument. The values are updated when the related row is retrieved using a fetch method. The maximum length of a value may be given in the third argument. Attributes may be added or the datatype may be given as a fourth argument.

can( )

$handle->can($*method_name*)

This returns true if the method named is implemented by the driver.

Perl API

clone( )

$database_handle->clone([\%*attributes*])

Use this to create a new database handle by copying the parameters of the database handle calling the method. Additional attributes may be given with the method.

    my $dbh1 = $dbh->clone({AutoCommit=>1});

column_info( )

$database_handle->column_info($*catalog*, $*schema*, $*table*, $*column*)

This returns a statement handle for fetching information about columns in a table.

commit( )

$database_handle->commit( )

This commits or makes permanent changes to a database. It's disregarded if AutoCommit is already enabled.

connect( )

DBI->connect(DBI:*server*:*database*[:*host*:*port*],

            username, password[, \%*attributes*])

Use this to establish a connection to MySQL and to select a database. The first argument includes a list of settings separated by colons. The name of the module (DBI), the type of server (mysql), and the name of the database to use are required. The hostname or IP address and port number are optional. The second argument is the username and the third is the user's password. You can substitute any of these settings or values with variables—just be sure to enclose each argument containing variables with double quotes so that the values will be interpolated. Finally, attributes may be given in the fourth argument.

```perl
my $dbh = DBI->connect('DBI:mysql:bookstore:localhost',
                       'jacinta','richardson',
                       {AutoCommit=>0});
```

In this excerpt, Perl is connecting to the MySQL server with the username of *jacinta* and the password of *richardson*, with the database *bookstore*. The attribute of AutoCommit is set to off so that changes to the data may be undone using rollback( ). See the end of this chapter for a list of attributes.

connect_cached( )

DBI->connect_cached(DBI:*server*:*database*[:*host*:*port*],

user, password[, \%attributes])

This is similar to connect( ), except that the database handle is stored in a hash with the given parameters. This allows the database handle to be reused if connect_cached( ) is called again. You can access and eliminate with the CachedKids attribute.

data_sources( )

DBI->data_sources([*driver*, \%attributes])

This returns a list of databases associated with a given driver. If none is specified, the driver named in the environment variable DBI_DRIVER is used. Attributes may be given as a second argument.

```perl
...
my @drivers = DBI->available_drivers( );
        || die "No drivers found.";
foreach my $driver(@drivers) {
   my @sources = DBI->data_sources($driver);
   foreach my $source(@sources) {
      print "$driver:  $source\n";
   }
}
```

disconnect( )

$*database_handle*->disconnect( )

This disconnects a Perl script from a database; it ends a MySQL session. There are no arguments for this function.

```perl
$sth->finish( );
$dbh->disconnect( );
```

It's appropriate to end all statement handles before disconnecting from MySQL using the finish( ) function as shown here.

do( )

$database_handle->do(statement[, \%attributes, @values])

This executes an SQL statement without having to use the prepare( ) method. It returns the number of rows changed. The first argument contains an SQL statement. If placeholders are used in the SQL statement, their values are provided in a comma-separated list or an array in the third argument. Statement handle attributes may be given for the second argument.

```
   ...
my $sql_stmnt = "UPDATE books SET publisher = ?
                  WHERE publisher = ?";
$dbh->do($sql_stmnt, '', 'Oxford Univ. Press', 'OUP');
$dbh->disconnect( );
```

In this example, the initials of a particular publisher are changed to the publisher's name. The SQL statement is executed without a prepare( ) or an execute( ). Therefore, a finish( ) isn't required, just a disconnect( ) is.

dump_results( )

$statement_handle->dump_results(length, row_delimiter,

column_delimiter, filehandle})

This displays the results of a statement using the neat_list( ) function on each row for the statement handle given. The first argument is the maximum length of each column's display. For columns containing more characters than the maximum length, the excess will be omitted and ellipses will be presented in its place. The default length is 35 characters. For the second argument, the delimiter for each row may be given—the default is \n. The delimiter for columns may also be changed from the default of a comma and a space in the third argument. In the last argument of the function, a file handle of where to direct the results of the function may be given. If one is not specified, stdout is used.

```
   ...
my $sql_stmnt = "SELECT title, authors
                  FROM books
                  WHERE author= 'Henry James' LIMIT 3";
my $sth = $dbh->prepare($sql_stmnt);
$sth->execute( );
$results = $sth->dump_results(10, "\n", '|');
   ...
```

The results of the preceding script would look like this:

```
'The Boston...'|'Henry James'
'The Muse'|'Henry James'
'Washington...'|'Henry James'
3 rows
```

err( )

$handle->err( )

This returns any error codes from the last driver method call.

```
    . . .
    my $dbh = DBI->connect('DBI:mysql:bookstore:localhost',
                           'username','password')
             || die 'Could not connect; Error Code: '
             . DBI->err;
```

errstr( )

$handle->errstr( )

This returns any error messages from the last driver method called.

```
    . . .
    my $dbh = DBI->connect('DBI:mysql:bookstore:localhost',
                           'username',"password')
             || die 'Could not connect to database: '
             . DBI->errstr;
```

The error message given in the die statement is joined to the DBI error message.

execute( )

$statement_handle->execute( )

This executes a statement handle that has been processed with the prepare( ) method. There are no arguments to this function.

```
    . . .
    my $dbh = DBI->connect ("$data_source","$user","$pwd")
    my $sql_stmnt = "SELECT * FROM books";
    my $sth = $dbh->prepare($sql_stmnt);
    $sth->execute( );
```

Although this excerpt will execute the given statement, it will not display the results. To do this, a method like fetchrow_array( ) is needed.

execute_array( )

$statement_handle->execute_array([\%attributes, @values)

Use this to execute a prepared statement multiple times, once for each set of values given either as the second argument of the method or from previous uses of the bind_param_array( ) method.

execute_for_fetch( )

execute_for_fetch($*fetch*[, \@*status*])

Use this to execute multiple statements given as the argument of the method.

fetch( )

$*statement_handle*->fetch( )

This returns a reference to an array of one row from the results of a statement handle. It's synonymous with fetchrow_arrayref( ). There are no arguments for this function.

fetchall_arrayref( )

$*statement_handle*->fetchall_arrayref( )

This captures the results of a statement and returns a reference to the data. The results is a complex data structure; an array of references to an array for each row of data retrieved.

```
...
my $sql_stmnt = "SELECT title, author FROM books";
my $sth = $dbh->prepare($sql_stmnt);
$sth->execute( );
my $books = $sth->fetchall_arrayref( );
$sth->finish( );
foreach my $book (@$books) {
   my ($title, $author) = @$book;
   print "$title by $author \n";
}
$sth->finish( );
```

fetchall_hashref( )

$*statement_handle*->fetchall_hashref(*key_column*)

This captures the result of a statement and returns a reference to the data. The result is a complex data structure: a hash of references to a hash of each row of data retrieved. By specifying the column to use as a key for the primary hash, a particular row may be accessed and thereby other columns.

```
...
my $sql_stmnt = "SELECT book_id, title, authors FROM books";
my $sth = $dbh->prepare($sql_stmnt);
$sth->execute( );
$books = $sth->fetchall_hashref('book_id');

foreach my $book_id (%$books) {
   print "$books->{$book_id}->{title} by
              $books->{$book_id}->{author} \n";
}
$sth->finish( );
```

fetchrow_array( )

$statement_handle->fetchrow_array( )

This returns one row from the results of a statement handle in the form of an array, each of whose element is a column.

```
...
my $sql_stmnt = "SELECT title, author FROM books";
my $sth = $dbh->prepare($sql_stmnt);
$sth->execute( );
while (my ($title, $author) = $sth->fetchrow_array( )){
    print "$title by $author \n";
}
$sth->finish( );
```

fetchrow_arrayref( )

$statement_handle->fetchrow_arrayref( )

This returns a reference to a place in memory containing an array of one row from the results of a statement handle. There are no arguments for this function. It's synonymous with fetch( ).

```
...
my $sql_stmnt = "SELECT title, author FROM books";
my $sth = $dbh->prepare($sql_stmnt);
$sth->execute( );
while (my $book = $sth->fetchrow_arrayref( )) {
    my ($title, $author) = @$book;
    print "$title by $author \n";
}
$sth->finish( );
```

Notice that fetchrow_arrayref( ) is reused at the beginning of each pass through the while statement. This is because a reference to one row is retrieved at a time.

fetchrow_hashref( )

$statement_handle->fetchrow_hashref( )

This returns a reference to a place in memory containing a hash of keys and values for one row from the results of a statement handle. There are no arguments for this function.

```
...
my $sql_stmnt = "SELECT title, author FROM books";
my $sth = $dbh->prepare($sql_stmnt);
$sth->execute( );
while (my $book_ref = $sth->fetchrow_hashref( )) {
    print "$book_ref->{'title'} by $book_ref->{'author'} \n";
}
$sth->finish( );
```

finish( )

*$statement_handle->*finish( )

This ends a statement handle given that was established by the prepare( ) method. There are no arguments to the method.

    $sth->finish( );

Although a statement handle may have been closed with finish( ), more statement handles may be created and executed as long as the database handle has not been closed using disconnect( ).

foreign_key_info( )

*$database_handle->*foreign_key_info(

                    $pk_catalog, $pk_schema, $pk_table,

                    $fk_catalog, $fk_schema, $fk_table

                    [, *\%attributes*])

This returns a handle for fetching information about foreign keys in a given table.

func( )

*$handle->*func(*@arguments, function_name*)

This calls private nonportable and nonstandard methods for handles. The name of the function is given as the second argument. Any arguments for the function specified are given in the first argument of this method.

get_info( )

*$database_handle->*get_info(*type*)

This returns information about the database handle for the numeric code type (based on SQL standards) given as an argument to the method. Information can include the driver and the capabilities of the data source. The function returns undef for an unknown type.

installed_versions( )

DBI->installed_versions( )

This returns a list of installed drivers. There are no arguments to this method. Enter the following from the command line to see results:

    perl -MDBI -e 'DBI->installed_versions'

last_insert_id( )

*$database_handle->*last_insert_id( )

This returns the value stored in the row identification column of the most recent row inserted for the current MySQL session, provided the identification number was incremented using AUTO_INCREMENT in MySQL. It works like the LAST_INSERT_ID( ) function in MySQL. No arguments for this function are necessary with MySQL. This function doesn't work with MySQL before Version 1.45 of DBI.

looks_like_number( )

DBI::looks_like_number(*@array*)

This returns 1 for each element in an array that appears to be a number.

neat( )

DBI::neat(*string*[, *length*])

This returns a string given as the first argument of the function, placed in quotes, for an optional maximum length given as the second argument.

```
#!/usr/bin/perl -w
use DBI;

my $test = "This is a test.";
print "Test: " . DBI::neat($test, 8) . "\n\n";
exit;
```

Here are the results of running this script:

```
Test: 'This is...'
```

Notice that the results are in single quotes, that the text was truncated based on the maximum length given, and that ellipses were automatically placed at the end of the string. To neaten a list of strings, use the neat_list( ) function.

neat_list( )

DBI::neat_list(\@*strings*[, *length, delimiter*])

This returns a list of strings given as the first argument of the function, placed in quotes, each truncated to an optional maximum length given as the second argument. An optional third argument can specify a delimiter to place between the elements of the list or array given in the first argument. A comma and a space will be used by default if no delimiter is specified.

```
#!/usr/bin/perl -w
use DBI;

my @test = ("This is a test.", "Another test");
print "Test: " . DBI::neat_list(\@test, 8);
exit;
```

Here are the results of this script:

```
Test: 'This is...', 'Another...'
```

parse_dsn( )

DBI->parse_dsn($*data_source_name*)

This returns the components of the DBI Data Source Name (DSN) values: the scheme (i.e., dbi); the driver (i.e, $ENV{DBI_DRIVER}); an optional attribute string; a reference to a hash with the attribute names and values; and the DSN DBI string.

```
...
my ($scheme, $driver, $attributes_string,
        $attributes_hash, $driver_dsn) = DBI->parse_dsn($dsn);
```

parse_trace_flag( )

$*handle*->parse_trace_flag($*settings*)

This returns a bit flag for a trace flag name given as an argument to this method. To parse a list of trace flags, see parse_trace_flags( ).

parse_trace_flags( )

$*handle*->parse_trace_flags($*settings*)

Use this to parse a string given as an argument that contains a list of trace settings. These settings are either trace flag names or integers representing trace levels.

ping( )

$*database_handle*->ping( )

Use this to determine if a MySQL server is still running and the database connection is still available. There are no arguments for this method.

```
...
$results = $dbh->ping( );
print "Results:  $results";
...
```

prepare( )

$*statement_handle* = $*database_handle*->prepare(*statement*[, \%*attribute*])

This creates a statement handle by preparing an SQL statement given as the first argument for subsequent execution with execute( ). It returns a reference to the statement handle. The second argument of this function is a hash of attributes.

```
my $dbh = DBI->connect ("$data_source","$user","$pwd")
my $sql_stmnt = "SELECT * FROM books";
my $sth = $dbh->prepare($sql_stmnt,
                    {RaiseError => 1, ChopBlanks => 1});
```

In this example, warning messages are enabled and trailing spaces of fixed-width character columns are trimmed. See the end of this chapter for a list of attributes.

prepare_cached( )

$database_handle->prepare_cached($sql_standard[, \%attribute, $active])

This creates a statement handle like prepare( ), but stores the resulting statement handle in a hash. Attributes for a statement handle may be given in the second argument in the form of a hash. The third argument of the method changes the behavior of the handle if an active statement handle is already in the cache. Table 12-1 lists the four choices for this argument.

Table 12-1. Active argument for prepare_cached( )

Active value	Result
0	Warning messages will be issued, and finish( ) for the statement handle will be employed.
1	No warning will be displayed, but finish( ) will be executed.
2	Disables checking for an active handle.
3	Causes the new statement handle to replace the active one.

primary_key( )

$database_handle->primary_key($catalog, $schema, $table)

This returns a list of primary key column names for a given table.

primary_key_info( )

$database_handle->primary_key_info($catalog, $schema, $table)

This returns a statement handle for fetching information about primary key columns for a table.

quote( )

$database_handle->quote(string)

Use this to escape special characters contained in a given string. It's useful in SQL statements particularly for unknown user input that might contain metacharacters that would cause undesirable behavior by MySQL.

```
...
my $comment = "Henry James' book \"The Muse\" is wonderful!";
my $quoted_comment = $dbh->quote($comment);
my $sql_stmnt = "UPDATE books SET comment = ?";
my $sth = $dbh->prepare($sql_stmnt);
$sth->execute($quoted_comment);
```

quote_identifier( )

$database_handle->quote_identifier($name)

$database_handle->quote_identifier($catalog, $schema,

$table, \%attributes)

Use this to escape special characters of an identifier for use in an SQL statement. In the first syntax, the one parameter could be an identifier such as a table name. For the second syntax, the catalog name or link is given for the first parameter, a schema for the second, a table name for the third, and database attributes for the fourth. Here is an example of the first syntax:

```
my $sql_stmnt = "SHOW indexes FROM "
                 . $dbh->quote_identifier($table);
```

Below is an example of the second syntax:

```
my $table_identifier = $dbh->quote_identifier('link', 'schema', 'table');
```

The value of $table_identifier would be "schema"."table"@"link".

rollback( )

$database_handle->rollback( )

Use this to undo the last change to an InnoDB or BDB table. It requires that the database handle was created with the attribute of AutoCommit set to false or 0, and that the change was not committed using the commit( ) function.

rows( )

$statement_handle->rows( )

This returns the number of rows affected by the last statement handle executed. It works with UPDATE, INSERT, and DELETE dependably. It doesn't work effectively with SELECT statements unless they select all rows in a table. If the number of rows is unknown, -1 is returned. There are no arguments to this method.

```
...
my $sql_stmnt = "UPDATE books SET author = 'Robert B. Parker'
                 WHERE author = 'Robert Parker'";
my $sth = $dbh->prepare($sql_stmnt);
$sth->execute( );
my $change_count = $sth->rows( );
print "$change_count rows were changed.";
```

This script displays the following when run:

```
2 rows were changed
```

selectall_arrayref( )

$database_handle*->selectall_arrayref(*$statement, \%*attributes*, @*bind_values*)

This returns a reference to an array of references to arrays containing data for each row retrieved from the results of an SQL statement given. This method combines prepare( ), execute( ), and fetchall_arrayref( ). An optional second argument can specify any of the attributes allowed for a statement handle. If placeholders are used in the SQL statement, their values must be given as an array for the third argument.

```
my $sql_stmnt = "SELECT title, author
                   FROM books WHERE book_id = ?";
my $books = $dbh->selectall_arrayref($sql_stmnt,
              undef, '1234');
foreach my $book (@$books) {
   my ($title, $author) = @$book;
   print "$title by $author \n";
}
```

selectall_hashref( )

$database_handle*->selectall_hashref(*$statement, *$key_field*,

\%*attributes*, @*bind_values*)

This returns a reference to a hash of references to hashes, one for each row from the results of an SQL statement given. This method combines prepare( ), execute( ), and fetchall_hashref( ). An optional second argument can specify any of the attributes allowed for a statement handle. If placeholders are used in the SQL statement, their values must be given as an array for the third argument.

```
...
my $sql_stmnt = "SELECT rec_id, title, author
                   FROM books";
my $books = $dbh->selectall_hashref($sql_stmnt, 'book_id');

foreach my $book_id (keys %$books) {
   print "$books->{$book_id}{title}
          by $books->{$book_id}{author} \n";
}
```

selectcol_arrayref( )

$database_handle*->selectcol_arrayref(*$sql_statement[,

\%*attributes*, @*bind_values*])

This returns a reference to an array containing a value in the first column of each row selected. The SQL statement is given as the first argument of the function. This can be particularly useful if the first column is a key field. This function performs prepare( ) and execute( ) on the SQL statement.

```
...
my $sql_stmnt = "SELECT * FROM books";
my $book = $dbh->selectcol_arrayref($sql_stmnt);
```

```
foreach my $author_id (@$book){
    print "$author_id \n";
}
```

selectrow_array( )

$*database_handle*->selectrow_array($*sql_statement*[,

$\%attributes, @values$])

This returns one row from the results of an SQL statement in the form of an array, where each column returned is represented by an element of the array, in order. This method combines prepare( ), execute( ), and fetchrow_array( ). No statement handle is created, so finish( ) is unnecessary. An optional second argument can specify any of the attributes allowed for a statement handle. If placeholders are used in the SQL statement, their values must be given as an array for the third argument.

```
...
my $sql_stmnt = "SELECT title, author
                 FROM books WHERE book_id = ?";
my ($title, $author) = $dbh->selectrow_array(
        $sql_stmnt, undef, '1234');
print "$title by $author \n";
```

No attributes are given for the SQL statement, so undef is used for the second argument. The third argument provides the *book_id* number for the placeholder in the SQL statement.

selectrow_arrayref( )

$*database_handle*->selectrow_arrayref($*sql_statement*[,

$\%attributes, @values$])

This returns a reference to an array of one row from the results of an SQL statement given. This method combines prepare( ), execute( ), and fetchrow_arrayref( ). An optional second argument can specify any of the attributes allowed for a statement handle. If placeholders are used in the SQL statement, their values must be given as an array for the third argument.

```
...
my $sql_stmnt = "SELECT title, author
                 FROM books WHERE book_id = ?";
my $book = $dbh->selectrow_arrayref($sql_stmnt,
                          undef, '1234');

my ($title, $author) = @$book;
print "$title by $author \n";
```

selectrow_hashref( )

$database_handle->selectrow_hashref($sql_statement[,

\%attributes, @values])

This returns a reference to a hash of one row from the results of an SQL statement given. This method combines prepare( ), execute( ), and fetchrow_hashref( ). Attributes that may be given for a statement handle may be provided in a hash for the second argument of this method. If placeholders are used in the SQL statement, their values may be given as an array for the third argument.

```
...
my $sql_stmnt = "SELECT title, author
                 FROM books WHERE book_id = ?";
my $book_ref = $dbh->selectrow_hashref($sql_stmnt,
              undef, '1234');
print "$book_ref->{title} by $book_ref->{author} \n";
```

Notice that the method captures the names of the columns as the keys to the values in the hash generated.

set_err( )

$handle->set_err($err, $errstr[,

$state, $method, $return_value])

This sets the values for err, errstr, and state for the handle.

state( )

$handle->state( )

This returns the error code of an error in a five-character format.

table_info( )

$database_handle->table_info($catalog, $schema, $table,

$type[, \%attributes])

This returns a statement handle for fetching information about a table in a database.

```
...
my $dbinfo = $dbh->table_info( );
while( my($qualifier,$owner,$name,$type,$remarks) =
      $dbinfo->fetchrow_array( )) {
    foreach ($qualifier,$owner,$name,$type,$remarks) {
      $_ = '' unless defined $_;
    }
    print "Info:  $qualifier $owner $name $type $remarks \n";
}
```

table_info_all( )

$database_handle->table_info_all($catalog, $schema, $table,

$type[, \%attributes])

This returns a statement handle for fetching information about a table in a database.

tables( )

$database_handle->tables($catalog, $schema, $table, $type)

This returns a list of tables for a database handle.

trace( )

$handle->trace(level[, log])

This sets the trace level for a handle. A level of 0 disables tracing; level 1 traces the execution of the database handle; level 2 provides more details including parameter values. If a filename is given as the second argument, trace information will be appended to that logfile instead of stderr.

trace_msg( )

$handle->trace_msg(message[, level])

This adds text given in first argument to trace data. A minimum trace level (see trace( ) method) required for the message to be used may be specified as a second argument.

type_info( )

$database_handle->type_info([$data_type])

This returns a hash containing information on a given datatype.

```
...
my $dbinfo = $dbh->type_info( );
while(my($key, $value) = each(%$dbinfo)){
   print "$key => $value\n";
}
```

type_info_all( )

$database_handle->type_info_all( )

This returns a reference to an array of all datatypes supported by the driver.

Attributes for Handles

This section lists the values that can be added to the optional %attributes hash that appears in many Perl DBI methods. The basic syntax to set an attribute is `$handle->{attribute} = 'setting';` to retrieve a setting use `$handle->{attribute}`.

Attributes for All Handles

You can use the following attributes with both database handles and statement handles.

Active
: Instructs the server that the handle should remain open until terminated explicitly by `finish()` or `disconnect()` depending on the handle type.

ActiveKids
: Provides the number of active handles under the handle that employed the attribute. If it's set by a database handle, then the number of active statement handles will be returned. If it's called by a database handle, the number of active statement handles will be returned. If set by a driver handle, the number of database handles will be returned.

CacheKids
: Returns a reference to a hash containing child handles for a driver or a database handle that was created by the `connect_cached()` or `prepare_cached()` methods, respectively.

ChopBlanks
: Trims trailing spaces from fixed-width character columns.

CompatMode
: Makes emulation layers compatible with a driver handle.

ErrCount
: Counts the number of errors logged by `set_err()`.

Executed
: Determines whether a handle or one of its children has been executed.

FetchHashKeyName
: Instructs `fetchrow_hashref()` calls to convert column names to either all lowercase (`NAME_lc`) or all uppercase (`NAME_uc`) letters.

HandleError
: Customizes the response to an error caused by the handle. You could use this attribute to run a subroutine in the event of an error.

HandleSetErr
: Customizes the settings of an error caused by the handle. It's similar to the `HandleError` attribute, but it relates to `set_err()`.

InactiveDestroy
: Prevents the server from destroying a handle that is out of scope, unless it is closed intentionally with a function like `finish()` or `disconnect()`.

Kids
>   Provides the number of all handles (active and inactive) under the handle that
>   employed the attribute. If it's called by a database handle, the number of
>   statement handles will be returned. If it's called by a driver handle, the
>   number of database handles will be returned.

LongReadLen
>   Sets the maximum length of data retrieved from long datatype columns (i.e.,
>   BLOB and TEXT).

LongTruncOK
>   Prevents a fetch method from failing if a column's data exceeds the maximum
>   length by the LongReadLen attribute.

PrintError
>   Obtains error codes and error messages associated with the handle.

PrintWarn
>   Controls the warning messages that are logged.

private_*
>   Stores information on the handle as a private attribute with a customized
>   name starting with private_.

Profile
>   Enables logging of method call timing statistics.

RaiseError
>   Raises exceptions when errors are associated with the handle.

ShowErrorStatement
>   Specifies text to append to error messages caused by the PrintError,
>   PrintWarn, and RaiseError attributes.

Taint
>   Combines TaintIn and TaintOut attributes.

TaintIn
>   Instructs DBI to check if method calls are tainted, when Perl is run in taint
>   mode.

TaintOut
>   Instructs DBI to assume that data fetched is tainted, when Perl is running in
>   taint mode.

TraceLevel
>   Sets trace levels and flags for a handle. It's an alternative to the trace( )
>   method.

Warn
>   Enables or disables warning messages for poor database procedures.

Attributes Only for Database Handles

AutoCommit
>   Allows the rollback( ) function to be used if attribute is 0.

Driver
> Provides the name of the parent driver.

Name
> Provides the name of the database for the database handle.

RowCacheSize
> Provides a suggested cache size for rows generated for SELECT statements. If it's 0, DBI automatically determines the cache size. A value of 1 disables local row caching.

Statement
> Provides the last SQL statement prepared with the database handle regardless of whether it succeeded.

Username
> Provides the name of the user for the database handle.

Attributes Only for Statement Handles

CursorName
> Sets the name of the cursor for the statement handle.

Database
> Provides the database handle of the statement handle.

Name
> Contains a reference to an array containing the names of the columns of the SQL statement from the statement handle.

NULLABLE
> Contains a reference to an array indicating whether each column in the SQL statement of the handle may contain a NULL value.

NUM_OF_FIELDS
> Returns the number of columns in the SQL statement of the handle.

NUM_OF_PARAMS
> Returns the number of placeholders in the SQL statement of the handle.

ParamValues
> Returns a reference to a hash of bound parameters and their values.

Statement
> Is the SQL statement passed to prepare( ).

TYPE
> Contains a reference to an array of codes for international standard values for data-types (e.g., 1 for SQL_CHAR, 4 for SQL_INTEGER).

PRECISION
> Contains a reference to an array containing the length of columns (as set in the table definition) in the SQL statement of the handle.

SCALE
> Contains a reference to an array containing the number of decimal places for columns in the SQL statement of the handle.

DBI Dynamic Attributes

These attributes are related to the last handle used, regardless of the type of handle. The syntax of each of these is `$DBI::`*`attribute`*.

err
> Is synonymous with `$handle->err`.

errstr
> Is synonymous with `$handle->errstr`.

lasth
> Returns the handle used by the last method call.

rows
> Is synonymous with `$handle->rows`.

state
> Is synonymous with `$handle->state`.

Perl API

13

PHP API

One of the most popular programming language and database engine combinations for the Web is PHP with MySQL. This combination works well for many reasons: primarily the speed, stability, and simplicity of both applications. The first part of this chapter provides a basic tutorial on how to connect to MySQL and how to query MySQL with PHP. Following the tutorial is a reference of PHP MySQL functions in alphabetical order. For the examples in this chapter, a database for a fictitious computer support business is used. The database contains one table with client work requests (*workreq*) and another with client contact information (*clients*).

Using PHP with MySQL

This section presents the basic tasks you need to query a MySQL database from PHP.

Connecting to MySQL

For a PHP script to interface to MySQL, first you must make a connection to it, thus establishing a MySQL session. To connect to the *workrequests* database, a PHP script might begin like so:

```
<?php

$host = 'localhost';
$user = 'russell';
$pw = 'dyer';
$db = 'workrequests';

mysql_connect($host, $user, $pw)
    or die(mysql_error);
mysql_select_db($db);

?>
```

This section of PHP code starts by establishing the variables with information necessary for connecting to MySQL and the database. After that, PHP connects to MySQL by giving the host and user variables. If it's unsuccessful, the script dies with an error message. If the connection is successful, though, the *workrequests* database is selected for use. Each PHP script example in this chapter begins with a section of code like this one.

Querying MySQL

In the fictitious database is a table called *workreq* that contains information on client work requests. To retrieve a list of work requests and some basic information on clients, a PHP script begins by connecting to MySQL, as shown in the previous script excerpt. That is followed by the start of a web page and then the invocation of an SQL statement to retrieve and display the data. You can achieve this with code such as the following:

```
...  // Connect to MySQL

<html>
<body>
<h2>Work Requests</h2>

<?php
$sql_stmnt = "SELECT wrid, client_name,
              wr_date, description
              FROM workreq, clients
              WHERE status = 'done'
              AND workreq.clientid = clients.clientid";

$results = mysql_query($sql_stmnt)
           or printf("%s", mysql_error());

while(mysql_fetch_row($results)) {
   list($wrid, $client_name, $wr_date, $description) = $row;
   print "<a href='detail.php?wrid=$wrid'>$client_name -
           $desription ($wr_date)</a><br/>";
}

mysql_close();
?>
</body>
</html>
```

After connecting to MySQL (substituted with ellipses here) and starting the web page, a variable ($sql_stmnt) containing the SQL statement is created. Then the database is queried with the SQL statement and a reference to the results set is stored in a variable ($results). The query is followed by an or statement, a common PHP syntax for error checking. The print statement executes only if no results were found.

Assuming PHP was successful in querying the database, a while statement is used to loop through each row of data retrieved from MySQL. With each pass, using the mysql_fetch_row( ) function, PHP will temporarily store the fields of data for each row in an array ($row). Within the code block of the while statement, the PHP list( ) function parses the elements of the $row array into their respective variables. The variables here are named to match their column counterparts. This is not necessary, though. They may be named anything. The array could even be used as it is and the appropriate sequence number referred to retrieve data. For instance, for the date of the work request, $row[2] could be used, because it's the third in the sequence (0 is first). Naming the variables as they are here, though, makes it easier to read the code and easier for others to follow later.

The second line of code within the while statement displays the data in the format required for the web page. The data is wrapped in a hyperlink with a reference to another PHP script (*details.php*), which will retrieve all of the details for the particular work request selected by a user. That work request will be identified by the work request number (i.e., *wrid*), which is a key column for the *details.php* PHP script. The value for *wrid* typically will automatically be placed in a variable by the same name ($wrid) regardless of what the variable is named in this script. It's based on the name given in the hyperlink or anchor tag. This will happen if the *php.ini* configuration file has *register_globals* set to *on*, something which is not the case in recent versions of PHP. On Unix and Linux systems, this file is located in the */etc* directory. On a Windows system, it's usually found in the *c:\windows* directory. If not, the value can be referenced using the $_POST associative array, which is describe in PHP's online documentation (*http://www.php.net*).

The output of this script is a line for each uncompleted work request found in the database. Each line will be linked to another script that presumably would provide details on the work request selected. In this simple example, only a few of the many PHP MySQL functions are used to display data. In the next section of this chapter, each function is described with script excerpts as examples of their use.

PHP MySQL Functions in Alphabetical Order

The rest of this chapter contains a list of PHP MySQL functions in alphabetical order. Each function is given with its syntax and an explanation. An example script, or script excerpt, is provided to show how you can use the function. To save space, almost all of the script excerpts are shown without the lines of code necessary to start a PHP script and to connect to MySQL, or following code to close the connection and to end the script. For an example showing how you would write these opening and closing lines, see the tutorial in the previous section.

mysql_affected_rows( )

```
mysql_affected_rows([connection])
```
This returns the number of rows affected by a previous SQL statement that modified rows of data for the current MySQL session. The function returns -1 if the previous statement failed. It works only after INSERT, UPDATE, and DELETE statements. See mysql_num_rows( ) for the number of rows returned by a SELECT statement. The connection identifier may be given as an argument to retrieve the number of rows affected by a different connection.

```
...
$sql_stmnt = "UPDATE workreq
                SET due_date = ADDDATE(due_date, INTERVAL 1 DAY)
                WHERE due_date = '2004-07-28'";
mysql_query($sql_stmnt);

$updated = mysql_affected_rows();
print "Number of Rows Updated: $updated \n";
...
```

This script changes the due dates for all work requests by one day.

mysql_change_user( )

mysql_change_user(*user, password*[, *database, connection*])

Use this to change the username for a MySQL connection. The new username is given as the first argument and the password for that user as the second. A different database from the one in use may be given as a third argument. The user information may be changed for a different MySQL connection by specifying it as the fourth argument. If the function is successful, true is returned; false is returned if it's unsuccessful. This function is no longer available as of Version 4 of PHP. Instead, a new connection should be established with a different user by using the mysql_connect( ) function:

```
...
mysql_connect('localhost', 'hui', 'shorty');
...
mysql_change_user('russell','dyer');
...
```

In this example, we needed to change the user in the script from *hui* to *russell*. If there had been a third argument, we would have changed to another database.

mysql_client_encoding( )

mysql_client_encoding([*connection*])

This returns the name of the default character set for the current MySQL connection or, if *connection* is supplied, for that connection.

```
...
$info = mysql_client_encoding();
print "Encoding in Use: $info \n";
...
```

Here are the results of this script on my computer:

```
Encoding in Use:  latin1
```

mysql_close( )

mysql_close([*connection*])

This closes the current or last MySQL connection, or a given connection. The function returns true if it's successful; false if unsuccessful. This function will not close persistent connections started with mysql_pconnect( ).

```
...
$connection = mysql_connect('localhost', 'russell', 'dyer');
mysql_select_db('workrequests', $connection);
...
mysql_close($connection);
...
```

If a script has opened only one connection to MySQL, it's not necessary to specify the connection link to close as shown here.

mysql_connect( )

```
mysql_connect(server[:port|socket], user, password[,

            new_link, flags])
```

Use this to start a MySQL connection. The first argument of the function is the server name. If none is specified, *localhost* is assumed. A port may be specified with the server name (separated by a colon) or a socket along with its path. If no port is given, port 3306 is assumed. The username is to be given as the second argument and the user's password as the third. If a connection is attempted that uses the same parameters as a previous one, the existing connection will be used and a new connection link will not be created unless *new_link* is specified as the fourth argument of this function. As an optional fifth argument, client flags may be given for the MySQL constants MYSQL_CLIENT_COMPRESS, MYSQL_CLIENT_IGNORE_SPACE, MYSQL_CLIENT_INTERACTIVE, and MYSQL_CLIENT_SSL. The function returns a connection identifier if successful; it returns false if it's unsuccessful. Use mysql_close( ) to close a connection created by mysql_connect( ).

```
#!/usr/bin/php -q
<?
    mysql_connect('localhost', 'russell', 'dyer');
    mysql_select_db('workrequests');
...
```

To be able to identify the connection link later, especially when a script will be using more than one link, capture the results of mysql_connect( ). Here is a complete script that sets up two connections to MySQL and captures the resource identification number for each link:

```
#!/usr/bin/php -q
<?
$user1 = 'hui';
$user2 = 'russell';
$connection1 = mysql_connect('localhost', $user1, 'shorty');
$connection2 = mysql_connect('localhost', $user2, 'dyer');
mysql_select_db('workrequests');

counter($connection1,$user1);
counter($connection2,$user2);

function counter($connection,$user) {
    $sql_stmnt = "SELECT * FROM workreq";
    $results = mysql_query($sql_stmnt, $connection);
    if(mysql_errno($connection)){
        print "Could not SELECT with $connection for $user. \n";
        return;
```

```
      }
      $count = mysql_num_rows($results);
      print "Number of Rows Found with $connection for $user:
            $count. \n";
   }

   mysql_close($connection1);
   mysql_close($connection2);
   ?>
```

In this example, two links are established with different usernames. The counter( ) subroutine is called twice, once with each connection identifier and username passed to the user-defined function. For the first connection, the user *hui* does not have SELECT privileges, so the SQL statement is unsuccessful. An error is generated and the number of rows is not determined due to the return ending the function call. For the second connection, the user *russell* has the necessary privileges, so the function is completed successfully. The output from running this script on my server follows. Notice in the script that although a separate mysql_close( ) statement is necessary to close each connection, one mysql_select_db( ) is applied to both connections—there's no ambiguity.

```
Could not SELECT with Resource id #1 for hui.
Number of Rows Found with Resource id #2 for russell:   528.
```

mysql_create_db( )

mysql_create_db(*database*[, *connection*])

Use this to create a database in MySQL for the current connection. The name of the database to create is given as the first argument of the function. A different MySQL connection identifier may be given as a second argument. The function returns true if it's successful, false if unsuccessful. This function is deprecated. Use the mysql_query( ) function with a CREATE DATABASE statement instead.

```
...
mysql_create_db('new_db');

$databases = mysql_list_dbs( );
while($db = mysql_fetch_row($databases)) {
   print $db[0] . "\n";
}
...
```

This script will create a new database and then display a list of databases to allow the user to confirm that it was successful.

mysql_data_seek( )

mysql_data_seek(*connection*, *row*)

Use this in conjunction with the mysql_fetch_row( ) function to change the current row being fetched to the one specified in the second argument of this function. The connection identifier is given as the first argument. The function returns true if it's successful; it returns false if it's unsuccessful.

```
...
$sql_stmnt = "SELECT wrid, clientid, description
              FROM workreq";
$results = mysql_query($sql_stmnt);
$count = mysql_num_rows($results);

mysql_data_seek($results, $count - 6);
$row = mysql_fetch_row($results);

while($row = mysql_fetch_object($results)) {
  print "WR-" . $row->wrid . " Client-" . $row->clientid .
        " - " . $row->description .  "\n";
}
...
```

In this script excerpt, the SQL statement is selecting the work request identification numbers for all rows in the table. The results set is stored in $results. Using mysql_num_rows( ) function, the number of rows is determined and placed in the $count variable. To be able to display only the last five work requests, the script calls mysql_data_seek( ). The results set is given as the first argument. In order to get the first row of a results set, the offset would be set to 0: so if a results set contains only one row, the row count of 1 less 1 would need to be given as the second argument of mysql_data_seek( ). For the example here, to get the last five records of the results set, the number of rows is reduced by six to move the pointer to the row before the fifth-to-last row. Here is the last line of the output of this script:

```
WR-5755 Client-1000 - Can't connect to network.
```

mysql_db_name( )

mysql_db_name(*databases, number*)

This returns the name of the database from the results of the mysql_list_dbs( ) function, which returns a pointer to a results set containing the names of databases for a MySQL server. The reference to the list of databases is given as the first argument. A number identifying the row to retrieve from the list is the second argument.

```
...
$databases = mysql_list_dbs( );
$dbs = mysql_num_rows($databases);

for($index = 0; $index < $dbs; $index++) {
    print mysql_db_name($databases, $index) . "\n";
}
...
```

In this script excerpt, a results set containing a list of databases is retrieved and stored in the $databases variable using the mysql_list_dbs( ) function. That results set is analyzed by mysql_num_rows( ) to determined the number of records (i.e., the number of database names) that it contains. Using a for statement and the number of databases ($dbs), the script loops through the results set contained in $databases. With each pass, mysql_db_name( ) extracts the name of each database by changing the second argument of the function as the value of $index increments from 0 to the value of $dbs.

mysql_db_query( )

mysql_db_query(*database, sql_statement*[, *connection*])

Use this to query the database given, for the current MySQL connection (unless another is specified), and to execute the SQL statement given as the second argument. If there isn't currently a connection to the server, it will attempt to establish one. For SQL statements that would not return a results set (e.g., UPDATE statements), true will be returned if the function is successful and false if it's unsuccessful. The mysql_query( ) function may be used instead if the statement is to be executed on the current database.

```
...
$sql_stmnt = "SELECT wrid, clientid, description
              FROM workreq";
$results = mysql_db_query('workrequests', $sql_stmnt);

while($row = mysql_fetch_object($results)) {
  print "WR-" . $row->wrid . ",
         Client-" . $row->clientid . " " .
         $row->description . "\n";
}
...
```

Basically, using mysql_db_query( ) eliminates the need to use mysql_select_db( ) and mysql_query( ).

mysql_drop_db( )

mysql_drop_db(*database*[, *connection*])

Use this to delete the database given from the MySQL server. A different connection identifier may be given as a second argument. The function returns true if it's successful; it returns false if it's unsuccessful. This function has been deprecated. Use the mysql_query( ) function with a DROP DATABASE statement instead.

```
...
mysql_dropdb('old_db');
...
```

mysql_errno( )

mysql_errno([*connection*])

This returns the error code number for the last MySQL statement issued. The function returns 0 if there was no error. Another MySQL connection identifier may be given as an argument for the function.

```
...
$sql_stmnt = "SELECT * FROM workreqs";
$results = mysql_db_query('workrequests', $sql_stmnt)
           or die (mysql_errno() . " " . mysql_error() . "\n");

$count = mysql_num_rows($results);
print "Number of Rows Found:  $count \n";
...
```

I've intentionally typed the name of the table incorrectly in the preceding SQL statement. It should read *workreq* and not *workreqs*. The result of this script follows:

```
1146 Table 'workrequests.workreqs' doesn't exist
```

Notice that the error number code is given by mysql_errno( ) and the message that follows it is given by mysql_error( ), which provides an error message rather than a code.

mysql_error( )

mysql_error([*connection*])

This returns the error message for the last MySQL statement issued. The function returns nothing if there was no error. Another MySQL connection identifier may be given as an argument for the function. See mysql_errno( ) for an example of how mysql_error( ) may be used.

mysql_escape_string( )

mysql_escape_string(*string*)

This returns the string given with special characters preceded by backslashes so that they are protected from being interpreted by the SQL interpreter. This function is used in conjunction with mysql_query( ) to help make SQL statements safe. It's similar to mysql_real_escape_string( ).

```
...
$clientid = '1000';
$description = "Can't connect to network.";
$description=mysql_escape_string($description);

$sql_stmnt = "INSERT INTO workreq
              (date, clientid, description)
              VALUES(NOW( ), '$clientid', '$description')";
mysql_query($sql_stmnt);
...
```

The string contained in the $description variable contains an apostrophe, which would cause the SQL statement to fail. It will fail because the related value in the SQL statement is surrounded by single quotes; an apostrophe would be mistaken for a single quote, which has special meaning in MySQL.

mysql_fetch_array( )

mysql_fetch_array(*results*[, *type*])

This returns an array containing a row of data from an SQL query results set. Data is also stored in an associative array containing the field names as the keys for the values. Field names are derived from either column names or aliases. To choose whether only an array is returned or only an associative array is returned, or both, one of the following may be given as a second argument to the function, respectively: MYSQL_NUM, MYSQL_ASSOC, or MYSQL_BOTH. This function is typically used with a loop statement to work through a results set containing multiple rows of data. When there are no more rows to return, false is returned, which typically triggers the end of the loop.

```
...
$sql_stmnt = "SELECT wrid, clientid, description
                FROM workreq";
$results = mysql_db_query('workrequests', $sql_stmnt);

while($row = mysql_fetch_array($results)) {
  print "WR-" . $row[0] . ", Client-" .
        $row[clientid] . " " . $row[description] . "\n";
}
...
```

Notice that both methods of extracting data from the row fetched are used here: the work request number is retrieved using a standard array data retrieval method (i.e., placing the index number of the array element in square brackets); the other pieces of data are retrieved using the associative array method (i.e., placing the field name and the key name in brackets).

mysql_fetch_assoc( )

mysql_fetch_assoc(*results*)

This returns an associative array containing a row of data from an SQL query results set. Field names of the results set are used as the keys for the values. Field names are derived from column names unless an alias is employed in the SQL statement. This function is typically used with a loop statement to work through a results set containing multiple rows of data. When there are no more rows to return, false is returned, which will end a loop statement. This function is synonymous with mysql_fetch_array( ) with MYSQL_ASSOC as its second argument.

```
...
$sql_stmnt = "SELECT wr_id, client_id, description
                FROM workreq";
$results = mysql_db_query('workrequests', $sql_stmnt);

while($row = mysql_fetch_assoc($results)) {
  print "WR-" . $row[wr_id] . ", Client-" .
        $row[client_id] . " " . $row[description] . "\n";
}
...
```

This loop is identical to the one for mysql_fetch_array( ) except that with the mysql_fetch_assoc( ) function, the index for a standard array could not be used to get the work request number—the wr_id key for the associative array stored in $row has to be used instead.

mysql_fetch_field( )

mysql_fetch_field(*results*[, *offset*])

This returns an object containing information about a field from a results set given. Information is given on the first field of a results set waiting to be returned; the function can be called repeatedly to report on each field of a SELECT statement. A number may be given as the second argument to skip one or more fields. The elements of the object are as follows: *name* for column name; *table* for table name, *max_length* for the maximum length of the column; *not_null*, which has a value of 1 if the column may not have a NULL value; *primary_key*, which has a value of 1 if the column is a primary key column; *unique_key*, which returns 1 if it's a unique key; *multiple_key*, which returns 1 if it's not unique; *numeric*, which returns 1 if it's a numeric datatype; *blob*, which returns 1 if it's a BLOB datatype; *type*, which returns the datatype; *unsigned*, which returns 1 if the column is unsigned; and *zerofill*, which returns 1 if it's a zero-fill column.

```
...
$sql_stmnt = "SELECT * FROM workreq LIMIT 1";
$results = mysql_db_query('workrequests', $sql_stmnt);
$num_fields = mysql_num_fields($results);

for ($index = 0; $index < $num_fields; $index++) {
  $info = mysql_fetch_field($results, $index);
  print "$info->name  ($info->type $info->max_length) \n";
}
...
```

Here all of the columns for one record are selected and placed in $results. The number of fields is determined by mysql_num_fields( ) for the for statement that follows. The for statement loops through each field of the results set and uses mysql_fetch_field( ) to return the field information in the form of an object. Then the example prints out the name of the field, the datatype, and the maximum length. Here are the first few lines of the output from this script:

```
wr_id   (int 4)
wr_date  (date 10)
clientid  (string 4)
...
```

mysql_fetch_lengths( )

mysql_fetch_lengths(*results*)

This returns an array containing the length of each field of a results set from a MySQL query.

```
...
$sql_stmnt = "SELECT wr_id, description, instructions
              FROM workreq";
$results = mysql_db_query('workrequests', $sql_stmnt);

while($row = mysql_fetch_object($results)) {
  $length = mysql_fetch_lengths($results);
  print "$row->wr_id: description: $length[1],
         instructions: $length[2] \n";
}
...
```

In this example, each work request number is selected, along with the brief description and the lengthy instructions. Looping through each row that is retrieved as an object with mysql_fetch_object( ) and a while statement, the code determines the length of the data for all three fields with mysql_fetch_lengths( ) and places them in an array. Within the statement block of the while statement, the value of the *wr_id* field is extracted, and the length of the *description* field and the *instructions* field is pulled out of the $length array using the relative index number for each. Here are a few lines from the output of this script:

```
...
5753: description: 26, instructions: 254
5754: description: 25, instructions: 156
5755: description: 25, instructions: 170
```

mysql_fetch_object( )

mysql_fetch_object(*result*)

This returns a row of data as an object from the results set given. The function returns false if there are no more rows to return. The field names of the results set are used to retrieve data from the object returned.

```
...
$sql_stmnt = "SELECT count(wrid) AS wr_count, client_name
              FROM workreq, clients
              WHERE status <> 'done'
              AND workreq.clientid = clients.clientid
              GROUP BY workreq.clientid
              ORDER BY wr_count DESC";
$results = mysql_db_query('workrequests', $sql_stmnt);

while($row = mysql_fetch_object($results)) {
  print $row->client_name . " " . $row->wr_count . "\n";
}
...
```

This script is written to generate a list of clients that have outstanding work requests and to give a count of the number of requests for each, in descending order. Within the while statement that follows, each row of the results set is processed with mysql_fetch_object( ). The values of each element of the object created for each row is displayed by calls using the field names, not the column names. For instance, to get the data from the field with the number of work requests, the wr_count alias is used. Here are a few lines from the output of this script:

```
...
Bracey Logistics 3
Neumeyer Consultants 2
Farber Investments 4
```

mysql_fetch_row( )

mysql_fetch_row(*results*)

This returns an array containing a row of data from a results set given. This function is typically used in conjunction with a loop statement to retrieve each row of data in a results set. Each loop retrieves the next row. Individual fields appear in the array in the order they appeared in the SELECT statement, and can be retrieved by an array index. The loop ends when rows are used up, because the function returns NULL.

```
...
```

```
$sql_stmnt = "SELECT wr_id, client_name, description
              FROM workreq, clients
              WHERE workreq.clientid = clients.clientid";
$results = mysql_db_query('workrequests', $sql_stmnt);

while($row = mysql_fetch_row($results)) {
  print "WR-$row[0]: $row[1] - $row[2] \n";
}
...
```

To get the data for each element of the $row array created by mysql_fetch_row( ), the number corresponding to each element must be known. The index of the elements begins with 0, so $row[0] is the first element and, in this case, the work request number, because *wr_id* was the first field requested by the SELECT statement. Here's one line of the output from the previous script:

```
WR-5755: Farber Investments - Can't connect to Internet.
```

mysql_field_flags( )

mysql_field_flags(*results, offset*)

This returns the field flags for a field of a results set given. See mysql_fetch_field( ) for a description of the flags. Specify the desired field through the offset in the second argument.

```
...
$sql_stmnt = "SELECT * FROM workreq LIMIT 1";
$results = mysql_db_query('workrequests', $sql_stmnt);
$num_fields = mysql_num_fields($results);

for ($index = 0; $index < $num_fields; $index++) {
  $field_name = mysql_field_name($results, $index);
  $flags = explode(' ', mysql_field_flags($results, $index));

  print "$field_name \n";
  print_r($flags);
  print "\n\n";
}
...
```

After retrieving one row as a sampler, using a for statement and the number of fields in the results set, this example determines the field name with mysql_field_name( ) and the flags for each field using mysql_field_flags( ). The mysql_field_flags( ) function assembles the flags into an array in which the data is separated by spaces. By using the explode( ) PHP function, the elements of the array are retrieved without having to know the number of elements, and they are stored in $flags. Next, the field name is displayed and the flags are printed out using print_r( ). Here is the output of the script for the first field:

```
wrid
Array
(
    [0] => not_null
    [1] => primary_key
    [2] => auto_increment
)
```

mysql_field_len( )

mysql_field_len(*results*, *index*)

This returns the length from a field of the results set given. Specify the desired field, through the index in the second argument.

```
...
$sql_stmnt = "SELECT * FROM workreq LIMIT 1";
$results = mysql_db_query('workrequests', $sql_stmnt);
$num_fields = mysql_num_fields($results);

for ($index = 0; $index < $num_fields; $index++) {
  $field_name = mysql_field_name($results, $index);
  print "$field_name - " .
        mysql_field_len($results, $index) . "\n";
}
...
```

Here, one row has been retrieved from a table and the number of fields in the results set is determined by mysql_num_fields( ). With a for statement, each field is processed to determine its name using mysql_field_name( ) and the length of each field is ascertained with mysql_field_len( ). Here are a few lines of the output of this script:

```
wrid - 9
wr_date - 10
clientid - 4
...
```

mysql_field_name( )

mysql_field_name(*results*, *index*)

This returns the name of a field from the results set given. To specify a particular field, the index of the field in the results set is given as the second argument—0 being the first field.

```
...
$sql_stmnt = "SELECT * FROM workreq LIMIT 1";
$results = mysql_db_query('workrequests', $sql_stmnt);
$num_fields = mysql_num_fields($results);

for ($index = 0; $index < $num_fields; $index++) {
  $field_name = mysql_field_name($results, $index);
  print $field_name . "\n";
}
...
```

The SQL statement in this example selects one row from the table. Then the results of the query are examined by mysql_num_fields( ) to determine the number of fields. The loop processes each field, starting with field 0 using the mysql_field_name( ) function to extract each field name. The second argument is changed as the $index variable is incremented with each loop.

mysql_field_seek( )

mysql_field_seek(*results*, *index*)

Use this to change the pointer to a different field from the results set given. The amount by which to offset the pointer is given as the second argument.

```
...
$sql_stmnt = "SELECT * FROM workreq LIMIT 1";
$results = mysql_db_query('workrequests', $sql_stmnt,
                          $connection);
$num_fields = mysql_num_fields($results);
mysql_field_seek($results, $num_fields - 3);

for ($index = 0; $index < 3; $index++) {
  $field = mysql_fetch_field($results, $index);
  print "$field->name \n";
}
...
```

This example determines the number of fields and that value, then gives the result as the second argument of the mysql_field_seek( ) function to choose the last three fields of the results set. The for statement prints out the field names of the last three fields using mysql_fetch_field( ).

mysql_field_table( )

mysql_field_table(*results*, *index*)

This returns the name of the table that contains a particular field from the results set given. An offset for the field is given as the second argument. This is useful for a results set derived from an SQL statement involving multiple tables.

```
...
$sql_stmnt = "SELECT wrid, client_name, description
              FROM workreq, clients
              WHERE workreq.clientid = clients.clientid";
$results = mysql_db_query('workrequests', $sql_stmnt);
$num_fields = mysql_num_fields($results);

for ($index = 0; $index < $num_fields; $index++) {
  $table = mysql_field_table($results, $index);
  $field = mysql_field_name($results, $index);
  print "$table.$field  \n";
}
...
```

The SQL statement in this example selects columns from two different tables. Using mysql_field_table( ) inside of the for statement, the code determines the name of the table from which each field comes. The mysql_field_name( ) function gets the field's name. Here are the results of the previous script:

```
workreq.wrid
clients.client_name
workreq.description
```

mysql_field_type( )

mysql_field_type(*results, index*)

This returns the column datatype for a field from the results set given. To specify a particular field, an offset is given as the second argument.

```
...
$sql_stmnt = "SELECT * FROM workreq LIMIT 1";
$results = mysql_db_query('workrequests', $sql_stmnt);
$num_fields = mysql_num_fields($results);

for ($index = 0; $index < $num_fields; $index++) {
  $name = mysql_field_name($results, $index);
  $type = mysql_field_type($results, $index);
  print "$name - $type \n";
}
...
```

In this example, after one row of data is selected as a sample, the number of rows in the results set is determined using mysql_num_fields( ) so that a counter limit may be set up ($num_fields) in the for statement that follows. Within the for statement, the name of the field is extracted using mysql_field_name( ) and the datatype using mysql_field_type( ). Here are a few lines of the output of this script:

```
wrid - int
wr_date - date
clientid - string
...
```

mysql_free_result( )

mysql_free_result(*results*)

Use this to free the memory containing the results set given. The function returns true if it's successful; it returns false if it's unsuccessful.

```
...
mysql_free_result($results);
mysql_close( );
?>
```

There's not much to this function. It merely flushes out the data for the location in memory referenced by the variable given.

mysql_get_client_info( )

mysql_get_client_info( )

This returns the library version of the MySQL client for the current connection.

```
...
$info = mysql_get_client_info( );
print "Client Version:  $info \n";
...
```

Here are the results of this script on one of my computers:

```
Client Version:  3.23.40
```

mysql_get_host_info( )

```
mysql_get_host_info([connection])
```

This returns information on the host for the current connection to MySQL. An identifier may be given to retrieve information on a host for a different connection.

```
...
$info = mysql_get_client_info( );
print "Connection Info:  $info \n";
...
```

Here are the results of this script when you run it on the host containing the server:

```
Connection Info:   127.0.0.1 via TCP/IP
```

mysql_get_proto_info( )

```
mysql_get_proto_info([connection])
```

This returns the protocol version for the current connection to MySQL. An identifier may be given to retrieve the protocol version for a different connection.

```
...
$info = mysql_get_proto_info( );
print "Protocol Version:  $info \n";
...
```

Here are the results of running this script:

```
Protocol Version:   10
```

mysql_get_server_info( )

```
mysql_get_server_info([connection])
```

This returns the MySQL server version for the current connection to MySQL. An identifier may be given to retrieve the server version for a different connection.

```
...
$info = mysql_get_server_info( );
print "MySQL Server Version:  $info \n";
...
```

Here are the results of running this script:

```
MySQL Server Version:   4.1.1-alpha-standard
```

mysql_info( )

```
mysql_info([connection])
```

This returns information on the last query for the current connection to MySQL. An identifier may be given to retrieve information on a query for a different connection.

```
...
$sql_stmnt = "SELECT * FROM workreq";
$results = mysql_query($sql_stmnt);
print mysql_info( );
...
```

Here are the results of this script:

```
String format: 528 rows in set
```

mysql_insert_id( )

```
mysql_insert_id([connection])
```

This returns the identification number of the primary key of the last record inserted using INSERT for the current connection, provided the column utilizes AUTO_INCREMENT and the value was not manually set. Otherwise, 0 is returned.

```
...
$sql_stmnt = "INSERT INTO workreq
                (date, clientid, description)
                VALUES(NOW( ), '1000', 'Network Problem')";
mysql_query($sql_stmnt);

$wrid = mysql_insert_id( );
print "Work Request ID:  $wrid \n";
...
```

Here is the output of this script:

```
Work Request ID:  5755
```

mysql_list_dbs( )

```
mysql_list_dbs( )
```

This returns a pointer to a results set containing the names of databases hosted by the MySQL server. The mysql_db_name( ) function or any function that extracts data from a results set may be used to retrieve individual database names.

```
...
$databases = mysql_list_dbs( );
$dbs = mysql_num_rows($databases);

for($index = 0; $index < $dbs; $index++) {
    print mysql_db_name($databases, $index) . "\n";
}
...
```

mysql_list_fields( )

```
mysql_list_fields(database, table[, connection])
```

This returns a results set containing information about the columns of a table given for a database specified. The mysql_field_flags( ), mysql_field_len( ), mysql_field_name( ), and mysql_field_type( ) functions can be used to extract information from the results set. An identifier may be given as a third argument to the function to retrieve information for a different MySQL connection.

```
...
$fields = mysql_list_fields('workrequests', 'workreq');
$num_fields = mysql_num_fields($fields);
```

```
for ($index = 0; $index < $num_fields; $index++) {
    print mysql_field_name($fields, $index) . "\n";
}
...
```

After connecting to MySQL, in the first line the example uses `mysql_list_fields()` to retrieve a list of column names from the database and table given as arguments. To assist the for statement that follows, the `mysql_num_fields()` function determines the number of fields in the results set, returning a field for each column. Then PHP loops through the for statement for all the fields and displays the name of each column using `mysql_field_name()`. Here are a few lines from the output of this script:

```
wrid
wr_date
clientid
...
```

mysql_list_processes( )

`mysql_list_processes([connection])`

This returns a results set containing information on the server threads for the current connection: the connection identifier, the hostname, the database name, and the command. An identifier may be given to retrieve information for a different connection.

```
...
$processes = mysql_list_processes($connection);

while ($row = mysql_fetch_array($processes)){
    print "$row['Id'], $row['Host'],
           $row['db'], $row['Command']";
}
...
```

mysql_list_tables( )

`mysql_list_tables(database[, connection])`

This returns a results set containing a list of tables for *database*. An identifier may be given as a second argument to the function to retrieve information for a different connection. The `mysql_tablename()` function can be used to extract the names of the tables from the results set of this function.

```
...
$tables = mysql_list_tables('workrequests');
$num_tables = mysql_num_rows($tables);

for($index = 0; $index < $num_tables ; $index++) {
    print mysql_tablename($tables, $index) . "\n";
}
...
```

The first line shown here gives the database name as an argument for the mysql_list_tables( ) function. The results are stored in the $tables variable. Next the number of rows and the number of tables found are determined and stored in $num_tables. Using a for statement to loop through the list of tables in the results set, each table name is printed out with the assistance of mysql_tablename( ). The second argument of mysql_tablename( ) is adjusted incrementally by using the $index variable, which will increase from 0 to the value of $num_tables variable.

mysql_num_fields( )

mysql_num_fields(*results*)

This returns the number from fields of the results set given.

```
...
$fields = mysql_list_fields('workrequests', 'workreq');
$num_fields = mysql_num_fields($fields);

for ($index = 0; $index < $num_fields; $index++) {
  print mysql_field_name($fields, $index) . "\n";
}
...
```

As this example shows, mysql_num_fields( ) can be useful in conjunction with other functions. Here a list of fields for a table is retrieved using mysql_list_fields( ). In order to help the code display the names of the fields using a for statement, the number of fields needs to be determined. The mysql_num_fields( ) function is handy for figuring out this bit of information.

mysql_num_rows( )

mysql_num_rows(*results*)

This returns the number of rows in the results set given, generated by issuing a SELECT statement. For other types of SQL statements that don't return a results set, use mysql_affected_rows( ).

```
...
$sql_stmnt = "SELECT * FROM workreq";
$results = mysql_query($sql_stmnt);

$count = mysql_num_rows($results);
print "Number of Rows Found:  $count \n";
...
```

mysql_pconnect( )

mysql_pconnect(*server[:port|socket], user, password[, flags]*)

Use this to open a persistent connection to MySQL. The connection will not end with the closing of the PHP script that opened the connection, and it cannot be closed with mysql_close( ). The first argument of the function is the server name. If none is specified, *localhost* is assumed. A port may be specified with the server name (separated by a colon) or a socket along with its path. If no port is given, port 3306 is assumed. The username is to be given as the second argument and the user's password as the third. If a connection is attempted that uses the same parameters of a previous one, the existing connection is used instead of creating a new connection. As an optional fourth argument, client flags may be given for the MySQL constants MYSQL_CLIENT_COMPRESS, MYSQL_CLIENT_IGNORE_SPACE, MYSQL_CLIENT_INTERACTIVE, and MYSQL_CLIENT_SSL. The function returns a connection identifier if it's successful; it returns false if it's unsuccessful.

```
mysql_pconnect('localhost', 'russell', 'dyer');
```

mysql_ping( )

mysql_ping([connection])

Use this to determine if the current MySQL connection is still open. If it's not open, the function attempts to reestablish the connection. If the connection is open or reopened, true is returned. If the connection is not open and cannot be reestablished, false is returned. An identifier may be given to ping a different connection.

```
...
$ping = mysql_ping($connection);
print "Info:  $ping \n";
...
```

This function is available as of Version 4.3 of PHP.

mysql_query( )

mysql_query(sql_statement[, connection])

Use this to execute an SQL statement given. An identifier may be given as a second argument to query through a different connection. The function returns false if the query is unsuccessful. For SQL statements not designed to return a results set (e.g., INSERT), true is returned when the function is successful. Otherwise, a reference to a results set is returned.

```
...
$sql_stmnt = "SELECT wrid, client_name, description
              FROM workreq, clients
              WHERE workreq.clientid = clients.clientid";
$results = mysql_query($sql_stmnt, $connection);

while($row = mysql_fetch_row($results)) {
  print "WR-$row[0]: $row[1] - $row[2] \n";
}
...
```

Here's one line from the output of this script:

```
WR-5755: Farber Investments - Can't connect to network.
```

mysql_real_escape_string( )

```
mysql_real_escape_string(string[, link])
```

This returns the string given with special characters preceded by backslashes so that they are protected from being interpreted by the SQL interpreter. Use this in conjunction with the mysql_query( ) function to make SQL statements safe. This function does not escape % or _ characters, but does take into account the character set of the connection. A different connection may be specified as the second argument to the function. This function is similar to mysql_escape_string( ), but it escapes a string based on the character set for the current connection.

mysql_result( )

```
mysql_result(results, row[, field|offset])
```

This returns the data from one field of a row from results. Normally, this statement returns the next row and can be reused to retrieve results sequentially. As a third argument, either a field name (i.e., the column or alias name) or an offset may be given to change the pointer for the function. This function is typically used in conjunction with a loop statement to process each field of a results set.

```
...
$sql_stmnt = "SELECT client_name FROM clients";
$results = mysql_query($sql_stmnt);
$num_rows = mysql_num_rows($results);

for ($index = 0; $index < $num_rows; $index++) {
   print mysql_result($results, $index) . "\n";
}
...
```

This script queries the database for a list of client names. Using the mysql_num_row( ) function, the number of rows contained in the results set is determined. Using that bit of data, a for statement is constructed to loop through the results set using mysql_ result( ) to extract one field of data per row. Otherwise, a function such as mysql_ fetch_array( ) would have to be used in conjunction with the usual method of retrieving data from an array (e.g., $row[0]).

mysql_select_db( )

```
mysql_select_db(database[, connection])
```

This sets the database to be used by the current MySQL connection, but you also can use it to set the database for another connection by supplying it as a second argument. The function returns true if it's successful; it returns false if it's unsuccessful.

```
...
$connection = mysql_connect('localhost','tina','muller');
mysql_select_db('workrequests', $connection);
...
```

mysql_stat( )

mysql_stat([connection])

This returns the status of the server for the current MySQL connection, but you also can use it to get the status for another connection. The function returns, as a space-separated list, the flush tables, open tables, queries, queries per second, threads, and uptime for the server. This function is available starting with Version 4.3 of PHP.

```
...
$connection = mysql_connect('localhost',
                           'jacinta', 'richardson');
$info = explode(' ', mysql_stat($connection));
print_r($info);
...
```

Using the explode( ) PHP function, the elements of the space-separated values contained in the associative array generated by mysql_stat( ) are listed along with their respective keys.

mysql_tablename( )

mysql_tablename(results, index)

This returns the table name for a particular table in the results set given by mysql_list_tables( ). An index may be specified to retrieve a particular element of the results set.

```
...
$tables = mysql_list_tables('workrequests');
$tbs = mysql_num_rows($tables);

for($index = 0; $index < $tbs; $index++) {
    print mysql_tablename($tables, $index) . "\n";
}
...
```

mysql_thread_id( )

mysql_thread_id([connection])

This returns the thread identification number for the current MySQL connection. An identifier for another connection may be given. This function is available starting with Version 4.3 of PHP.

```
...
$connection = mysql_connect('127.0.0.1', 'russell', 'spenser');
$info = mysql_thread_id($connection);
print "Thread ID:  $info \n";
...
```

mysql_unbuffered_query( )

mysql_unbuffered_query(*sql_statement*[, *connection*])

Use this to execute an SQL statement given without buffering the results so that you can retrieve the data without having to wait for the results set to be completed. An identifier may be given as a second argument to the function to interface with a different connection. The function returns false if the query is unsuccessful. For SQL statements that would not return a results set based on their nature (e.g., INSERT), true is returned when the function is successful. This function should be used with care, because an enormous results set could overwhelm the program's allocated memory.

```
...
$sql_stmnt = "SELECT wrid, client_name, description
              FROM workreq, clients
              WHERE workreq.clientid = clients.clientid";
$results = mysql_unbuffered_query($sql_stmnt, $connection);

while($row = mysql_fetch_row($results)) {
  print "WR-$row[0]: $row[1] - $row[2] \n";
}
...
```

There's no difference in the syntax for mysql_unbuffered_query( ) and mysql_query( ), nor in the handling of the results. The only differences in this function are the speed for large databases and the fact that functions such as mysql_num_row( ) and mysql_data_seek( ) cannot be used, because the results set is not buffered and therefore cannot be analyzed by these functions.

14

C API

This chapter covers the C API provided by MySQL. The first part provides a basic tutorial on how to connect to MySQL and how to query MySQL with C and the C API. Following the tutorial is an alphabetical listing of MySQL functions in the C API with explanations and, in most cases, examples. At the end of this chapter is a listing of special datatypes for the C API. For the examples in this chapter, a database for a fictitious computer support business used. The database contains one table with client work requests (*workreq*) and another with client contact information (*clients*).

Using C with MySQL

This section presents the basic tasks you need to perform use the C API.

Connecting to MySQL

When writing a C program to interact with MySQL, first make a connection to MySQL. To do this easily, you need to include a couple of C header files: *stdio.h* for basic C functions and variables, and *mysql.h* for special MySQL functions and definitions. These two files come with C and MySQL, respectively; you shouldn't have to download them from the Web if both were installed properly.

```
#include <stdio.h>
#include "/usr/include/mysql/mysql.h"

int main(int argc, char *argv[ ])
{
        MYSQL *mysql;
        MYSQL_RES *result;
        MYSQL_ROW row;
```

Because of the < and > symbols surrounding *stdio.h*, C is instructed to look for it in the default location for C header files (e.g., */usr/include*), or in the user's path.

Because *mysql.h* may not be in the default locations, with the aide of double quotes, the absolute path is given. An alternative here would have been *<mysql/mysql.h>*, because the header file is in a subdirectory of the default directory.

Within the standard main function just shown, the connection to MySQL is established. The first line sets up the definition for MySQL, with mysql, which will be referenced by mysql later. The second line defines and names a results set based on the definitions for MYSQL_RES in *mysql.h*. The results are to be stored in the result array, which will be an array of rows from MySQL. The third line of main uses the definition for MYSQL_ROW to establish the row variable, which will be used later to contain an array of columns from MySQL.

Having set up the header files and initial variables, set up an object in memory for interacting with the MySQL server using mysql_init( ):

```
if(mysql_init(mysql) == NULL)
   {
       fprintf(stderr, "Cannot initialize MySQL");
       exit( );
   }
```

The if statement here is testing whether a MySQL object can be initialized. If the initialization fails, a message is printed and the program ends. The mysql_init( ) function initializes the MySQL object using the MYSQL structure declared at the beginning of the main function called by convention, mysql. If C is successful in initializing the object, it will go on to attempt to establish a connection to MySQL:

```
if(!mysql_real_connect(mysql, "localhost",
   "user", "password", "db1", 0, NULL, 0))
   {
       fprintf(stderr, "%d: %s \n",
           mysql_errno(mysql), mysql_error(mysql));
       exit(EXIT FAILURE);
   }
```

The elements of the mysql_real_connect( ) function here are fairly obvious: first the MySQL object is referenced; next the hostname or IP address; then the username and password; and finally the database to use. The three remaining items are the port number, the Unix socket filename, and a client flag, if any. Passing zeros and NULL tells the function to use the defaults for these. If the program cannot connect, it is to print the error message generated by the server to the standard error stream, along with the MySQL error number (hence the %d format instruction for displaying digits or a number) and finally a string (%s) containing the MySQL error message and then a line feed or a newline (\n). The actual values to plug into the format follow, separated by commas.

The program so far only makes a connection to MySQL. Now let's look at how you can add code to the program to run an SQL statement with the C API.

Querying MySQL

If the MySQL connection portion of the program is successful, the program can query the MySQL server with a query function such as mysql_query( ):

```
if(mysql_query(mysql, "SELECT col1, col2 FROM table1"))
{
    fprintf(stderr, "%d:  %s\n",
    mysql_errno(mysql), mysql_error(mysql));
}
else
{
    result = mysql_store_result(mysql);
    while(row = mysql_fetch_row(result))
        { printf("\%d - \%s \n", row[0], row[1]]); }
    mysql_free_result(result);
}
    mysql_close(mysql);
    exit(EXIT_SUCCESS);
}
```

Incidentally, this excerpt is using mysql_query( ), but you could use the mysql_real_query( ) function instead. The main difference between the two is that mysql_real_query( ) allows the retrieval of binary data, which may not be necessary, but it's safer to use. mysql_query( ) returns 0 if it's not successful, so if the preceding SQL statement does not succeed in selecting data from MySQL, an error message will be printed. However, if the query is successful, it will return a 0 and the else statement to be executed. In the else statement block, the first line captures the results of the query and stores them in memory with the use of the mysql_store_result( ) function. Later, the memory will be freed when mysql_free_result( ) is issued with the variable name result in the parentheses.

Before letting go of the data, though, you must loop through each row of it and display results from each row for the user. Do this with a while statement and the mysql_fetch_row( ) function. This function retrieves one row of the results at a time and in this particular program, it stores each row in the row variable. Then the printf statement prints to the screen the value of each field in the format shown. Notice that each field is extracted by typical array syntax (i.e., array [n]). The formatting instructions for printf are in double quotes, the same method as with fprintf in the if statement earlier. Once C has gone through each row of the results, it will stop and then free up the buffer of the data, concluding the else statement. This brief program ends with a mysql_close( ) call to finish the MySQL session and to disconnect from MySQL. The final closing curly brace ends the main function.

To compile the program with the GNU C Compiler (*gcc*), you can enter something such as the following from the command line:

```
gcc -o mysql_c_prog mysql_c_prog.c \
    -L/usr/include/mysql -L/usr/lib/mysql -lmysqlclient
```

Notice that the paths to the MySQL header file and the MySQL data directory are given as well, and the name of the client library, *mysqlclient*, is also given. These paths may be different on your system. When the compiler attempts to compile the program (*mysql_c_prog.c* here), it will check for syntax errors in the code. If it finds any, it will fail to compile and will display error messages. If its successful, the resulting compiled program (*mysql_c_prog*) may be executed.

Functions in Alphabetical Order

The bulk of this chapter consists of a list of C API functions in alphabetical order. Each function is given with its syntax and an explanation. For almost all functions, an example program, or excerpt, is provided to show how you can use the function. To save space, almost all of the excerpts are shown without the lines of code necessary to start a C program and to connect to MySQL, as well as to close the connection and to end the program. For an example on how you would write opening and closing lines, see the tutorial in the previous section. The examples in this section will tend to be more succinct and won't usually include typical error checking. It's assumed that the reader has a basic understanding of C. For the syntax of each function, the datatype expected is given before each parameter or argument.

mysql_affected_rows( )

```
my_ulonglong mysql_affected_rows(MYSQL *mysql)
```

This returns the number of rows affected by the most recent query for the current session. This function is meaningful only for INSERT, UPDATE, and DELETE statements. For SQL statements that don't affect rows (e.g., SELECT), this function will return 0. For errors, it will return -1.

```
...
mysql_query(mysql,"UPDATE workreq
                  SET tech_person_id = '1015'
                  WHERE tech_person_id = '1012'");
my_ulonglong chg = mysql_affected_rows(mysql);
printf("Number of requests reassigned: %ul \n", chg);
...
```

In this example, an UPDATE statement is issued and the number of rows changed is extracted with the function and stored in the chg variable, which is then printed. For REPLACE statements, rows that are replaced are counted twice: once for the deletion and once for the insertion.

mysql_autocommit( )

```
my_bool mysql_autocommit(MYSQL *mysql, my_bool mode)
```

Use this to set auto-commit mode on the MySQL server. A value of 1 for the second argument of this function sets the server's auto-commit mode to on. A value of 0 sets it to off. The autocommit causes the server to update the database after each INSERT, UPDATE, or DELETE statement, essentially running each in its own transaction. The default is on.

```
...
mysql_autocommit(mysql, 0);
...
```

mysql_change_user( )

```
my_bool mysql_change_user(MYSQL *mysql, const char *user,

                          const char *password,

                          const char *database)
```

Use this to change the current user for the MySQL session to the one given as the second argument. The password of the new user is given in the third argument. This function will end the current session if successful, so it will need to issue a new USE statement. Therefore, a database to use is to be given as the fourth argument.

```
...
mysql = mysql_init(NULL);
mysql_connect(mysql,"localhost","hui","shorty");
mysql_select_db(mysql,"workrequests");
...
mysql_change_user(mysql,"russell","password","workrequests");
mysql_query(mysql, "UPDATE workreq
                    SET tech_person_id = '1015'
                    WHERE tech_person_id = '1012'");
...
```

In this example, the program begins with one user for running SQL statements, which are replaced with ellipses. However, for changing a sensitive data column (i.e., the person assigned to perform the work requests), the user is changed to one who has the proper authority.

mysql_character_set_name( )

```
const char *mysql_character_set_name(MYSQL *mysql)
```

This returns the name of the default character set in use by the MySQL server.

```
...
MYSQL *mysql;
const char *char_set;
mysql = mysql_init(NULL);
mysql_connect(mysql,"localhost","russell","password");

char_set = mysql_character_set_name(mysql);
printf("Character Set: %s \n", char_set);
...
```

To get just the character set name, it's not necessary to select a database. Here are what the results of running this program might look like:

```
Character Set: latin1
```

mysql_close( )

```
void mysql_close(MYSQL *mysql)
```

Use this to close the connection to the MySQL serve. It releases the MYSQL object if allocated by mysql_init( ). It does not return a value.

```
...
mysql = mysql_init(NULL);
mysql_connect(mysql,"localhost","russell","password");
...
mysql_close(mysql);
...
```

mysql_commit( )

```
my_bool mysql_commit(MYSQL *mysql)
```

Use this to commit the current transaction. After this function is executed, INSERT, UPDATE, and DELETE statements are written to the database, and you cannot use the mysql_rollback( ) function to undo them. The function returns 0 if successful, nonzero if unsuccessful.

```
    mysql_commit(mysql);
```

mysql_connect( )

```
MYSQL *mysql_connect(MYSQL *mysql, const char *host,

                  const char *user, cont char *password)
```

Use this to establish a connection to a MySQL server. The first argument is an object by mysql_init( ). The second argument for the function is the hostname. If NULL is given, the default of *localhost* is used. The third argument is the username for connecting and the fourth is the user's password in plain text. The return value for the function, if successful, is a MYSQL structure and is saved to the variable named in the first argument. This variable should be used in subsequent functions to access the server. NULL is returned if the connection fails.

This function is deprecated in favor of mysql_real_connect( ). The mysql_close( ) function is used to end a connection:

```
    int main( )
    {
        MYSQL *mysql;
        const char *host = "localhost";
        const char *user = "russell";
        const char *password = "password";

        mysql = mysql_init(NULL);
        mysql_connect(mysql,host,user,password);
        ...
        mysql_close(mysql);
        exit(EXIT_SUCCESS);
    }
```

Notice that datatypes for the variables set up in the first few lines coincide with the data types shown in the function prototype. Instead of variables, the actual values may be given within the function. Each value must be contained within double quotes.

C API

mysql_create_db( )

int mysql_create_db(MYSQL *mysql, const char *database)

Use this to create a new database on the MySQL server. The new database's name is given as the second argument. This function has been deprecated. Instead, a CREATE DATABASE statement should be given with mysql_query( ) or mysql_real_query( ).

```
...
mysql_real_connect(mysql,host,user,password,NULL,0,NULL,0);
mysql_create_db(mysql, "new_database");
mysql_select_db(mysql, "new_database");
...
```

This program excerpt creates a database named *new_database*. The parameters for the mysql_real_connect( ) function are variables declared earlier in the program. Notice that the fifth argument (the parameter for the initial database to use) is set to NULL.

mysql_data_seek( )

void mysql_data_seek(MYSQL_RES *result, my_ulonglong offset)

Use this in conjunction with mysql_store_result( ) and a fetch function such as mysql_fetch_row( ) to change the current row being fetched to the one specified in the second argument of this function.

```
...
mysql_query(mysql, "SELECT client_id, client_name
                    FROM clients ORDER BY start_date");
result = mysql_store_result(mysql);
num_rows = mysql_num_rows(result);

mysql_data_seek(result, (num_rows - 8));

while((row = mysql_fetch_row(result)) != NULL)
  { printf("%s (%s) \n", row[1], row[0]); }
...
```

This program excerpt retrieves a list of client names along with their respective IDs. Using the mysql_data_seek( ) function in conjunction with mysql_fetch_row( ) and a while statement, the last eight clients who started with the company will be displayed.

mysql_debug( )

void mysql_debug(const char *debug)

Use this to set debugging if the client was compiled with debugging.

```
...
mysql_debug("d:t:o,filename");
...
```

The filename given could include the path to the logfile where debugging information is to be written.

mysql_drop_db( )

`int mysql_drop_db(MYSQL *mysql, const char *database)`

Use this to delete the database named in the second argument of the function from the MySQL server. It returns 0 if successful and nonzero if not. This function has been deprecated. Use `mysql_query( )` or `mysql_real_query( )` with a `DROP DATABASE` statement instead.

```
...
mysql = mysql_init(NULL);
mysql_real_connect(mysql,host,user,password,NULL,0,NULL,0);
...
mysql_drop_db(mysql, "db5");
...
```

This returns a nonzero if it fails, so a program that uses it should include error checking for the function. Otherwise, the program may hang if the function is unsuccessful.

mysql_dump_debug_info( )

`int mysql_dump_debug_info(MYSQL *mysql)`

Use this to write debugging information about the current connection to the MySQL server's logfile. The user must have administrative privileges. It returns 0 if successful, nonzero if unsuccessful.

```
...
if(!mysql_dump_debug_info(mysql))
    { printf("Debugging Info. Written. \n"); }
...
```

mysql_eof( )

`my_bool mysql_eof(MYSQL *result)`

Use this to determine whether the last row of the results set has been fetched. It returns 0 until end of file is reached and nonzero at end of file. This function has been deprecated. Use `mysql_errno( )` and `mysql_error( )`, or `mysql_more_results( )`, instead to check for an error indicating that the last row has been reached.

mysql_errno( )

`unsigned int mysql_errno(MYSQL *mysql)`

This returns the error number for the last function executed that failed. After a successfully executed function, 0 is returned from this function.

```
...
if(mysql_real_connect(mysql,host,"goofy",
                      password,database,0,NULL,0) == NULL)
  {
   printf("Error %d \n", mysql_errno(mysql));
   exit(EXIT FAILURE);
  }
...
```

In this example, the program is attempting to connect to the MySQL server with a user who is not in the *mysql* database.

mysql_error( )

char *mysql_error(MYSQL *mysql)

This returns the error message for the last function executed that failed. After a successfully executed function, an empty string is returned from this function.

```
...
if(!mysql_real_connect(mysql,host,"goofy",
                       password,database,0,NULL,0))
  {
    printf("Error Message: %s \n", mysql_error(mysql));
    exit(EXIT FAILURE);
  }
...
```

In this example, the program is attempting to connect to the MySQL server with a user who is not in the *mysql* database.

mysql_escape_string( )

unsigned int mysql_escape_string(char *destination,

const char *source,

unsigned int length)

This returns a string given as the second argument with special characters escaped by adding backslashes in front of them. The number of bytes to be copied from the source string is given for the third. When declaring the two strings, the destination must be double the source string, plus one byte. This function does not include a MYSQL object (which includes knowledge of the current character set), so it may not be comprehensive. This is a security problem. Use the mysql_real_escape_string( ) function instead, which does this job properly and safely.

```
...
char client_name[ ] = "O'Reilly Media";
unsigned int bytes = strlen(client_name);
char client_name_esc[(2 * bytes) + 1];

mysql_escape_string(client_name_esc, client_name, bytes);

char *sql_stmnt;
sprintf(sql_stmnt, "INSERT INTO clients (client_name)
                    VALUES('%s')", client_name_esc);
printf("SQL Statement:\n%s", sql_stmnt);

mysql = mysql_init(NULL);
mysql_real_connect(mysql,host,user,password,database,
                   port,socket,flag);
mysql_real_query(mysql, sql_stmnt, strlen(sql_stmnt));
...
```

In this example, the client name is first stored in the client_name variable. Next, the number of bytes contained in the variable is calculated with the C function strlen( ) and stored in the bytes variable. Then the client_name_esc variable is declared with a size of the value contained in bytes doubled, plus one, per the requirements of the mysql_escape_string( ) function. Then the mysql_escape_string( ) is run to convert the string contained in client_name and save it to client_name_esc. Then the program creates an SQL statement, inserting the escaped client name where the %s is shown. To see the results, a print statement is issued before the SQL statement is executed.

```
SQL Statement:
INSERT INTO clients (client_name)
VALUES('O\'Reilly Media')
```

mysql_fetch_field( )

MYSQL_FIELD *mysql_fetch_field(MYSQL_RES *result)

This returns a MYSQL_FIELD structure that provides information on a given field of a results set. If you use it in conjunction with a loop statement, you can extract information on each field.

```
...
MYSQL_FIELD *field;
...
mysql_query(mysql, "SELECT * FROM clients LIMIT 1");
result = mysql_store_result(mysql);

while((field = mysql_fetch_field(result)) != NULL)
   { printf("%s \n", field->name);  }
...
```

The wildcard in the SELECT statement selects all columns in the table. The loop therefore lists the name of each column. The other possibilities are field->table for the table name and field->def for the default value of the column.

mysql_fetch_field_direct( )

MYSQL_FIELD *mysql_fetch_field_direct(MYSQL_RES *result,

                              unsigned int field_nbr)

This returns a MYSQL_FIELD structure that provides information on a given field of a results set referred to in the first argument of the function. The particular field is given as the second argument.

```
...
MYSQL_FIELD *field;
...
mysql_query(mysql, "SELECT * FROM clients LIMIT 1");
result = mysql_store_result(mysql);
field = mysql_fetch_field_direct(result, 0);
printf("%s \n", field->name);
...
```

This function is similar to mysql_fetch_field( ) except that information on just one specified field can be obtained. In the example here, the name of the first field (0 being the first) will be displayed.

mysql_fetch_fields( )

MYSQL_FIELD *mysql_fetch_fields(MYSQL_RES *result)

This returns an array of information about the fields in a results set.

```
...
mysql_query(mysql, "SELECT * FROM clients");
result = mysql_store_result(mysql);
num_fields = mysql_field_count(mysql);

MYSQL_FIELD *field;
field = mysql_fetch_fields(result);

for(i = 0; i < num_fields; i++)
    { printf("%u. %s \n", i, &field[i].name); }
...
```

In addition to the .name key to extract the column name, a program can specify .table for the table name and .def for the default value of the column.

mysql_fetch_lengths( )

unsigned long *mysql_fetch_lengths(MYSQL *result)

This returns the length of each column within a particular row of a results set. The values returned can vary for each row fetched, depending on the data contained in the columns.

```
...
mysql_query(mysql, "SELECT * FROM clients");
result = mysql_store_result(mysql);
row = mysql_fetch_row(result);

unsigned int num_fields = mysql_num_fields(result);
unsigned long *lengths = mysql_fetch_lengths(result);

for(i = 0; i < num_fields; i++)
    {
     field = mysql_fetch_field(result);
     printf("%s %lu \n", field->name, lengths[i]);
    }
...
```

This example retrieves one row of the results and checks the lengths of the fields in that row. To retrieve each field, the SELECT statement would need to be altered and a while statement would be wrapped around the for statement to loop through each row.

mysql_fetch_row( )

`MYSQL_ROW mysql_fetch_row(MYSQL_RES *result)`

Use this to retrieve the next row of a results set. When there are no more rows to retrieve, the function returns NULL. Here is a fairly complete example using this function:

```c
#include <stdio.h>
#include <stdlib.h>
#include <mysql/mysql.h>

int main( )
 {
    MYSQL *mysql;
    MYSQL_RES *result;
    MYSQL_ROW row;
    MYSQL_FIELD *field;
    int i, num_fields;

    mysql = mysql_init(NULL);
    mysql_real_connect(mysql,"localhost","user","password",
                             "workrequests",0,NULL,0);
    mysql_query(mysql,"SELECT * FROM users");
    result = mysql_store_result(mysql);
    num_fields = mysql_field_count(mysql);

    while((row = mysql_fetch_row(result)) != NULL)
      {
        for(i = 0; i < num_fields; i++)
          {
            field = mysql_fetch_field_direct(result, i);
            printf("%s: %s, ", field->name, row[i]);
          }
        printf("\n");
      }
    mysql_free_result(result);
    mysql_close(mysql);
    exit(EXIT_SUCCESS);
 }
```

Although this example is a complete program, it's missing the usual error checking.

mysql_field_count( )

`unsigned int mysql_field_count(MYSQL *mysql)`

This returns the number of columns in a results set. You can also use this function to test whether there was an error in a SELECT query. A SELECT query will return at least one blank field when there is an error, resulting in a value of 0 for the function.

```c
...
if(!result)
  {
    if(mysql_field_count(mysql) == 0)
```

```
            {
            printf("Error \n");
            exit(EXIT FAILURE);
            }
        }
    ...
```

See the entry for the mysql_fetch_row( ) function for another example involving this function.

mysql_field_seek( )

```
MYSQL_FIELD_OFFSET mysql_field_seek(MYSQL_RES *result,

                            MYSQL_FIELD_OFFSET offset)
```

Use this in conjunction with mysql_fetch_field( ) to change the current field being fetched to the one specified in the second argument of this function. The function returns the offset of the field that was current before the function was invoked. A reference to the results set must be passed as the first argument.

```
...
mysql_query(mysql, sql_stmnt);
MYSQL_FIELD_OFFSET offset = 2;
mysql_field_seek(result, offset);

while((field = mysql_fetch_field(result)) != NULL)
    {
     printf("%d: %s \n", mysql_field_tell(result), field->name);
    }
...
```

Using mysql_field_seek( ) here and an offset of 2, the first two rows of the results set are skipped The mysql_field_tell( ) function is used to ascertain the index of the field being displayed within each loop of the while statement. The mysql_field_seek( ) function will return the offset prior to invoking the function. If you change the mysql_field_seek( ) call in the program to the following, the old_offset variable would contain 0, the starting point for a row.

```
...
MYSQL_FIELD_OFFSET old_offset = mysql_field_seek(result, offset);
...
```

You can use this for notating a point in a results set before moving the pointer. The program can later return to that point using the old offset.

mysql_field_tell( )

```
MYSQL_FIELD_OFFSET mysql_field_tell(MYSQL_RES *result)
```

This returns the value of the field pointer for the current row in use by a fetch function such as mysql_fetch_field( ). The field pointer starts at 0 for the first field when a row is retrieved and advances by one as each field is retrieved in order. See mysql_field_seek( ) for an example of this function.

mysql_free_result( )

```
void mysql_free_result(MYSQL_RES *result)
```

Use this to free memory allocated by a function such as `mysql_store_result( )` in which a MYSQL_RES element was employed to store a results set.

```
...
result = mysql_query(mysql, sql_stmnt);
...
mysql_free_result(result);
...
```

Not freeing allocated memory or attempting to access allocated memory after it's freed can cause problems.

mysql_get_client_info( )

```
char *mysql_get_client_info(void)
```

This returns the client library version.

```
...
const char *info;
info = mysql_get_client_info( );
printf("Client Library Version: %s \n", info);
...
```

mysql_get_client_version( )

```
unsigned long *mysql_get_client_version(void)
```

This returns the client library version in a numeric format. For example, for Version 4.1.7, the function will return 40107.

```
...
unsigned long version;
version = mysql_get_client_version( );
printf("Client Version: %d \n", version);
...
```

mysql_get_host_info( )

```
char *mysql_get_host_info(MYSQL *mysql)
```

This returns the hostname and the connection type for the current connection.

```
...
MYSQL *mysql;
mysql = mysql_init(NULL);
mysql_real_connect(mysql,"localhost","marie","password",
                   NULL,0,NULL,0);
printf("Host Info: %s \n", mysql_get_host_info(mysql));
mysql_close(mysql);
...
```

The results of this program excerpt will look something like the following:

```
Host Info: Localhost via UNIX socket
```

mysql_get_proto_info( )

unsigned int mysql_get_proto_info(MYSQL *mysql)

This returns the protocol version for the current connection.

```
...
MYSQL *mysql;
mysql = mysql_init(NULL);
mysql_real_connect(mysql,"localhost","root","password",
                   NULL,0,NULL,0);
printf("Protocol: %u \n", mysql_get_proto_info(mysql));
mysql_close(mysql);
...
```

mysql_get_server_info( )

char *mysql_get_server_info(MYSQL *mysql)

This returns a string containing the version of MySQL running on the server for the current connection.

```
...
MYSQL *mysql;
mysql = mysql_init(NULL);
mysql_real_connect(mysql,"localhost","root","password",
                   NULL,0,NULL,0);
printf("Server Version: %s \n", mysql_get_server_info(mysql));
mysql_close(mysql);
...
```

mysql_get_server_version( )

unsigned long mysql_get_server_version(MYSQL *mysql)

This returns the version of the server for the current connection in a numeric format. For example, for Version 4.1.7, the function will return 40107.

```
...
MYSQL *mysql;
mysql = mysql_init(NULL);
mysql_real_connect(mysql,"localhost","root","password",
NULL,0,NULL,0);
printf("Server Version: %ul \n",
        mysql_get_server_version(mysql));
mysql_close(mysql);
...
```

mysql_info( )

char *mysql_info(MYSQL *mysql)

This returns a string containing information provided by MySQL when certain SQL statements are executed. This function works only with five types of SQL statements: INSERT INTO...SELECT..., INSERT INTO... VALUES..., LOAD DATA INFILE, ALTER TABLE, and UPDATE. For all other statements, this function typically returns NULL.

```
...
mysql_query(mysql, "UPDATE clients
                    SET telephone_areacode = '985'
                    WHERE city = 'Hammond'");
printf("Query Info: %s \n", mysql_info(mysql));
...
```

The results of the previous program excerpt will look like the following:

```
Query Info: Rows matched: 3   Changed: 3   Warnings: 0
```

mysql_init( )

MYSQL *mysql_init(MYSQL *mysql)

This function optionally allocates, and then initializes, a MYSQL object suitable for connecting to a database server and subsequently performing many of the other operations described in this chapter. If the function's parameter is NULL, the library allocates a new object from the heap; otherwise, the user's pointed-to local MYSQL object is initialized.

The return value is a pointer to the object however obtained, and a NULL indicates a failure of allocation or initialization. Calling mysql_close( ) with this pointer not only releases the connection-related resources, but also frees the object itself if the library had allocated it in the first place.

It's generally safer to allow the library to allocate this object rather than to do so yourself: it avoids hard-to-debug complications that can arise if certain compiler options are not in effect while building the *application* as were when building the *library*.

Though this function prepares a handle for a database connection, no connection is attempted.

```
...
MYSQL *mysql;

if(mysql_init(mysql) == NULL)
        {
          printf("Could not initialize MySQL object. \n");
          exit(EXIT FAILURE);
        }
...
```

mysql_insert_id( )

my_ulonglong mysql_insert_id(MYSQL *mysql)

This returns the identification number issued to the primary key of the last record inserted using INSERT in MySQL for the current connection. This works provided the column utilizes AUTO_INCREMENT and the value was not manually set. Otherwise, 0 is returned.

```
...
const char *sql_stmnt =  "INSERT INTO workreq
                          (req_date, client_id, description)
                          VALUES(NOW( ), '1000', 'Net Problem')";
mysql_query(mysql, sql_stmnt);
my_ulonglong wr_id = mysql_insert_id(mysql);
printf("Work Request ID: %ld \n", wr_id);
...
```

mysql_kill( )

int mysql_kill(MYSQL *mysql, unsigned long *identifier*)

Use this to terminate a thread on the server. The thread identifier is passed as the second argument to the function. If you're attempting to kill the current connection, you can use the mysql_thread_id( ) function with the session handle.

```
...
if(!mysql_kill(mysql, mysql_thread_id(mysql)))
    { printf("Terminated Current Thread. \n"); }
...
```

To kill a thread other than the current one, you can use the mysql_list_processes( ) function to list all threads to determine which one to terminate.

mysql_list_dbs( )

MYSQL_RES *mysql_list_dbs(MYSQL *mysql, const char *wild)

This returns a results set containing a list of databases found for the current connection. An expression may be given to select databases whose names match a certain pattern. The % or _ characters may be used as wildcards. If NULL is given for the second argument, the names of all databases on the server will be selected in the results set.

```
...
MYSQL_RES *result;
MYSQL_ROW row;
...
result = mysql_list_dbs(mysql, NULL);

while((row = mysql_fetch_row(result)) != NULL)
{ printf("%s \n", row[0]);  }
mysql_free_result(result);
...
```

This excerpt extracts a list of databases from the server using the mysql_list_dbs( ) function and stores the results. Using the mysql_fetch_row( ) function, each row of the results set is stored temporarily for printing. To extract a list of databases with "work" in the name, NULL would be replaced with "%work%". As with all results sets, release the resources with mysql_free_result( ) when finished.

mysql_list_fields( )

```
MYSQL_RES *mysql_list_fields(MYSQL *mysql, const char *table,
                             const char *wild)
```

This returns a results set containing a list of fields found for the table given as the second argument to the function. An expression may be given as the third argument to select fields whose names match a certain pattern. The % or may be used as wildcards. If NULL is given for the third argument, all fields for the table are returned. The results set must be freed when finished.

```
...
result = mysql_list_fields(mysql, "stores", "s%");
num_rows = mysql_num_rows(result);
printf("Rows: %d \n", num_rows);

while((row = mysql_fetch_row(result)) != NULL)
   {
     for(i = 0; i < num_rows; i++)
       { printf("%s \n", row[i]); }
   }
mysql_free_result(result);
...
```

mysql_list_processes( )

```
MYSQL_RES *mysql_list_processes(MYSQL *mysql)
```

This returns a results set containing a list of MySQL server processes or server threads found for the handle given as the argument to the function.

```
...
result = mysql_list_processes(mysql);

while((row = mysql_fetch_row(result)) != NULL)
   {
     printf("Thread ID: %s \n", row[0]);
     printf("User: %s, Host: %s \n", row[1], row[2]);
     printf("Database: %s, Command: %s \n", row[3], row[4]);
     printf("Time: %s, State: %s, Info: %s \n\n",
            row[5],row[6],row[7]);
   }
mysql_free_result(result);
...
```

Using the mysql_fetch_row( ) function, each row of the results set is read and each field displayed with its related label. The results are the same as the SHOW PROCESSES query in

MySQL. It's important to run the `mysql_free_result( )` function when finished with a results set, as shown here.

mysql_list_tables( )

```
MYSQL_RES .*mysql_list_tables(MYSQL *mysql,

                              const char *expression)
```

This returns a results set containing a list of tables in the currently selected database. An expression may be given as the second argument of the function to select tables whose names match a certain pattern. The % or _ may be used as wildcards. If NULL is given for the second argument, all tables in the database will be returned.

```
...
MYSQL_RES *result;
MYSQL_ROW row;
...
result = mysql_list_tables(mysql, "w%");

while((row = mysql_fetch_row(result)) != NULL)
{ printf("%s \n", row[0]);  }
mysql_free_result(result);
...
```

This excerpt extracts a list of tables beginning with the letter "w" using the `mysql_list_tables( )` function and stores the results in the `result` variable. Using the `mysql_fetch_row( )` function, each row of the results set is stored temporarily in the `row` variable for printing.

mysql_more_results( )

```
my_bool mysql_more_result(MYSQL *mysql)
```

Use this to determine whether more results remain in a results set when using the `mysql_next_result( )` function to retrieve data. It returns 1 if there are more results, 0 if not.

mysql_next_result( )

```
int mysql_next_result(MYSQL *mysql)
```

Use this to read the next row of data from a results set. It returns 0 if successful and if there are more results to retrieve and -1 if it was successful in retrieving data, but there are no further rows to retrieve. It returns an error (or a value greater than 0) if it's unsuccessful because the results set was not loaded with the data. You can use the `mysql_more_results( )` function to check for more results before invoking this function.

mysql_num_fields( )

unsigned int mysql_num_fields(MYSQL_RES *result)

This returns the number of fields in each row of a results set. This function is similar to mysql_field_count( ) except that function operates on the MYSQL handle and not the results set.

```
...
unsigned int num_fields = mysql_num_fields(result);
...
```

See mysql_fetch_lengths( ) for a more elaborate example that uses this function.

mysql_num_rows( )

int mysql_num_rows(MYSQL_RES *result)

This returns the number of rows in the results set when issued after the mysql_store_result( ) function. When issued after mysql_use_result( ), it returns the number of rows already fetched.

```
...
my_ulonglong num_rows = mysql_num_rows(result);
...
```

See mysql_list_fields( ) for a more elaborate example that uses this function.

mysql_options( )

int mysql_options(MYSQL *mysql, enum mysql_option *option*,

const char *value*)

Use this to set connection options before a connection has been established with a function such as mysql_real_connect( ) or mysql_connect( ). This function may be used multiple times to set additional options before connecting. For the second argument of the function, specific options for the connection may be given. A value associated with the chosen option may be given for the third argument.

```
...
mysql = mysql_init(NULL);
mysql_options(mysql, MYSQL_OPT_COMPRESS, NULL);
mysql_real_connect(mysql,host,user,password,NULL,0,NULL,0);
...
```

The options permitted for the second argument of the function follow, along with the type of variable or value for the third argument in parentheses and a brief explanation of each:

MYSQL_OPT_CONNECT_TIMEOUT *(unsigned int *)*
  Sets the number of seconds for connection timeout.

MYSQL_OPT_READ_TIMEOUT *(unsigned int *)*
  Sets the timeout for reads from a Windows MySQL server.

MYSQL_OPT_WRITE_TIMEOUT *(unsigned int *)*
  Sets the timeout for writes to a Windows MySQL server.

MYSQL_OPT_COMPRESS (NULL)
Compresses communications between the client and server if supported by both.

MYSQL_OPT_LOCAL_INFILE *(pointer to unsigned integer)*
Runs on a file pointed to in the argument. If the pointer is NULL, the LOAD LOCAL INFILE statement is run when connecting.

MYSQL_OPT_NAMED_PIPE (NULL)
Instructs the client to use named pipes for connecting to a Windows NT MySQL server.

MYSQL_INIT_COMMAND *(char *)*
Instructs the server on connecting to execute an initial SQL statement given as the third argument to the function.

MYSQL_READ_DEFAULT_FILE *(char *)*
Instructs the server to read a configuration text file named in the third argument of the function instead of the default *my.cnf* configuration file for the client.

MYSQL_READ_DEFAULT_GROUP *(char *)*
Instructs the server to read a server section or group (e.g., [special_client]) from either the default *my.cnf* configuration file or the one specified by the MYSQL_READ_DEFAULT_FILE option to this function.

MYSQL_OPT_PROTOCOL *(unsigned int *)*
Specifies the default protocol for communicating with the server.

MYSQL_SHARED_MEMORY_BASE_NAME *(char *)*
Names the shared memory object for connecting to the server.

mysql_ping( )

int mysql_ping(MYSQL *mysql)

Use this to determine whether the current MYSQL connection is still open. If it's not open, the function attempts to reestablish the connection. If the connection is open or is reestablished, 0 is returned. Otherwise, nonzero is returned.

```
...
MYSQL *mysql;

int main( )
{
...
    test_connection( );
    mysql_close(mysql);
    test_connection( );
}

test_connection( )
{
    int live;
    live = mysql_ping(mysql);
    if(live){ printf("Connection not alive. \n");  }
    else { printf("Connection alive. \n"); }
}
```

This excerpt employs a user function to test for a MySQL connection.

mysql_query( )

int mysql_query(MYSQL *mysql, const char *query)

Use this to execute the SQL query given as the second argument of the function. Only one SQL statement may be given. For queries containing binary data, use the mysql_real_query( ) function instead. If successful, this function will return 0; otherwise, nonzero.

```
...
MYSQL *mysql;
MYSQL_RES *result;
MYSQL_ROW row;
MYSQL_FIELD *field;
int i, num_fields;
...
mysql = mysql_init(NULL);
mysql_real_connect(mysql,host,user,password,database,0,NULL,0);
const char *sql_stmnt = "SELECT * FROM workreq";

mysql_query(mysql, sql_stmnt, bytes);

result = mysql_store_result(mysql);
num_fields = mysql_field_count(mysql);

while((row = mysql_fetch_row(result)) != NULL)
  {
  for(i = 0; i < num_fields; i++)
    { printf("%s, ", row[i]); }
  printf("\n");
  }
mysql_free_result(result);
mysql_close(mysql);
...
```

Although this example is fairly complete, the lines declaring the variables containing the connection information are not shown. See the example for the msyql_real_connect( ) function for those details. The SQL statement in the previous example is given through a variable, but could be given within the function if enclosed within double quotes. The results of the query are stored in the result variable by way of the mysql_store_result( ) function. Incidentally, it's important to free the memory allocated for the results with the mysql_free_result( ) function when finished.

mysql_real_connect( )

MYSQL *mysql_real_connect(MYSQL *mysql, const char *host,

const char *user, const char *password,

const char *database, uint port,

const char *unix_socket, uint flag)

Use this to establish a connection to a MySQL server. The MYSQL structure created by mysql_init( ) is given as the first argument to the function. The hostname, username, and user's password for connecting to the server are given next. The name of the database is given as the fifth argument. The port, the socket file path and name for Unix systems, and any client flags are given as the sixth, seventh, and eighth arguments, respectively. For any parameter requiring a *char* pointer, a value of NULL may be given to instruct the server to use the default setting. For unsigned int variables, a value of 0 may be given to rely on the default value.

```c
#include <stdio.h>
#include <stdlib.h>
#include <mysql/mysql.h>

int main(void)
{
  MYSQL *mysql;
  MYSQL_RES *result;
  MYSQL_ROW row;
  MYSQL_FIELD *field;

  const char *host = "localhost";
  const char *user = "root";
  const char *password = "my_password";
  const char *database = "workrequests";
  unsigned int port = 3306;
  const char *socket = NULL;
  unsigned long flag = 0;
  int i, num_fields;

  mysql = mysql_init(NULL);
  mysql_real_connect(mysql,host,user,password,database,
                     port,socket,flag);

  const char *sql_stmnt = "SELECT * FROM stores";
  ulong bytes = strlen(sql_stmnt);

  mysql_real_query(mysql, sql_stmnt, bytes);
  result = mysql_store_result(mysql);
  num_fields = mysql_field_count(mysql);

  while((row = mysql_fetch_row(result)) != NULL)
    {
      for(i = 0; i < num_fields; i++)
        { printf("%s, ", row[i]); }
      printf("\n");
    }
  mysql_free_result(result);
  mysql_close(mysql);
  exit(EXIT_SUCCESS);
}
```

This example is fairly complete. Each variable is declared at the beginning based on the type called for by the function, along with their respective values. Without having to disconnect and reconnect, you can change the database with the mysql_select_db( ) function.

mysql_real_escape_string( )

```
unsigned long mysql_real_escape_string(MYSQL *mysql,

                                       char *result_string,

                                       char *original_string,

                                       unsigned long src length)
```

This writes a string given as the third argument, to a string named in the second argument, but with special characters escaped by adding backslashes in front of them. The number of bytes to be copied from the source string is given for the fourth argument. When declaring the two strings, the destination string must be double the size of the source string, plus one byte.

```
...
const char client_name[ ] = "O'Reilly Media";
ulong bytes = strlen(client_name);
char client_name_esc[(2 * bytes)+1];
mysql_real_escape_string(mysql, client_name_esc,
                         client_name, bytes);
char *sql_stmnt;
sprintf(sql_stmnt, "INSERT INTO clients (client_name)
                    VALUES('%s')", client_name_esc);
mysql_real_query(mysql, sql_stmnt, strlen(sql_stmnt));
...
```

After establishing the initial variable for storing the client's name, the C function strlen( ) is used to determine the number of bytes contained in the string. Next the second variable to hold the client's name is declared with a size double the size of the first variable, plus one byte. The mysql_real_escape_string( ) function is run with both variables and the size of the first. In this example, the function will place a backslash in front of the apostrophe in the client's name so as not to cause an error when the query is run later. Using the C function sprintf( ), the escaped client name is inserted into the SQL statement given. Finally, the SQL statement is run with mysql_real_query( ).

mysql_real_query( )

```
int mysql_real_query(MYSQL *mysql, const char *query,

                     unsigned int length)
```

Use this to execute the SQL query given as the second argument of the function. Only one SQL statement may be given. Unlike mysql_query( ), this function can execute queries containing binary data. Because of this feature, the number of bytes contained in the query needs to be given for the third argument. This can be determined with the C function strlen( ). If successful, the function will return 0; otherwise, nonzero.

```
...
mysql = mysql_init(NULL);
mysql_real_connect(mysql,host,user,password,database,port,socket,flag);

const char *sql_stmnt = "SELECT * FROM stores";
ulong bytes = strlen(sql_stmnt);
```

```
mysql_real_query(mysql, sql_stmnt, bytes);
result = mysql_store_result(mysql);
num_fields = mysql_field_count(mysql);

while((row = mysql_fetch_row(result)) != NULL)
  {
  for(i = 0; i < num_fields; i++)
    { printf("%s, ", row[i]); }
  printf("\n");
  }
...
```

In this example, the number of bytes of the variable containing the SQL statement is determined with the C function strlen( ) and is stored in a separate variable called bytes. In turn, the bytes variable is given as the third argument to the mysql_real_query( ) function. As an alternative, strnlen(sql_stmnt) could be given as the third argument instead.

mysql_reload( )

```
int mysql_reload(MYSQL *mysql)
```

This instructs the MySQL server to reload the grants table. It returns 0 if successful and nonzero if unsuccessful. This function has been deprecated. Use mysql_query( ) or mysql_real_query( ) with a FLUSH PRIVILEGES statement instead.

mysql_rollback( )

```
my_bool mysql_rollback(MYSQL *mysql)
```

Use this to roll back or reverse the current transaction. This will not work if the mysql_commit( ) function has already been called for the transaction. The function returns 0 if successful, nonzero if unsuccessful.

mysql_row_seek( )

```
MYSQL_ROW_OFFSET mysql_row_seek(MYSQL *result,

                                MYSQL_ROW_OFFSET offset)
```

Use this to move the pointer of a result set to the row given as the second argument of the function. The pointer given must use the MYSQL_ROW_OFFSET structure. Use a function such as mysql_row_tell( ) to determine the offset in the proper format.

```
...
MYSQL_ROW_OFFSET special_location;

while((row = mysql_fetch_row(result)) != NULL)
  {
  if(strcmp(row[1], "1000") == 0)
    {
      special_location = mysql_tell_row(result);
```

```
         continue;
      }
   if(!mysql_more_results(mysql))
      {
        mysql_row_seek(result, special_location);
        printf("%s (%s) \n", row[1], row[0]);
        break;
      }
   printf("%s (%s) \n", row[1], row[0]);
   }
...
```

In this example, a list of clients has been retrieved, but the developer wants the row with a client identification number of 1000 to be displayed last. So, an if statement is used to check for the special record. When it finds the row for which it's looking, the mysql_row_tell( ) function is used to make a note of the point in the results set in which it was found. The remainder of the while statement in which the row is to be printed is then skipped. Using the mysql_more_results( ) function, another if statement watches for the end of the results set. If it determines that there are no more rows in the results set to print, it will move the pointer back to the special client using the mysql_row_seek( ) function and the pointer saved with mysql_row_tell( ), print out that particular row's data, and then end the while statement with break.

mysql_row_tell( )

MYSQL_ROW_OFFSET mysql_row_tell(MYSQL_RES *result)

This returns the pointer for the current position in a results set generated from the mysql_store_result( ) function. The value obtained can be used with mysql_row_seek( ) for changing the pointer while fetching rows. See the mysql_row_seek( ) function for an example of its use.

mysql_select_db( )

int mysql_select_db(MYSQL *mysql, const char *database)

Use this to select a different database for the current connection. The name of the new database to use is given as the second argument of the function. It returns 0 if successful, nonzero if unsuccessful.

```
...
mysql = mysql_init(NULL);
mysql_connect(mysql,"localhost","hui","shorty");
mysql_select_db(mysql,"workrequests");
...
```

mysql_set_server_option( )

```
int mysql_set_server_option(MYSQL *mysql,

                            enum mysql_set_option option)
```

Use this to enable or disable a server option. The only options currently available are MYSQL_OPTION_MULTI_STATEMENTS_ON and MYSQL_OPTION_MULTI_STATEMENTS_OFF, to enable and disable multiple SQL statements, respectively. It returns 0 if successful, nonzero if not successful.

mysql_shutdown( )

```
int mysql_shutdown(MYSQL *mysql)
```

Use this to shut down the MySQL server. It returns 0 if successful and nonzero if unsuccessful.

```
...
if(!mysql_ping(mysql))
  {
    mysql_shutdown(mysql);
    printf("Shutting down server \n");
    if(mysql_ping(mysql))
      { printf("MySQL server is down.\n"); }
  }
...
```

The mysql_ping( ) function in the example checks if the server is alive. Recall that a zero, not a TRUE, return signifies a live server.

mysql_sqlstate( )

```
const char *mysql_sqlstate(MYSQL *mysql)
```

This returns the SQLSTATE error code for the last error that occurred for the current connection. The string will contain five characters and is terminated with a NULL character. A lack of error is signified by "00000" and unmapped errors by "HY000".

mysql_stat( )

```
char * mysql_stat(MYSQL *mysql)
```

This returns a character string containing information about the status of the MySQL server for the current connection.

```
...
printf("Server Status \n %s \n", mysql_stat(mysql));
...
```

mysql_store_result( )

`MYSQL_RES *mysql_store_result(MYSQL *mysql)`

Use this to read and store all of a results set in a `MYSQL_RES` structure. When finished with these results, it's necessary to use the `mysql_free_result( )` function to free the memory allocated for storing the results set. The function returns NULL if it's unsuccessful or if the query is not the type that would return any results (e.g., an UPDATE statement).

```
...
mysql = mysql_init(NULL);
mysql_real_connect(mysql,"localhost","user","password",
                    "workrequests",0,NULL,0);
mysql_query(mysql,"SELECT * FROM users");
result = mysql_store_result(mysql);
num_fields = mysql_field_count(mysql);

while((row = mysql_fetch_row(result)) != NULL)
   {
     for(i = 0; i < num_fields; i++)
       {
         field = mysql_fetch_field_direct(result, i);
         printf("%s: %s, ", field->name, row[i]);
       }
      printf("\n");
    }
mysql_free_result(result);
...
```

See the example for the `mysql_fetch_row( )` function for an alternative method.

mysql_thread_id( )

`unsigned long mysql_thread_id(MYSQL *mysql)`

This returns the thread identifier number for the current connection to MySQL. Thread identifiers can change if a connection is closed or restarted.

```
...
int thread = mysql_thread_id(mysql);
printf("Thread ID: %d \n", thread);
...
```

mysql_thread_safe( )

`unsigned int mysql_thread_safe(void)`

Use this to determine whether the MySQL client library is safe for a threaded environment. It returns 1 if safe, 0 if not.

```
...
if(mysql_thread_safe( ))
   { printf("Safe Environment \n"); }
else{ printf("Unsafe Environment \n"); }
...
```

mysql_use_result( )

MYSQL_RES *mysql_use_result(MYSQL *mysql)

Use this to read the results of a query, one row at a time. This functions in a way similar to the mysql_store_result( ) function, except that function retrieves all of the data at once and stores it for later use. The mysql_use_result( ) function is best used when a results set would be large and speed of processing is a concern. With this function, processing may be started sooner, without having to wait for all of the data to be retrieved. One drawback to this function is that other queries cannot be run without finishing with the results that are in use from the first query. Also, functions such as mysql_data_seek( ) cannot be used and the return value from running mysql_num_rows( ) is altered, because the complete size of the results set is unknown.

```
...
mysql_query(mysql, "SELECT * FROM clients");
result = mysql_use_result(mysql);
num_fields = mysql_field_count(mysql);

while((row = mysql_fetch_row(result)) != NULL)
   {
     for(i = 0; i < num_fields; i++)
       {
         field = mysql_fetch_field_direct(result, i);
         printf("%s: %s, ", field->name, row[i]);
       }
     printf("\n");
}
mysql_free_result(result);
...
```

See the example for the mysql_fetch_row( ) function for an alternative method.

mysql_warning_count( )

unsigned int mysql_warning_count(MYSQL *mysql)

This returns the number of warning messages encountered from the previous query. This can be useful, for instance, when performing multiple INSERT statements with the IGNORE flag.

```
...
MYSQL *mysql;
mysql = mysql_init(NULL);
mysql_real_connect(mysql,"localhost","root","password",
                                 "workrequests",0,NULL,0);
...
unsigned int warnings = mysql_warning_count(mysql);
printf("Number of Warnings: %d \n", warnings);
...
```

C API Datatypes

Here is a list of C API datatypes from the *mysql.h* header file:

MYSQL

> A database handle structure created by mysql_init( ) and released with mysql_close( ).

MYSQL_RES

> A structure for a results set from an SQL query. This structure is used by fetch functions and is released with mysql_free_result( ).

MYSQL_ROW

> A structure for holding a row of data from a results set. The data is retrieved from this structure by using the mysql_fetch_row( ) function.

MYSQL_FIELD

> A structure for holding an array of information about a field of a results set. The array may be set with the mysql_fetch_field( ) function. The elements include name, table, and def for default value.

MYSQL_FIELD_OFFSET

> Used for recording a pointer location for a results set. The offset value can be retrieved by the mysql_row_tell( ) function and deployed with mysql_row_seek( ).

my_ulonglong

> A variable type for storing the number of rows for functions such as mysql_affected_rows( ), mysql_num_rows( ), and mysql_insert_id( ). To print the value of a variable using this type, the value should be copied to another variable that uses the *unsigned long* type.

C API

A

Datatypes

Every column in a table must be declared as one of the datatypes supported by MySQL. Datatypes can be organized into three basic groups: numeric, date and time, and string. This appendix provides a listing of datatypes along with their limitations.

Numeric Datatypes

Standard SQL numeric datatypes are allowed: accurate numeric (i.e., BIGINT, DECIMAL, INTEGER, MEDIUMINT, NUMERIC, SMALLINT, and TINYINT) and approximate numeric datatypes (i.e., DOUBLE PRECISION, FLOAT, and REAL).

For all numeric datatypes, you can use the UNSIGNED and ZEROFILL flags depending on your needs. If UNSIGNED is omitted, SIGNED is assumed. A numeric datatype has different allowable ranges based on whether it's SIGNED or UNSIGNED. The ZEROFILL flag instructs MySQL to pad the unused spaces to the left of a number with spaces. For example, a column with a datatype set to INT(10) will display the number 5 as 0000000005. If the ZEROFILL flag is used, UNSIGNED is assumed for the column. When subtracting values where one is UNSIGNED, the results will become UNSIGNED.

For several of the numeric datatypes, a width for displaying may be specified. This cannot exceed 255. The display width is a factor only when ZEROFILL is used for the column. You may also specify the number of digits allowed for the decimals, including the decimal point.

Accurate Numeric Types

Table A-1 lists accurate numeric types. A few of these types have synonyms for compatibility. A synonym for INTEGER is INT. Synonyms for TINYINT are BIT, BOOL, and BOOLEAN. The datatypes DEC, NUMERIC, and FIXED are synonyms for DECIMAL. If

UNSIGNED is used with DECIMAL, negative values are not allowed. The DECIMAL datatype is similar to floating-point numbers, but it's a fixed-point number. MySQL stores numbers in DECIMAL columns as strings. Therefore, although a numeric range appears in Table A-1, a larger number may be stored in a DECIMAL column. It may be retrieved and displayed as a string, but in a numeric context (i.e., as part of a calculation), it cannot exceed the values shown in the table.

Table A-1. Accurate numeric types

TINYINT[(*width*)] [UNSIGNED] [ZEROFILL]	
0 bytes	Unsigned: 0 to 255
	Signed: -128 to 127
SMALLINT[(*width*)] [UNSIGNED] [ZEROFILL]	
2 bytes	Unsigned: 0 to 65535
	Signed: -32768 to 32767
MEDIUMINT[(*width*)] [UNSIGNED] [ZEROFILL]	3 bytes
Unsigned: 0 to 16777215	
Signed: -8388608 to 8388607	INTEGER[(width)] [UNSIGNED] [ZEROFILL]
4 bytes	
Unsigned: 0 to 4294967295	
Signed: -2147483648 to 2147483647	BIGINT[(width)] [UNSIGNED] [ZEROFILL]
8 bytes	
Unsigned: 0 to 18446744073709551615	
Signed: -9223372036854775808 to 9223372036854775807	DECIMAL[(*width*[,*digits*])] [UNSIGNED] [ZEROFILL]
-3.402823466E+38 to -1.175494351E-38	
0	
1.175494351E-38 to 3.402823466E+38	

Approximate Numeric Datatypes

Approximate numeric datatypes store floating-point numbers like fractions where an approximation must be made. For instance, an accurate number, per se, cannot be stored for 1/3, because the decimal point for 3 continues on endlessly. Table A-2 lists approximate numeric datatypes. There are synonyms for a few of these types. DOUBLE and REAL are synonyms for DOUBLE PRECISION. However, if the SQL mode for the server has the REAL_AS_FLOAT option enabled, REAL is a synonym for FLOAT. For FLOAT, a level of precision may be specified. It may be from 0 to 24 for single-precision floating-point numbers and from 25 to 53 for double-precision floating-point numbers. If a precision isn't given with FLOAT, a single-precision floating point is assumed. With DOUBLE, if UNSIGNED is specified, negative values are not allowed.

Table A-2. Approximate numeric datatypes

FLOAT(***precision***) [UNSIGNED] [ZEROFILL]	
FLOAT[(*width*,*digits*)] [UNSIGNED] [ZEROFILL]	
	-3.402823466E+38 to -1.175494351E-38
	0
	1.175494351E-38 to 3.402823466E+38
DOUBLE PRECISION[(*width*,*digits*)] [UNSIGNED] [ZEROFILL]	
	-3.402823466E+38 to -1.175494351E-38
	0
	1.175494351E-38 to 3.402823466E+38

Date and Time Datatypes

There are a few column datatypes for storing date and time values. They are listed in Table A-3. The table also lists the valid ranges for each datatype. If a value is inserted that is not permitted, or is outside of the acceptable range for the datatype, zeros are used instead. You can override this by starting the server with --sql-mode='ALLOW_INVALID_DATES'. Starting in Version 5.0.2 of MySQL, warnings will be generated when inserting invalid dates or times. For dates that are inserted with only two digits for the year, values from 00 to 69 are assumed to be in the 21st century. For years from 70 to 99, they are assumed to be in the 20th century.

Table A-3. Date and time data types

Data type	Format	Range
DATE	yyyy-mm-dd	1000-01-01 *to* 9999-12-31
DATETIME	yyyy-mm-dd hh:mm:ss	1000-01-01 00:00:00 *to* 9999-12-31 00:00:00
TIMESTAMP[(*width*)]	yyyymmddhhmmss	1970-01-01 00:00:00 *to* 2037-12-31 23:59:59
TIME	hh:mm:ss	-838:59:59 *to* 838:59:59
YEAR[(2|4)]	yy *or* yyyy	1970 *to* 2069 *or* 1901 *to* 2155

Times values may be given as either a string, or numerically. As a string, you may enter a value as d hh:mm:ss.f. In this format, d stands for the number of days, with an allowable range of 0 to 34. The f stands for a fractional number of seconds. This value will not be stored, though. Storing fractional seconds is expected to be added in future releases of MySQL. You don't have to specify values for all elements of a time. Instead, you can enter a time value using one of these formats: hh:mm:ss.f, or hh:mm:ss, hh:mm, or just ss. If you want to include the number of days you can use these formats: d hh:mm:ss, d hh:mm, or d hh. You can also drop the colons and just enter hhmmss, but you can't add minutes onto the end of that format. The datatype TIMESTAMP stores the date and time in a format of yyyymmddhhmmss, but displays it with the format of yyyy-mm-dd hh:mm:ss. MySQL will automatically convert a date or time to its numeric equivalent when it is used in a numeric context, and it will do the reverse as well.

Datatypes

String Datatypes

These datatypes are case-sensitive. So, lowercase and uppercase letters remain unchanged when stored or retrieved. For a few of the string datatypes, a maximum column width may be specified. If a string is entered in a column that exceeds the width set for the column, the string will be right-truncated when stored. The CHAR datatype is a fixed-width column. Columns are right-padded with spaces when stored. The VARCHAR datatype adjusts its width and does not pad the strings stored. Any trailing spaces contained in a string that is stored are removed.

As of Version 4.1 of MySQL, the ASCII attribute may be specified for use with the CHAR datatype. This will set the column to the latin1 character set. As of Version 4.1 of MySQL, the UNICODE attribute may be specified for use with the CHAR datatype. This will set the column to the ucs2 character set.

The BINARY and VARBINARY datatypes store data as binary strings and not character strings like CHAR. Table A-4 lists the various types and their maximum sizes. Some types are listed together: BLOB (Binary Large Object) and TEXT. They have the same maximum value, but TEXT-type columns are handled based upon their character set, whereas BLOB types are not; they're handled as binary strings. This becomes a factor in sorting and comparing data. Binary strings are case-sensitive. As of Version 4.1 of MySQl, you can assign a character set to a TEXT type of column. Values are sorted based on the collation of the character set for the column if one is assigned, or, if not, on the server's character set.

The datatype of BINARY replaces CHAR BINARY. The datatype of VARBINARY replaces VARCHAR BINARY. Before Version 4.1.2 of MySQL, adding the BINARY flag after CHAR or VARCHAR instructed MySQL to treat the values as byte strings for sorting and comparisons. If a BINARY column is used in an expression, all elements of the expression are treated as a binary.

Table A-4. Maximum sizes od MySQL datatypes

Datatype	Maximum size
CHAR(*width*) [BINARY|ASCII|UNICODE]	255 *characters*
VARCHAR(*width*) [BINARY]	255 *characters*
BINARY(*width*)	255 *characters*
VARBINARY(*width*)	255 *characters*
TINYBLOB, TINYTEXT	255 *bytes*
BLOB, TEXT	65535 *bytes*
MEDIUMBLOB, MEDIUMTEXT	16777215 *bytes*
LONGBLOB, LONGTEXT	4294967295 *bytes*
ENUM('*value*', ...)	65535 *elements*
SET('*value*', ...)	64 *elements*

An ENUM column is one in which all possible choices are enumerated (e.g., ENUM('yes', 'no', 'maybe')). It's possible for it to contain a blank value (i.e., ") and NULL. If an ENUM column is set up to allow NULL values, NULL is allowed and will be the default value. If an ENUM column is set up with NOT NULL, NULL isn't allowed and the default value becomes the first element given. MySQL stores a numeric index of the enumerated values in the column: 1 being the first value. The values can be retrieved when the column is used in a numeric context (e.g., SELECT col1 + 0 FROM table1;). The reverse may be performed when entering data into a column (e.g., UPDATE table1 SET col1 = 3;) to set the value to the third element. The column values are sorted in ascending order based on the numeric index, not their corresponding enumerated values. The SET datatype is similar to ENUM, except that a SET column can hold multiple values (e.g., UPDATE table1 SET col1 = 'a, b';). For the SET datatype, values may be filtered with the FIND_IN_SET( ) function.

B

Operators

Operators are used in mathematical or logical operations. An operator is typically placed between two values (i.e., numbers, strings, columns, or expressions) for comparing or evaluating them. There are four types of operators: arithmetic, relational, logical, and bitwise. This appendix provides a listing of operators grouped by these four types.

Arithmetic Operators

The arithmetic operators in MySQL work only on numbers, and not on strings. However, MySQL will convert a string as a number when in a numeric context if it can. If it can't convert a particular string, it will convert it to 0. The arithmetic operators allowed are listed in Table B-1.

Table B-1. Arithmetic operators

Operator	Use
+	Addition
-	Subtraction and negation
*	Multiplication
/	Division
DIV	Division of integers
%	Modulo division

The minus sign may be used for subtracting numbers or for setting a number to a negative. The DIV operator converts values to integers and returns only integers. It doesn't round fractions that would be returned, but truncates them.

Relational Operators

Relational operators are used for comparing numbers and strings. If a string is compared to a number, MySQL will try to convert the string to a number. If a TIMESTAMP column is compared to a string or a number, MySQL will attempt to convert the string or number to a timestamp value. If it's unsuccessful at converting the other value to a timestamp, it will convert the TIMESTAMP column's value to a string or a number. TIME and DATE columns are compared to other values as strings. The logical and relational operators allowed are listed in Table B-2.

Table B-2. Relational operators

Operator	Use
<	Less than
>	Greater than
<=	Less than or equal to
>=	Greater than or equal to
expression BETWEEN n AND n	Between first and second number
expression NOT BETWEEN n AND n	Not between first and second number
IN (...)	In a set
NOT IN (...)	Not in a set
=	Equal to
<=>	Equal to (for comparing NULL values)
LIKE	Matches a pattern
NOT LIKE	Doesn't match a pattern
REGEXP, RLIKE	Matches a regular expression
!=	Not equal to
<>	Not equal to
IS NULL	NULL
IS NOT NULL	Not NULL

The minus sign may be used for subtracting numbers or for setting a number to a negative. The equals sign is used to compare two values. If one is NULL, though, NULL will be returned. The <=> operator is used to compare for equality and it's NULL-safe. For example, an SQL statement containing something like IF(col1 <=> col2) where the values of both are NULL will return 1 and not NULL.

Logical Operators

Logical operators are used for evaluating values or expressions for true, false, or unknown. Table B-3 lists allowable logical operators.

Table B-3. Logical operators

Operator	Use
AND	Logical *AND*
&&	Logical *AND*
IS *boolean*	Logical *equal*
IS NOT *boolean*	Logical *equal*
OR	Logical *OR*
||	Logical *OR*
NOT	Logical *NOT*
!	Logical *NOT*
XOR	Logical *XOR*

The operators IS and IS NOT are being added in Version 5.0.2 of MySQL. A boolean value of TRUE, FALSE, or UNKNOWN should immediately follow these operators.

Bitwise Operators

Bitwise operators are used for comparing numbers based on their binary digits. These operators are listed in Table B-4.

Table B-4. Bitwise operators

Operator	Use
|	OR
&	AND
<<	*Shift bits to left*
>>	*Shift bits to right*
~	*NOT or invert bits*

The tilda (~) may be used to invert the bits of a value.

Environment Variables

The MySQL server, and many of its clients and utilities, use several environment variables provided by the operating system. For some programs, the user can override some of these variables by command-line options or values set in an option file (i.e., *my.cnf* or *my.ini*). Table C-1 lists the variables used.

Table C-1. Variables and their uses

Variable	Use
CC	C compiler
CXX	C++ compiler
CFLAGS	C compiler flags
CXXFLAGS	C++ compiler flags
DBI_USER	Default username for Perl DBI applications
DBI_TRACE	Perl DBI trace options
HOME	Default path for `mysql` client program history file
LD_RUN_PATH	Path for *libmysqlclient.so* file
MYSQL_DEBUG	Debug trace options
MYSQL_HISTFILE	Default path for *mysql* client program history file
MYSQL_HOST	Default host for *mysql* client program
MYSQL_PS1	Command-line prompt for first line of a statement for *mysql* client program
MYSQL_PWD	Default password for connecting to server
MYSQL_TCP_PORT	Default TCP/IP port number
MYSQL_UNIX_PORT	Default Unix socket filename
PATH	Path for the MySQL programs
TMPDIR	Path for temporary directory
TZ	Time zone of server
UMASK_DIR	Permissions settings for creating directories
UMASK	Permissions settings for creating files
USER	Default username for connecting to server running on MS Windows or Novell NetWare

Index

Symbols

( ) parentheses, 26, 59, 60
& (ampersand), 7
\ (backslash), 6, 76, 111
, (comma) (see comma)
% (percent sign) (see percent sign)

A

ABS( ) function, 143
ACOS( ) function, 144
Active attribute (Perl DBI), 226
ActiveKids attribute (Perl DBI), 226
ActivePerl, 2
ADD clause (ALTER TABLE), 35, 36
ADD COLUMN clause (ALTER
          TABLE), 35
ADD INDEX clause (ALTER
          TABLE), 35
ADDDATE( ) function, 118, 122, 135
--add-drop-table option
          (mysqldump), 195, 197
--add-locks option (mysqldump), 195,
          197
ADDTIME( ) function, 119, 136
--addtodest option (mysqlhotcopy), 199
AES algorithm, 96
AES_DECRYPT( ) function, 96
AES_ENCRYPT( ) function, 96

AFTER keyword
     ADD COLUMN clause, 35
     CHANGE COLUMN clause, 36
aggregate functions, 143–155
aliases
     AS keyword and, 21, 22, 63, 67, 74
     example, 29
     HANDLER statement and, 58
ALL flag
     GRANT statement, 15, 55
     REVOKE statement, 53
     SELECT statement, 75
--all option (mysqldump), 195, 196, 197
ALL PRIVILEGES privilege (GRANT/
          REVOKE), 56
--all-databases option
     mysqlcheck utility, 193
     mysqldump utility, 195
--all-in-1 option (mysqlcheck), 193
--allow-keywords option
          (mysqldump), 195
--allowold option (mysqlhotcopy), 199
alphabetical order, 118–142
ALTER DATABASE statement, 34
ALTER privilege (GRANT/
          REVOKE), 56
ALTER TABLE statement
     adjusting variables, 89, 91
     changing values with, 48
     checksums and, 42

We'd like to hear your suggestions for improving our indexes. Send email to *index@oreilly.com*.

OPEN flag (SHOW TABLES), 91
--open-files-limit option
    mysqld program, 175
    mysqld_safe program, 179
--open_files_limit option
    (mysqlbinlog), 191
operators
    arithmetic, 290
    bitwise, 292
    logical, 291, 292
    relational, 291
--opt option (mysqldump), 197
--optimize option (mysqlcheck), 194
OPTIMIZE TABLE statement, 67, 68
OPTIONALLY flag (LOAD DATA
    INFILE), 65
OR operator, 292
OR REPLACE clause (CREATE
    VIEW), 49
ORD( ) function, 110, 116
ORDER BY clause
    ALTER TABLE statement, 37
    DELETE statement, 50
    HANDLER statement, 58
    SELECT statement, 22, 23, 37, 75,
        77, 78, 79, 94
ordering
    columns, 66
    data, 22, 23
OUTER keyword (JOIN clause), 63

P

package (PKG) files, 9, 10
--packlength option (myisampack), 186
--parallel-recover option
    (myisamchk), 183
ParamValues attribute (Perl DBI), 228
parentheses (), 26, 59, 60
parse_dsn( ) function (Perl DBI), 219
parse_trace_flag( ) function (Perl
    DBI), 219
parse_trace_flags( ) function (Perl
    DBI), 219
PASSWORD( ) function, 81, 102, 110
password command (mysqladmin), 190
--password option
    mysql program, 170
    mysqlaccess utility, 188
    mysqladmin utility, 189
    mysqlbinlog utility, 192

mysqlcheck utility, 194
mysqld_multi program, 178
mysqldump utility, 197
mysqlhotcopy utility, 200
mysqlimport utility, 202
mysqlshow utility, 203
passwords
    encrypting, 110
    entering, 17
    mysqladmin and, 178
    postinstallation adjustments, 14
    providing for servers, 170, 189
PATH environment variable, 293
percent (%) operator, 151
percent sign (%), 14, 28, 86, 91, 111
PERIOD_ADD( ) function, 132, 142
PERIOD_DIFF( ) function, 133, 142
Perl DBI
    mailing lists, 3
    methods and functions, 208–229
    overview, 204–208
Perl language, 2, 204
perror utility, 203
PHP
    functions, 232–253
    overview, 230–232
PI( ) function, 151
--pid-file option
    mysqld program, 175
    mysqld_safe program, 179
ping( ) function (Perl DBI), 219
ping command (mysqladmin), 190
PKG (package) files, 9, 10
--plan option (mysqlaccess), 188
--port option
    mysql program, 170
    mysqladmin utility, 189
    mysqlbinlog utility, 192
    mysqlcheck utility, 194
    mysqld program, 175
    mysqld_safe program, 179
    mysqldump utility, 197
    mysqlhotcopy utility, 200
    mysqlimport utility, 202
    mysqlshow utility, 203
POSITION( ) function, 110
--position option (mysqlbinlog), 192
POW( ) function, 151, 152
POWER( ) function, 151, 152
PRECISION attribute (Perl DBI), 228

T

--tab option (mysqldump), 196, 197
--table option
    mysql program, 171
    mysqlaccess utility, 188
    mysqlbinlog utility, 192
table types (see storage engines)
table_info( ) function (Perl DBI), 224
table_info_all( ) function (Perl
        DBI), 225
tables
    adding indexes, 35, 43
    adding rows, 59–62
    analyzing, 39
    backing up, 2, 39
    checksum values for, 42
    converting character sets, 38
    copying data between, 48
    creating, 17–19, 84
    creating based on other, 48
    creating within databases, 44
    deleting contents, 93
    deleting indexes, 52
    displaying information about, 51
    displaying status, 90
    flushing, 54
    joining, 18, 19, 21, 62, 63
    listing, 20, 91
    locking, 67
    manipulating, 34
    optimizing data in, 67
    renaming, 68
    repairing, 69
    restoring, 39, 72
    restricting access, 56
    ROLLBACK statement and, 73
    SQL statements, 33
    unlocking, 67, 94
tables( ) function (Perl DBI), 225
--tables option
    mysqlcheck utility, 193, 194
    mysqldump utility, 196, 198
table-spaces, 38
Taint attribute (Perl DBI), 227
TaintIn attribute (Perl DBI), 227
TaintOut attribute (Perl DBI), 227
TAN( ) function, 144, 154
tangent, 154
tar utility (GNU), 6, 8
--tcp-ip option (mysqld_multi), 178
--temp_dir option (myisampack), 186

TEMPORARY flag
    CREATE TABLE statement, 44
    DROP TABLE statement, 53
--temp-pool option (mysqld), 176
--test option (myisampack), 186
TEXT datatype, 35, 43, 67, 288
TEXT_FIELDS clause, 29
threads, displaying, 88
tilde (~), 292
TIME( ) function, 137
TIME datatype
    CAST( ) function, 162
    CONVERT( ) function, 163
    format, 117
    GET_FORMAT( ) and, 127
    overview, 287
time datatype, 128
time functions, 118–142
TIMEDIFF( ) function, 137
TIME_FORMAT( ) function, 123, 138
TIMESTAMP( ) function, 137
TIMESTAMP datatype
    format, 117
    GET_FORMAT( ) and, 127
    mysqlbinlog utility, 192
    overview, 287
TIMESTAMPADD( ) function, 138
TIMESTAMPDIFF( ) function, 138
TIME_TO_SEC( ) function, 139
--timezone option (mysqld_safe), 179
TINYBLOB datatype, 288
TINYINT datatype, 285, 286
TINYTEXT datatype, 288
TMPDIR environment variable, 293
--tmpdir option
    myisamchk utility, 184
    mysqld program, 177
    mysqlhotcopy utility, 200
TO keyword
    ALTER TABLE statement, 37
    BACKUP TABLE statement, 39
    PURGE MASTER LOGS
        statement, 68
    RENAME TABLE statement, 68
TO_DAYS( ) function, 126, 139
trace( ) function (Perl DBI), 225, 227
TraceLevel attribute (Perl DBI), 227
trace_msg( ) function (Perl DBI), 225
trademarks, 3
--transaction-isolation option
        (mysqld), 177

X

--xml option (mysqldump), 198
XOR operator, 292

Y

YEAR( ) function, 134, 142
YEAR datatype, 117, 287
YEAR interval
    DATE_ADD( ) function, 122
    TIMESTAMPADD( ) function, 138
YEAR_MONTH increment (DATE_
       ADD), 122
YEARWEEK( ) function, 142

Z

ZEROFILL flag, 285, 286, 287

About the Author

Russell J.T. Dyer has been a software developer since 1981, and in the past eight years has worked as an IT manager, a MySQL developer, and a Perl programmer. Since September 2002, he has worked as a freelance technical writer. He has also taught courses on Linux and other open source software at ITT Technical Institute in the New Orleans area where he currently lives. Russell writes a monthly column on MySQL and a series on Apache in *Unix Review*, and has contributed articles about MySQL and other open source topics to the *Linux Journal*, *ONlamp.com*, *The Perl Journal*, *Tech Republic*, *SysAdmin Magazine*, and *XML.com*.

Colophon

Our look is the result of reader comments, our own experimentation, and feedback from distribution channels. Distinctive covers complement our distinctive approach to technical topics, breathing personality and life into potentially dry subjects.

The animal appearing on the cover of *MySQL in a Nutshell* is the pied kingfisher (*Ceryle rudis*). At 80 grams and 28 centimeters in length, the pied kingfisher is the largest bird in the world capable of a true hover in still air. Like most kingfishers, it hunts small fish from a perch or by hovering over open water. But unlike others, the pied kingfisher often travels up to three miles from land. While the closely related giant kingfisher relies heavily on shoreline perching places, the pied kingfisher can hover above choppy water and swallow its prey on the wing. For this adaptive skill, the pied kingfisher is consider the most advanced of the 87 kingfisher species.

Pied kingfishers are common and widespread across much of Africa, the Middle East, and Southeast Asia, and are easily distinguishable from other kingfishers by their unique black and white markings. Never far from water, pied kingfishers breed in burrows excavated into riverbanks. These birds form family groups, with the previous season's offspring often helping to raise their parents' next brood. Additional male helpers may also contribute food depending on their availability. If food is scarce, the breeding male feeds its mate, while helpers feed both parents and chicks after hatching. Helpers may thus increase their chances of mating with a nesting female the following year.

Although kingfishers are known for their fishing skills, many kingfishers don't eat fish at all; among those that do, less than half of all dives are successful. kingfishers are apparently blind under water, so their survival depends on perfect aim from above. They are able to judge both the size and depth of fish swimming below—the two greatest factors in determining a likely and rewarding catch. The instant a kingfisher hits water, opaque, protective third eyelids called nictitating membranes cover the eyes. More than a few hungry kingfishers have been seen emerging with stones in their bills. Still, among piscivorous birds, the kingfisher has earned its name justly.

Sarah Sherman was the production editor and proofreader, and Audrey Doyle was the copyeditor for *MySQL in a Nutshell*. Adam Witwer and Mary Anne Weeks Mayo provided quality control. Lydia Onofrei provided production assistance. Lucie Haskins wrote the index.

Ellie Volckhausen designed the cover of this book, based on a series design by Edie Freedman. The cover image is a 19th-century engraving from the Dover Pictorial Archive. Karen Montgomery produced the cover layout with InDesign CS using Adobe's ITC Garamond font.

David Futato designed the interior layout. This book was converted by Joe Wizda to FrameMaker 5.5.6 with a format conversion tool created by Erik Ray, Jason McIntosh, Neil Walls, and Mike Sierra that uses Perl and XML technologies. The text font is Linotype Birka; the heading font is Adobe Myriad Condensed; and the code font is LucasFont's TheSans Mono Condensed. The illustrations that appear in the book were produced by Robert Romano, Jessamyn Read, and Lesley Borash using Macromedia FreeHand MX and Adobe Photoshop CS. This colophon was written by Lydia Onofrei.